THE BEDFORD SERIES IN

The Scopes Trial

A Brief History with Documents

Jeffrey P. Moran

University of Kansas

BEDFORD/ST. MARTIN'S Boston ♦ New York

For Bedford/St. Martin's

Publisher for History: Patricia A. Rossi
Director of Development for History: Jane Knetzger
Developmental Editor: Molly E. Kalkstein
Editorial Assistant, Publishing Services: Maria Teresa Burwell
Production Supervisor: Tina Cameron
Project Management: Books By Design, Inc.
Text Design: Claire Seng-Niemoeller
Indexer: Books By Design, Inc.
Cover Design: Billy Boardman
Cover Photo: Courtesy of Special Collections Library, University of Tennessee, Knoxville.
Composition: Stratford Publishing Services, Inc.
Printing and Binding: Haddon Craftsmen, an RR Donnelley & Sons Company

President: Charles H. Christensen
Editorial Director: Joan E. Feinberg
Director of Marketing: Karen R. Melton
Director of Editing, Design, and Production: Marcia Cohen
Manager, Publishing Services: Emily Berleth

Library of Congress Control Number: 2001093634

Manufactured in the United States of America.

7 6 5 4 3 2
f e d c b

For information, write: Bedford / St. Martin's, 75 Arlington Street, Boston, MA 02116 (617-399-4000)

ISBN: 0-312-24919-5 (paperback)
0-312-29426-3 (hardcover)

Acknowledgments

Vine Deloria Jr., from *Red Earth, White Lies: Native Americans and the Myth of Scientific Fact* (New York: Scribner, 1995). Used by permission of the author.

Foreword

The Bedford Series in History and Culture is designed so that readers can study the past as historians do.

The historian's first task is finding the evidence. Documents, letters, memoirs, interviews, pictures, movies, novels, or poems can provide facts and clues. Then the historian questions and compares the sources. There is more to do than in a courtroom, for hearsay evidence is welcome, and the historian is usually looking for answers beyond act and motive. Different views of an event may be as important as a single verdict. How a story is told may yield as much information as what it says.

Along the way the historian seeks help from other historians and perhaps from specialists in other disciplines. Finally, it is time to write, to decide on an interpretation and how to arrange the evidence for readers.

Each book in this series contains an important historical document or group of documents, each document a witness from the past and open to interpretation in different ways. The documents are combined with some element of historical narrative—an introduction or a biographical essay, for example—that provides students with an analysis of the primary source material and important background information about the world in which it was produced.

Each book in the series focuses on a specific topic within a specific historical period. Each provides a basis for lively thought and discussion about several aspects of the topic and the historian's role. Each is short enough (and inexpensive enough) to be a reasonable one-week assignment in a college course. Whether as classroom or personal reading, each book in the series provides firsthand experience of the challenge—and fun—of discovering, recreating, and interpreting the past.

Natalie Zemon Davis
Ernest R. May
Lynn Hunt
David W. Blight

Preface

In July 1925, the state of Tennessee placed a high school teacher named John Thomas Scopes on trial for violating a recent law against teaching the doctrine of human evolution. The charge was a misdemeanor, but for more than a month, the entire nation's attention remained fixed on Dayton, Tennessee, the scene of the trial.

This book situates the Scopes trial in the middle of the cultural conflicts of the 1920s. Running throughout the case were themes such as the moral decline of youth; the growing cleavages opened up by race, region, and urbanization; the struggle between majoritarianism and a nascent rights-based liberalism; and the clash between older religious attitudes and modern secularism. At the same time, the prosecution and defense wrangled over subtler points of constitutional interpretation—especially the separation of church and state—and of theology. The Scopes trial is a useful lens for bringing the cultural conflicts of the 1920s into focus.

A glance through recent newspapers, however, reveals that these issues are not confined to the 1920s. Shortly after I first proposed this book in 1999, the state board of education in Kansas deleted evolution from its statewide science requirements, reminding the nation that antievolutionism was still alive and well. Reporters in Kansas repeatedly invoked comparisons to the Scopes trial, and indeed the Kansas controversy revived many of the same themes of region, religion, local control, majority rule, and academic freedom that had convulsed the nation in 1925. Contrary to what many historians after the 1930s believed, these tensions never really went away. Indeed, conflicts over such issues are perhaps inherent in democracy, especially in the United States, with its peculiar political, religious, and cultural inheritances. I hope that this new examination of the Scopes trial will aid students and historians in their understanding not only of the 1920s but also of the decades that have passed since that "trial of the century."

This volume aims to clear away some of the clutter left by seventy-five years of historical interpretation of the Scopes trial. The introduction seeks to guide readers through the culture of the Jazz Age, the causes of the antievolution controversy, and the events of the trial itself. It also highlights areas of the trial that have received scant attention before, such as the relationship between antievolutionism and race and the importance of women and gender in the evolution dispute.

Then the reader's work of historical imagination takes over. The documents in parts two and three allow readers to go back to the Scopes trial so that they can hear for themselves the arguments of the prosecution and the defense and listen to the words of reporters who sat in Dayton during that hot summer. The main document in this book, presented in part two, is a transcript of the trial itself, edited to remove at least some of the courtroom tedium. By turns brilliant, pandering, humorous, and vicious, the courtroom testimony repays careful attention. At the end of each day's testimony stands a reporter's reflection on the events of the trial, just as newspaper accounts in 1925 juxtaposed testimony and reportage. Part three of the book contains supporting documents and cartoons organized by themes such as race, academic freedom, gender, and regionalism. The commentaries on the trial—the meanings various Americans attached to the struggle in Dayton—were at least as important as the trial itself. The introduction and the documents reflect on one another, and I hope that together they will provoke as many arguments as they will settle.

Acknowledgments

I am grateful to the General Research Fund at the University of Kansas for supporting this work.

In lieu of money, many scholars have been extremely generous with their time and care. My colleagues at the University of Kansas, Donald Worster and Peter Mancall, provided thorough and wise readings of the introduction, while the members of the history department's Junior League, Jonathan Earle foremost among them, gave good cheer mixed with sobering suggestions. Ronald Numbers, Beth Bailey, Jonathan Zimmerman, Dale Soden, and Larry Whitaker all offered careful evaluations of the entire project, and if I had incorporated more of their suggestions, this would undoubtedly be a much better book—and doorstop. I am grateful as well to Donald Fleming, James Ivy, Bruce Lieberman, Michael Vorenberg, Scott Hirons, the anonymous reader at Bedford/St. Martin's, the helpful people in Word Processing in Wescoe Hall, and the saving remnant of the Interlibrary Loan staff at the University of Kansas libraries.

I appreciate the way that David Blight, Ernest May, Patricia Rossi, Charles Christensen, and Katherine Kurzman at Bedford/St. Martin's took a leap of faith on this. Thank you very much to Molly Kalkstein, who is every writer's dream editor: conscientious, wise, and complimentary, all in one.

Finally, thank you to Susan, Hannah, and Rebecca. I can't say you suffered with me, because I quite enjoyed writing this book, but maybe you suffered anyway.

Jeffrey P. Moran

Contents

PART TWO

The Scopes Trial Day by Day: Transcript and Commentary 73

PART ONE

Introduction: The Scopes Trial and the Birth of Modern America

The only real victors in the Scopes antievolution trial of 1925 were the monkeys. As the state of Tennessee prepared to indict a schoolteacher, John Scopes, for violating a new law against teaching evolution, it seemed that everyone in the South who owned a monkey converged on the site of the trial in Dayton, Tennessee, to offer the pet as an exhibit for the prosecution or defense, to pose for reporters, or to parade the primate down Main Street. Most conspicuously, promoters brought Joe Mendi, the "$100,000 chimpanzee with the Intelligence of a Five-Year Old Child," from New York to tour Dayton and appear in his tailored suit at the sold-out Princess Theater in neighboring Nashville. "Take a look at 'Joe,'" advised his managers in advertisements throughout the region. "Every man has a perfect right to decide for himself as to whether his 'family tree' bore cocoanuts or not." Elsewhere in the South, zookeepers contended with record crowds as men, women, and children elbowed in to inspect their purported primate relatives. The Glendale Zoo in Nashville, for example, reported a 50 percent jump in attendance in the weeks leading up to the July trial. And by the time the Scopes trial began, Dayton flappers, young women who flouted convention, had launched a short-lived fashion trend for shoulder wraps made of toy monkeys.[1] If monkeys

[1] *Nashville Tennessean,* 14 June 1925, 9; *Nashville Banner,* 13 June 1925, 1; *Nashville Tennessean,* 11 July 1925, 5.

had not evolved by the time of the Scopes trial, they had at least ascended.

The trial went less well for the humans. The celebrity attorney for the prosecution, William Jennings Bryan, a three-time Democratic candidate for president, began the trial with a reputation as one of the nation's great reformers but by the end found himself branded an ignorant bigot. On the defense, Clarence Darrow came down to Dayton fresh from saving two notorious killers from the electric chair, but he was unable to prevent John Scopes's conviction on a mere misdemeanor and later found himself outfoxed on the appeal. And the leading citizens of Dayton, who had launched the trial as a way to gain favorable publicity for their town, instead heard the name "Dayton" transformed into a synonym for backwardness and religious fanaticism. Such ironies seemed to proliferate in the fertile Tennessee soil.

In a decade that gave birth to the phrase "trial of the century" and then immediately overworked the expression into a cliché, the Scopes trial nevertheless stood out. Nearly 200 journalists from throughout the United States and abroad filed on the order of 135,000 words daily during the trial. One sociologist estimated that the reportage would fill 3,000 volumes of 300 pages apiece. Every day, newsreel crews sent out miles of film from Dayton, and a Chicago newspaper created history's first radio network hookup to broadcast the trial to a waiting nation. To be sure, some of this interest was aroused by a lack of competing news—one front-page story about Calvin Coolidge on the eve of the trial bore the headline "President, Weary of Loafing, Looks for Something to Do"—but Americans also recognized that the Scopes trial raised critical questions for society in the 1920s, and it raised them with grand drama.[2]

The case erupted out of tectonic shifts in American culture. Millions of Americans in the 1920s were in revolt against the dominant Victorian morality and took their moral cues from advertising, Hollywood, scientists, and intellectuals rather than from the nation's Protestant establishment. In the vanguard of the revolt was the so-called New Woman, the model of the educated, independent feminist who repudiated the sexual morality of the past. The antievolution movement derived much of its moral fervor from the conviction that Darwinism was partly responsible for these Jazz Age rebellions. This war between the old culture and the new was also bound up with a grow-

[2]Howard Odum, "Editorial Notes," *Social Forces,* Sept. 1925, 190; *Baltimore Sun,* 3 July 1925, 1.

ing split between an older rural America and the nation's burgeoning cities, for the new culture was very much a product of city life. The antievolution movement was in many ways an expression of rural resentment toward the rise of the city. Further, in a way that is perhaps difficult to see today, when regional variations in the United States have been mostly ironed flat, the Scopes trial exposed a deep cleavage between the more traditional American South and a North that was rapidly growing more urban and diverse. Finally, even as the nation's religious leaders fretted about their loss of influence in the Jazz Age, their churches were shaking with a clash between theological liberals and a rising movement of fundamentalist Protestants—a war waged in part on the battleground of evolution. Culture, urbanism, regionalism, religion—all of these issues became entangled in the struggle over evolution at Dayton, Tennessee.

EVOLUTION BEFORE THE 1920s

Although the culture clash of the 1920s was the proximate cause of the Scopes trial, the ultimate cause, or primary mover, was Charles Darwin's publication in 1859 of *On the Origin of Species by Means of Natural Selection, or the Preservation of Favored Races in the Struggle for Life*. In this masterpiece of empirical observation and hypothetical deduction, the English naturalist wrought a revolution in science and helped touch off a radical revision in the status and content of Christianity. In a sense, Darwin and all he represented would sit next to Scopes in the courtroom at Dayton.

Scientifically, *Origin of Species* provided a powerful framework for explaining phenomena that had puzzled scientists for generations, particularly the exceptional diversity of living organisms and the history of life in the fossil record. Although some natural scientists during the early nineteenth century accepted that life on earth had existed for perhaps millions of years, they were prevented from developing greater insight into organic development by the general belief that species were fixed for all time, so that any variation within a species constituted merely a deviation from the species' "ideal form." Thus, natural scientists could attribute the appearance of new species in the fossil record only to separate, divine creations. A trilobite, in other words, was always a trilobite, and if a paleontologist discovered a trilobite fossil with twelve segments rather than eleven, that represented either an accidental deviation from the "true" trilobite form or a separate species of trilobite created by God. Many scientists were growing dissatisfied with this explanation, but Darwin was among the first to make the conceptual leap to the idea that a species constituted not a fixed platonic ideal, but rather a shifting, fluctuating population of closely related organisms. The rest of the so-called Darwinian revolution spread from this insight.[3]

Once he accepted that species were not fixed, Darwin was free to seek other explanations for the problem of the multiplication of species. Rather than having been created separately by God, could not species have evolved from common ancestors? Indeed, Darwin suggested that all organisms were related to one another at some early branching of the family tree.[4] Thus far, Darwin's ideas found ready acceptance. With the death in 1873 of Harvard's Louis Agassiz, the last major scientist to argue that God had separately created fixed species, virtually every American natural scientist of any repute had come to agree with Darwin that species were mutable and that the fossil record demonstrated the evolution of species from earlier species.[5] Freed from their belief in the fixity of species, natural scientists no longer focused on merely cataloging the earth's flora and fauna into static divisions, but instead they turned to the work of connecting species through history. Darwin's fundamental insight opened up for science what he called a "grand and almost untrodden field of inquiry."[6]

Accepting the fact of evolution, however, did not mean that scientists accepted Darwin's explanation of how evolution worked. For reasons both scientific and theological, Darwin's theory of natural selection—his proposal that species evolved because the "struggle for survival" made animals with certain traits more likely to survive and reproduce than others—would not find general scientific acceptance until the evolutionary synthesis of the 1930s and 1940s. Natural selection provided a powerful explanation for organic evolution and undoubtedly played a large role in the acceptance of Darwin's work, but it also became the focus of tremendous opposition. Even Darwin's scientific supporters were far from unanimous in their approval. Many

[3]Charles Darwin, *On the Origin of Species by Means of Natural Selection, or the Preservation of Favoured Races in the Struggle for Life* (1859; facsimile ed., with an introduction by Ernst Mayr, Cambridge: Harvard University Press, 1964); Ernst Mayr, *The Growth of Biological Thought: Diversity, Evolution, and Inheritance* (Cambridge: Belknap Press of the Harvard University Press, 1982), 405.

[4]Mayr, *Growth of Biological Thought,* 505–9.

[5]Ronald L. Numbers, *Darwinism Comes to America* (Cambridge: Harvard University Press, 1998), 47.

[6]Darwin, *Origin of Species,* 486.

produced technical objections to natural selection, questioning, for example, whether small, undirected changes could produce such complex structures as the eyeball.[7] Darwin himself sometimes wavered in his commitment to strict natural selection.

The objections were not merely technical. Many commentators also considered the theory to be a "moral outrage."[8] Darwinian natural selection, based on "the war of nature," seemed an immensely cruel process, a law that operated randomly and created tremendous waste by killing off the "unfit" by the millions. And for what? Darwin saw in the fossil record and the living world no overt evidence of an intervening intelligence, no indication of a trend toward greater perfection among organisms. Natural selection thus seemed to contradict the "argument from design" that had for decades unified theology and natural science. Scientists and ministers alike had been accustomed to viewing the natural world as a revelation of God's nature and purposes—the elegant "design" of life on earth seemed evidence of an equally elegant "Designer" in heaven above—but Darwin now seemed to be suggesting that nature revealed a God who was either cruel and wasteful or absent altogether.[9] Many evolutionists were as unwilling as their opponents to make this particular leap and give up the argument from design.

Darwin's theory also struck more directly at certain foundational Judeo-Christian beliefs.[10] Most obviously, the theory of evolution was incompatible with a literal reading of either of the two creation stories in Genesis, for it contradicted the story that God created the earth and subsequently stocked it with living creatures within seven days, and it contradicted the account of Adam and Eve as the first humans on earth. Darwin further undermined the Christian ideal of humanity's special relationship to God by lumping humans in with all other animals, rather implicitly in *Origin of Species* and then explicitly in *The Descent of Man,* published in 1871.[11] Finally, Darwin seemed to

[7]Mayr, *Growth of Biological Thought,* 513–25.

[8]Ibid., 510.

[9]For the most important expression of the argument from design, see William Paley, *Natural Theology: Or, Evidences of the Existence and Attributes of the Deity, Collected from the Appearances of Nature* (London: R. Faulder, 1802).

[10]James R. Moore, *The Post-Darwinian Controversies: A Study of the Protestant Struggle to Come to Terms with Darwin in Great Britain and America, 1870–1900* (New York: Cambridge University Press, 1979); Jon H. Roberts, *Darwinism and the Divine in America: Protestant Intellectuals and Organic Evolution, 1859–1900* (Madison: University of Wisconsin Press, 1988), 7–10, 91–117; Paul Conkin, *When All the Gods Trembled: Darwinism, Scopes, and American Intellectuals* (New York: Rowman & Littlefield, 1998), 37.

[11]Charles Darwin, *The Descent of Man* (London: Murray, 1871).

undermine Christianity simply by ignoring it as irrelevant to his scientific endeavor. In Darwin's opinion, the scientist's task was to seek out the natural causes of phenomena and not to fall back on supernatural explanations. Darwin followed his own rule and largely omitted God from his work. In this respect, *Origin of Species* was the culmination of a process of secularization that had been building for years in the scientific community, as scientists attempted to formulate hypotheses that, if they did not necessarily rule out God, at least did not directly invoke him as an explanatory mechanism.[12] But Darwin's challenge cut deeper. Strictly understood, Darwin's work seemed to make God, as Christians had long understood him, not merely unknowable but unnecessary. Such issues touched off repeated public debates and scholarly controversies in the decade after *Origin of Species* was published.

Nevertheless, by the turn of the twentieth century, most of the leading Protestant theologians in England and the United States had adapted to the Darwinian environment. They achieved this accommodation both by tailoring their own aspirations to fit the new evolutionary consensus and by adjusting Darwin's theories to suit them better. Instead of continuing to elaborate a "two-tiered worldview"—natural science below supporting biblical revelation above, as in the argument from design—leading Protestant theologians came to argue that religion and science occupied entirely separate spheres.[13] Theology was to give up its former status as arbiter of the natural and supernatural and henceforth confine itself more closely to the arenas of faith and morality. There, beyond the reach of scientific inquiry, religion could survive and perhaps, they hoped, even thrive. But this change also meant that religion was now in the position of accommodating scientific discoveries, rather than the other way around.

At the same time, theologians and natural scientists, the majority of whom remained pious Christians, chose selectively which elements of Darwin's theory to accommodate. Even as they accepted the fact of organic evolution, they generally threw aside the theory of natural selection, for its alleged cruelty and directionlessness contradicted their belief in a caring and immanent God. As historian Paul Conkin notes, Darwin in the first edition of *Origin of Species* left a narrow

[12]Numbers, *Darwinism Comes to America,* 48.

[13]George M. Marsden, *Understanding Fundamentalism and Evangelicalism* (Grand Rapids, Mich.: William B. Eerdmans Publishing, 1991), 130–31.

opening for a "Creator," and his American disciples crowded into the breach.[14] Theological liberals such as Henry Ward Beecher retreated to the shelter of "theistic evolution," claiming that evolution was merely the working out of God's blueprint for the universe and that natural history revealed clear evidence of organic progress toward perfection. The argument from design, they believed, still held.[15] Some went further and simply proclaimed that humans were not part of the evolutionary process at all, but a separate creation by God. Ironically, it would be evolution's detractors, and not its supporters, who would seek in the 1920s to identify evolution closely with Darwin's theory of natural selection and the brutal struggle for "survival of the fittest." Theistic evolutionists had made a separate peace.

The theistic, sanitized version of evolution began to make its way into textbooks and classrooms at the university and secondary levels in the 1880s. The generation of scientists and educators trained after *Origin of Species* began to write textbooks that discarded the older theory of special creation in favor of an evolutionary framework. Biology education at the college level, including that provided by institutions with a religious affiliation, rapidly reoriented itself around the central concept of organic evolution. High schools moved more slowly. Although none of the natural science books for the high school market around the turn of the century presented a particularly good explication of evolution, almost all of them included the concept. In general, public disputes over evolution seemed to belong to the past.[16]

Few observers at the time could have predicted that two decades later, the nation would witness an antievolution crusade popular enough to sponsor forty-one antievolution bills in twenty-one states

[14]Conkin, *When All the Gods Trembled,* 25–26.

[15]Moore, *The Post-Darwinian Controversies,* 216–51.

[16]Edward J. Larson, "Before the Crusade: Evolution in American Secondary Education before 1920," *Journal of the History of Biology* 20 (Spring 1987): 89–114; Edward J. Larson, *Trial and Error: The American Controversy over Creation and Evolution* (New York: Oxford University Press, 1985), 7–18; Judith V. Grabiner and Peter D. Miller, "Effects of the Scopes Trial: Was It a Victory for Evolutionists?" *Science,* 6 Sept. 1974, 832–37; Gerald Skoog, "Topic of Evolution in Secondary School Biology Textbooks: 1900–1977," *Science Education* 63 (1979): 624–27; Philip J. Pauly, "The Development of High School Biology, New York City, 1900–1925," *Isis* 82 (Dec. 1991), 685–87. The textbook at issue in the Scopes trial, George W. Hunter, *A Civic Biology* (New York: American Book Company, 1914), included marginally more evolutionary information than most of its competitors. For a few exceptions to acceptance of evolution, see Clement Eaton, "Professor James Woodrow and the Freedom of Teaching in the South," *Journal of Southern History* 28 (Feb. 1962): 3–17; and Numbers, *Darwinism Comes to America,* 67–70.

and powerful enough to suppress teaching of the subject in three states and countless localities. Fewer still would have guessed that the mantle of leadership for this crusade would come to rest on William Jennings Bryan, the "Boy Orator of the Platte" and Democratic voice of political reform. What had changed?

THE STRUGGLE AGAINST "MODERNITY" AND MODERNISM

To the casual observer, the simple answer is that *everything* had changed. Most critical for the emergence of the antievolution movement in the 1920s were what we might call the depredations of modernity—the twin novelties of a "modern" revolt against Victorian America and a "modernist" revolt against older forms of Christianity.[17] The United States was changing rapidly, and during and after the Great War, the specter of radical social and theological change inspired a deep sense of unease among millions of citizens. This broad anxiety about the future of the nation would find an outlet in the antievolution movement, and it would lend the crusade against Darwin its peculiar moral urgency.

To the millions of Americans who had grown accustomed to thinking of their country as a virtuous rural paradise for native-born white Protestants, life in the Jazz Age presented a series of painful shocks. The Jeffersonian ideal was the first to go. The 1920 census recorded that for the first time in history, more Americans lived in the city than in the country. Life in these burgeoning cities also seemed more remote than ever from the rural ideal. In the decades before the Great War, eastern and southern Europe had poured annually nearly a million immigrants—many of them Catholics and Jews—into American cities, and African Americans were slowly beginning their Great Migration from the rural South to destinations such as Chicago's South Side and New York's Harlem. The rise of the cities also allowed for the development of a class of artists and intellectuals, such as the denizens of New York's Greenwich Village, who, despite their native origins, defiantly proclaimed themselves to be outsiders and revolutionaries against America's genteel Protestant culture.

These polyglot city dwellers seemed to be developing a new "mongrel" culture of sensation. Whereas the inherited Victorian morality

[17]Larson, *Trial and Error,* 31.

held up the ideals of temperance, gentility, and sexual repression—ideals bequeathed to the nation by Protestant opinion leaders—the icons of the Jazz Age were the speakeasy, the tabloid press, and the sexually free flapper. A working-class culture built partly on "cheap amusements"—amusement parks such as Coney Island, jazz music, dance halls, and lurid motion pictures—seemed to be percolating upward socially to the "respectable" white middle class, especially the Jazz Age youth most memorably portrayed in F. Scott Fitzgerald's novel *The Beautiful and Damned.*[18] Young men and their flapper girlfriends began to give up supervised courtship for more openly sexual dating relationships. They listened to jazz, an African American music form, and engaged in such "tremendously suggestive" dances as the "fox trot" and the "shimmy."[19] They did so without apology. "Revolt has become characteristic of our age," observed a pair of prominent authors. "The intellectuals are in revolt against an entire civilization. The revolt against the old sex attitudes, with their silences and their stupidities, is a vital part of this entire revolt against a decaying culture."[20] The 1920 census suggested that this urban culture of revolt was likely to become the dominant way of life in America.

Equally alarming for many observers was the new independence of women. The youthful flappers were in some ways only mimicking the independence of their mothers and older sisters. White women had finally won the right to vote with the Nineteenth Amendment, and women in the 1920s were beginning to attend college and work outside the home in much greater numbers. With their sexual independence at least partly supported by education and income, as well as by a greater awareness of birth control, married women took the lead in calling for marriages to be more "companionate" and fulfilling, and feminist activists fought to make it easier for women to divorce husbands who could not live up to these new demands.[21] The New Woman of the 1920s—educated, independent, and feminist—may

[18]Lizabeth Cohen, *Making a New Deal: Industrial Workers in Chicago, 1919–1939* (New York: Cambridge University Press, 1990); Kathy Peiss, *Cheap Amusements: Working Women and Leisure in Turn-of-the-Century New York* (Philadelphia: Temple University Press, 1986).

[19]"Is the Younger Generation in Peril?" *Literary Digest,* 14 May 1921, 9–12. See also Paula Fass, *The Damned and the Beautiful: American Youth in the 1920's* (New York: Oxford University Press, 1977).

[20]V. F. Calverton and Samuel D. Schmalhausen, eds., *Sex in Civilization* (Garden City, N.Y.: Garden City Publishing, 1929), 12.

[21]Elaine Tyler May, *Great Expectations: Marriage and Divorce in Post-Victorian America* (Chicago: University of Chicago Press, 1980).

have been only an ideal, but she bore little resemblance to the thoroughly domestic archetype of the Victorian matron.

Nor was religion immune from the allure of the Jazz Age. Observing a weakening of elite Protestant leadership, many authors claimed that the moral slide of the 1920s was due to the "general abandonment of religion," but religion was occasionally a full participant in the new culture.[22] In Los Angeles, "Sister" Aimee Semple McPherson made a national name at the Church of the Foursquare Gospel by staging elaborate sermons with costumes, music, indoor blimps, and even scoreboards that kept tally for the forces of "good" against the forces of "evil." As "the world's most pulchritudinous evangelist," McPherson combined "sex appeal" with a sunny and sentimental theology. In New York, an advertising executive named Bruce Barton jazzed up the New Testament by retelling the life of Jesus as the "founder of modern business." In his best-selling book *The Man Nobody Knows,* Barton dressed the Messiah in all the trappings of 1920s business culture: He was a man who liked a cocktail party now and then, understood the importance of good advertising, and inspired his apostles to forge the greatest business concern ever—the Christian church. A Protestantism that needed to resort to such gimmicks seemed to be a Protestantism in decline.

The new urban culture did not go unchallenged. On the less coercive end of the spectrum, automaker Henry Ford offered his immigrant workers "Americanization" classes, as well as instruction in such old-fashioned American dances as the "Rye Waltz" and "Pop Goes the Weasel," in order to supplant "the sensuous jazz wriggling of the modern cabaret."[23] The Young Women's Christian Association (YWCA) and related groups attempted to instruct young ladies in the niceties of "proper" behavior. Less gently, the prohibition crusade aimed directly to impose a version of Protestant morality on liquor-drinking city dwellers and seemed to have victory in its hands with the passage of the Eighteenth Amendment in 1919. In the early years of the 1920s, the prohibition experiment boasted of significant support from middle-class city dwellers, but the sinews of the temperance movement had long been residents of rural states—especially "native-stock" Protestants—who were concerned about the immorality of the cities.[24]

[22]Katherine Fullerton Gerould, "Reflections of a Grundy Cousin," *Atlantic Monthly,* Aug. 1920, 158.

[23]*Baltimore Sun,* 16 July 1925, 1.

[24]Jack S. Blocker, *American Temperance Movements: Cycles of Reform* (Boston: Twayne, 1989).

On the right wing of reaction against the new culture marched the Ku Klux Klan. The Klan was reborn in 1915 to reassert the dominance of white Protestant leadership over the supposed immorality of urban ethnics, Jews, Catholics, and African Americans.[25] Note that "immorality" in this equation carried almost as much weight as racial or ethnic difference. In the Klan's vision, immigrants, labor radicals, and sexual "revolutionaries" together presented an indivisible challenge to white Protestant authority. Indeed, the Klan expended nearly as much energy policing the length of women's dresses and fighting "flapperism" as it did reinforcing the barriers of race. Although the Klan explicitly opposed evolution as a threat to Protestant belief—Klan strongholds were usually centers of antievolutionist sentiment—it is also worth noting that, in the early 1920s, the Klan tried to organize a klavern (local unit) in Dayton, Tennessee, but failed. Nevertheless, the Klan's aggressively traditional message attracted well over a million members and tens of millions of sympathizers. With the aid of its women's auxiliary, during stretches of the 1920s it ruled politics in much of the South and in states as far away as Colorado and Indiana. In the culture clash between the old and the new, the city and the country, each side had its partisans.

To many conservative Christians, the cultural degradation presented by modernity—urbanization, "mongrelization," sensationalism, and the flock of other "isms" that characterized life in the Jazz Age—had its theological counterpart in the threat posed by "modernism," a more liberal approach to interpreting the Bible. Thus, as conservative Protestants struggled to reassert their dominance in public life, they found that they also had to fight for dominance in their own churches against the modernist heresy. Like the clash over the direction of American culture, the battle over the soul of American Protestantism being waged by modernists and the growing ranks of their fundamentalist opponents was to spill over into the antievolution controversy.

The antievolution movement cannot be understood apart from its roots in the subvariety of Protestant Christianity that came to be known in 1919 as fundamentalism. Although the roots of fundamentalism were old and diverse, theological fundamentalism in the 1910s came to be associated with five or six central doctrines that all "true Christians"—especially ministers and faculty at the theological

[25] Nancy MacLean, *Behind the Mask of Chivalry: The Making of the Second Ku Klux Klan* (New York: Oxford University Press, 1994); Kathleen M. Blee, *Women of the Klan: Racism and Gender in the 1920s* (Berkeley: University of California Press, 1991).

seminaries—must believe, including the inerrancy of Scripture, the virgin birth of Jesus, the sacrifice of Jesus to atone for human sins, the bodily resurrection of Jesus, and either the authenticity of biblical miracles or the inevitability of Jesus' return to earth to usher in a millennium of peace. The doctrines made sense as an attempt by conservative theologians to shore up Christian belief where the progress of science seemed to threaten it most.[26]

The fundamentalist movement developed its theology and identity in opposition to modernism—the theological liberals' effort to reconcile science and faith after the Darwinian revolution. Modernists such as Shailer Mathews at the University of Chicago asserted that the Bible employed symbolic and allegorical language to convey God's meaning to the ancient chroniclers. Modernists thus accommodated what was known as the "higher criticism," which used historical and literary tools to uncover the Bible's historical context. Modernists also embraced scientific discoveries, including evolution, as part of God's continuing revelation to his followers, and they felt few qualms about leaving behind the Bible's literal descriptions of the natural world. Following the literal words of the Bible was less compelling for modernists than uncovering what Mathews called the "spirit and purpose" of Jesus Christ's moral teachings.[27]

Conservative believers argued that such claptrap substituted human whims for divine authority. "The Bible is either the Word of God or merely a man-made book," William Jennings Bryan explained in an article in 1923. "When all the miracles and all the supernatural are eliminated from the Bible it becomes a 'scrap of paper.'"[28] Bryan, a conservative Presbyterian, argued vigorously in favor of a fundamentalist approach to the Bible. Without miracles, without the literal truth of the Bible, fundamentalists believed, Jesus becomes a mere mortal, and his ideas carry no more weight, no more compelling authority, than any other teacher's lessons. The result of the modernists' campaign, therefore, would be moral anarchy. "When the Bible ceases to be an authority—a divine authority—the Word of God can be accepted, rejected, or mutilated, according to the whim or mood of the reader," Bryan concluded.[29] America in the 1920s seemed to be suffering from a kind of moral anarchy: Did not the immoral life in the cities

[26]Conkin, *When All the Gods Trembled*, 65.
[27]Shailer Mathews, *The Faith of Modernism* (New York: Macmillan, 1924), 36.
[28]William Jennings Bryan, "The Fundamentals," *Forum* 70 (July 1923): 1666, 1675.
[29]Ibid., 1668.

suggest that millions of Americans had already closed their ears to the divine authority of the Bible? Biblical literalists resolved to fight against any arguments that undermined the Bible's factual veracity.

In 1919, the uncoordinated struggle for conservative orthodoxy found an institutional home, as more than six thousand crusaders came together in Philadelphia for the first conference of the World's Christian Fundamentals Association (WCFA), an interdenominational organization created by William Bell Riley, a prominent Baptist minister in Minneapolis. As historian George Marsden has argued, these fundamentalists became distinct not so much for their theology as for their militancy in seeking to return the churches and the nation to righteousness.[30] But they awaited a legitimate leader and an issue powerful enough to unify their energies. They did not have to wait long.

WILLIAM JENNINGS BRYAN AND THE ANTIEVOLUTION ARGUMENT

At first, the militancy of the fundamentalists spent itself in scattershot crusades—the sins of the mainstream culture and the errors of the modernists were everywhere—but within three years of the first WCFA conference, the leading fundamentalists had united behind the conviction that Darwinian evolution was the one great evil that fed modernism, urbanism, sensationalism, and most of the other transgressions that seemed to be crowding in upon the faithful. To understand how cultural and religious discontent came to be harnessed in the antievolution movement of the 1920s, one must first understand the movement's leader, William Jennings Bryan.

Despite accusations that Bryan turned to antievolutionism only because he had failed as a politician, one thing is clear: The "Great Commoner" had not changed. The Bryan who called for public schools to measure their science teaching by the standards of the Bible was the same Bryan who in 1896 had fought Wall Street on behalf of the nation's farmers and debtors. He was the same Bryan who had demanded the direct election of senators and helped push women's suffrage into the Constitution. As with these other crusades for reform, Bryan was not the founder of the antievolution movement,

[30]George Marsden, "Fundamentalism as an American Phenomenon: A Comparison with English Evangelicalism," *Church History* 46 (June 1977): 225–28.

but he became its mouthpiece, his baritone voice amplifying the protests of millions of largely rural Protestants against an increasingly urban, secular culture.

Protestant Christianity was always the lamp by which Bryan guided his steps. Born in 1860 in Illinois, William Jennings Bryan grew up in an intensely pious household. Until the age of twelve, he attended Sunday school twice a week, once at his father's Baptist church and once at his mother's Methodist church. Bryan foreshadowed the dual importance of religion and politics in his life when he was converted at a Presbyterian revival in his fifteenth year. Not only did Presbyterianism fit well with the habits he had already learned in what he called his "Christian home," but the Presbyterian church was the largest church in town, and the budding politician was eager to accompany seventy of his classmates who joined the church at the same time.[31] Once in, Bryan stayed converted. He eventually became a lay elder of the Presbyterian church and worked as diligently at church politics as he did in the politics of the nation.

For Bryan, the two kinds of politics could not be separated. Bryan always interpreted political reform as part of the Christian mission to move man closer to God's vision of earthly perfection. Indeed, much of Bryan's strength as a politician lay in his ability to marshal the spirit and rhetoric of the nation's Christian heritage. "You shall not press down upon the brow of labor this crown of thorns," Bryan proclaimed during the 1896 Democratic convention, at the climax of his most famous speech. "You shall not crucify mankind upon a cross of gold!" At the height of his political power, Bryan also made a point of delivering purely religious lectures. The antievolution crusade was fully consistent with this vision. Conversely, he continued to be involved in the Democratic party even as he led the antievolution forces. The year before the Scopes trial, Bryan was still a potent force at the Democrats' marathon convention in New York, and during the 1924 campaign, he lectured vigorously on behalf of the ticket, which included his younger brother in the vice-presidential slot. Bryan continued comfortably to mix piety with politics; in his own mind, he had changed not at all.

And yet, on the long road from his first presidential candidacy to the Scopes trial, Bryan had witnessed an enormous shift in the character of his world. In response, he began to alter the emphasis, but not

[31] William Jennings Bryan and Mary Baird Bryan, *The Memoirs of William Jennings Bryan* (Philadelphia: United Publishers of America, 1925), 44–48.

Trial Participants
At center stands William Jennings Bryan. A spellbinding orator with strong roots in conservative Protestantism, Bryan led the antievolution charge in Tennessee. The presiding judge in the Scopes trial, John T. Raulston, is second from left.

the principles, of his public activity.[32] Shortly after the turn of the century, Bryan had announced his distaste for evolutionary theory, but at that time he did not find evolution troubling enough to "quarrel" about. During and after the Great War, however, Bryan increasingly focused his attention on what he considered evolutionary theory's three great crimes: It provided a rationale for warfare; it undercut the impulse for political reform; and, perhaps most important for his future fundamentalist allies, it contradicted biblical revelation.

Bryan had long believed that Darwinism constituted an endorsement of warfare, and the danger of this endorsement seemed more pressing after Europe marched into the slaughterhouse of the

[32]Lawrence W. Levine, *Defender of the Faith: William Jennings Bryan: The Last Decade, 1915–1925* (New York: Oxford University Press, 1965), 250.

Great War. As President Woodrow Wilson's secretary of state, Bryan vigorously opposed America's becoming entangled in the European conflict, and when Wilson seemed to tilt too consistently toward war, Bryan made that rarest of political maneuvers—a principled resignation from office. In office and out, Bryan searched for the causes of Europe's great conflagration, and he gradually became convinced that Germany's militarism and "barbarism" had grown directly from the German belief that a Darwinian "struggle for survival" applied not only to individuals but also to the nations of the world.[33] Darwin and his German acolyte, the philosopher Friedrich Nietzsche, supposedly had spurred the German high command into action.

Bryan also became convinced that Darwinism was an immediate threat at home. As early as his famous "Prince of Peace" speech in 1904, Bryan had fretted that Darwinism undermined the cause of social reform in the United States. "The Darwinian theory," he explained, "represents man as reaching his present perfection by the operation of the law of hate—the merciless law by which the strong crowd out and kill off the weak."[34] Bryan had heard far too many conservatives justify their opposition to reform by appealing to what came to be called "social Darwinism," with its claim that socialism, social uplift, and other forms of mutual aid interfered with the "laws of nature."[35] With the end of the Great War, the United States seemed to be withdrawing even further from the reform impulse. Bryan saw, for example, that many of Darwin's staunchest American defenders had also become committed eugenicists, calling for the imprisonment or sterilization of thousands of Americans whose mental weakness or "moral feebleness" made them unfit for the struggle for existence.[36] Rather than aiding the weak, as Bryan

[33]Levine, *Defender of the Faith,* 261–62. Bryan derived his conclusions largely from Vernon Kellogg, *Headquarters Nights: A Record of Conversations and Experiences at the Headquarters of the German Army in France and Belgium* (Boston: Atlantic Monthly Press, 1917), and Benjamin Kidd, *The Science of Power* (New York: G. P. Putnam's Sons, 1918).

[34]William Jennings Bryan, "The Prince of Peace," in *William Jennings Bryan: Selections,* ed. Ray Ginger (New York: Bobbs-Merrill Company, 1967), 138–41.

[35]The classic expression of this came in William Graham Sumner, *What Social Classes Owe to Each Other* (New York: Harper & Brothers, 1883); Richard Hofstadter, *Social Darwinism in American Thought: 1860–1915* (Philadelphia: University of Pennsylvania Press, 1944); Donald C. Bellomy, "Social Darwinism Revisited," *Perspectives in American History,* n.s., 1 (1984): 1–130.

[36]Kidd, *Science of Power,* 77–83. See Nicole Hahn Rafter, ed., *White Trash: The Eugenic Family Studies, 1877–1919* (Boston: Northeastern University Press, 1988); Daniel Kevles, *In the Name of Eugenics: Genetics and the Uses of Human Heredity,* new ed. (Cambridge: Harvard University Press, 1995), 3–19, 41–69, 110–12; John Higham,

sought to do for his entire career, many Darwinians seemed bent on eliminating them.[37]

And yet Bryan felt that warfare and social Darwinism were but secondary effects of Darwinism's greatest impact: its erosion of faith in God. Theories of evolution contradicted the miraculous account of creation in the Bible, and the scientific focus on mechanistic and naturalistic explanations seemed to leave no place, in Bryan's opinion, for those moments in which God suspended the laws of nature to allow for the virgin birth of Jesus, for example, or to raise Jesus from the dead three days after the Crucifixion. On theological grounds alone, Darwinism—and perhaps any modern science—posed a problem for Bryan's brand of faith in the Bible.

Further, Bryan uncovered empirical evidence that evolution and scientific education were weakening Christian belief. According to his memoirs, as Bryan lectured throughout the country during and after the Great War, many parents began to approach him to complain that something was happening to their children in college. "How I wish our son could have heard you," said one weeping mother. "He has lost his faith." A father told him that one of his lectures had been the only thing that had salvaged his daughter's belief while she was a university student.[38] At a time when the newspapers and magazines were clogged with articles about the revolt in manners and morals among Jazz Age youths, such stories about the decline in adolescent faith resonated deeply. Bryan found confirmation of his worst fears about the impact of higher education in James Leuba's *The Belief in God and Immortality,* a 1916 book that concluded that fully 40 to 45 percent of college students had given up their belief in the "fundamental" Christian doctrines of "a personal God" and "personal immortality" during their college years.[39] Conservative Christians were already fond of noting that Charles Darwin himself had moved reluctantly from orthodox Christian belief to what Bryan called "helpless and hopeless agnosticism." Now Bryan applied this knowledge to Leuba's findings and reached a clear conclusion: "The teaching of evolution as

Strangers in the Land: Patterns of American Nativism, 1860–1925, 2nd ed. (New Brunswick, N.J.: Rutgers University Press, 1988).

[37]On Bryan's (and others') misinterpretation of Darwin, see Stephen Jay Gould, *Bully for Brontosaurus: Reflections in Natural History* (New York: W. W. Norton & Co., 1991), 421, 426–27.

[38]Bryan and Bryan, *Memoirs,* 479.

[39]James H. Leuba, *The Belief in God and Immortality: A Psychological, Anthropological and Statistical Study* (Boston: Sherman, French & Co., 1916), 280.

a fact instead of theory caused the students to lose faith in the Bible."[40]

To Bryan, the Darwinian threats were all of a piece. Darwinism skulked behind German militarism and offered a mask of authority to those who would crush the weak in the name of the strong. Evolution shook believers' faith in the literal truth of Genesis and the Bible, and it provided models of scientific investigation and historical change that seemed heavily to influence modernist theology. "The unproven hypothesis of evolution," Bryan concluded in 1923, "is the root cause of nearly all the dissention in the church."[41] Finally, in the schools, Darwinism sapped the students' Christian spirit and turned them against their parents' faith. During the Great War and its aftermath, Bryan concluded that Darwinism was gaining the upper hand. He was not alone.

In the first years of the 1920s, millions of Americans began to heed Bryan's cry for a crusade against evolution. Typically less concerned than Bryan over Darwin's impact on social reform, many fundamentalists found much greater cause for alarm in the connection between evolutionary thought and Germany—the heartland of biblical criticism and the font of European militarism. "If you turn hell upside down," the evangelist Billy Sunday shouted in his sermons during the war, "you will find 'Made in Germany' stamped on the bottom!"[42] Darwinism's association with America's enemy in the Great War did little to recommend it to patriots. Further, as they surveyed the rapidly shifting culture in postwar America, conservative Protestants could readily believe that here, too, Darwinism was eroding the nation's moral foundations by substituting "materialism" and modernism for faith in the Bible.[43] In the first years of the 1920s, these preachers and theologians largely transformed the fundamentalist movement into an antievolution crusade.

[40]William Jennings Bryan, "Text of Bryan's Proposed Address in Scopes Case," in *The World's Most Famous Court Trial: Tennessee Evolution Case* (1925; reprint, Dayton, Tenn.: Rhea County Historical Society, 1979), 328; Bryan and Bryan, *Memoirs,* 479.

[41]Bryan, "The Fundamentals," 1675.

[42]Quoted in George M. Marsden, *Fundamentalism and American Culture: The Shaping of Twentieth-Century Evangelicalism: 1870–1925* (New York: Oxford University Press, 1980), 142.

[43]Bryan, "The Fundamentals," 1675; Edward J. Larson, *Summer for the Gods: The Scopes Trial and America's Continuing Debate over Science and Religion* (New York: Basic Books, 1997), 36–37; Ronald L. Numbers, *The Creationists* (New York: Alfred A. Knopf, 1992), 35–36.

For a while, antievolutionism would function very effectively as a unifying symbol for a wide variety of conservative Christians. Antievolutionism allowed fundamentalists of many stripes to join together in defense of the literal Bible. Presbyterians, Baptists, and innumerable nondenominational believers could at least agree that the Bible was the authoritative word of God and that evolution directly contradicted its message.[44] Further, fundamentalists could attack evolution as a symbol of social trends that threatened the traditional order of America. The *Nashville Tennessean* exemplified this approach when it lumped evolutionists together with "the liberals, the feminists, the radicals of all degrees and shades, the birth controlists [*sic*], the psycho-analysts, the agnostics . . . the Socialists, social service workers, professional 'causers.' "[45] Before this threat of radical social change, the antievolutionists' other doctrinal differences faded into the background.

Finally, the embrace of antievolutionism gave fundamentalism the enthusiastic participation of Bryan, a man with a national reputation, a weekly column syndicated in approximately one hundred newspapers, and an army of loyalists. Any crusade that Bryan endorsed immediately became a national force.[46] Antievolutionism galvanized other crusaders as well. Underlining the lack of organized church leadership on the issue, the layman Bryan was joined not by prominent theologians but by such popular evangelists as T. T. Martin, Dallas's J. Frank Norris, and the flamboyant former major-league ballplayer Billy Sunday.[47] These men crisscrossed the nation, especially the South, and as they delivered antievolution sermons to hundreds of thousands of the faithful, they hardened vague antievolution sentiment into militant resistance.

[44]Jeanette Keith, *Country People in the New South: Tennessee's Upper Cumberland* (Chapel Hill: University of North Carolina Press, 1995), 2–3.

[45]*Nashville Tennessean,* 21 June 1925, 11. See also Marsden, "Fundamentalism as an American Phenomenon," 215.

[46]Levine, *Defender of the Faith,* 272.

[47]Numbers, *Creationists,* 19. Some scholars have ascribed the birth of antievolutionism at this time in part to the death of such orthodox Christian evolutionists as Asa Gray, George Frederick Wright, and Joseph LeConte, but the decentralized nature of American Protestantism, especially in the South, would certainly have limited their influence even if they had lived into the 1920s. J. Gresham Machen, for example, seldom made his voice heard above Billy Sunday's simplistic roar. See Willard B. Gatewood Jr., *Preachers, Pedagogues, and Politicians: The Evolution Controversy in North Carolina* (Chapel Hill: University of North Carolina Press, 1966), 9–10.

THE BUTLER BILL AND THE FIGHT FOR THE PUBLIC SCHOOLS

With evolution replacing modernism as the fundamentalists' central concern, the battleground shifted from the denominations to the public schools. "The teaching of Evolution," complained the evangelist T. T. Martin in *Hell and the High Schools,* "is being drilled into our boys and girls in our High Schools during the most susceptible, dangerous age of their lives."[48] For the sake of their children and their faith, antievolutionists drew a line against evolution at the schoolhouse door.

Education's impact on faith had become a pressing question by the 1920s because of the massive expansion of public secondary education. Teaching Darwin in the high schools had been hardly a public issue in the late nineteenth century, when each year only about 200,000 youths, or less than 5 percent of high-school-age children, attended secondary school. By 1920, however, attendance had shot up to nearly 2 million students per year, making the public schools a central object of political and social concern.[49] Intense public controversies broke out over topics such as sex education, teacher radicalism, and the patriotism of history textbooks, for now the content of the curriculum affected so many more children and their families.[50] The proliferation of public schools similarly brought thousands of "impressionable" youths into contact with evolutionary science for the first time, alarming many parents and religious conservatives. Thus, when the antievolution movement around 1922 made the teaching of evolution in the schools its central theme, many Americans were ready to listen.

Under inspiration from the Kentucky General Assembly, antievolutionists turned to legislation to rescue the schools from Darwinism. In the winter of 1921–22, the Kentucky General Assembly considered the nation's first law to ban the teaching of Darwinian evolution in the

[48]T. T. Martin, *Hell and the High Schools: Christ or Evolution: Which?* (Kansas City, Mo.: Western Baptist Publishing Co., 1923).

[49]Larson, "Before the Crusade," 112–13.

[50]Jeffrey P. Moran, "'Modernism Gone Mad': Sex Education Comes to Chicago, 1913," *Journal of American History* 83 (Sept. 1996): 481–513; Jonathan Zimmerman, "'Each "Race" Could Have Its Heroes Sung': Ethnicity and the History Wars in the 1920's," *Journal of American History* 87 (June 2000): 92–111; American Civil Liberties Union (ACLU) Committee on Academic Freedom, *The Gag on Teaching* (New York: ACLU, 1931).

public schools. Such moralistic legislation was in some ways a natural tool for the antievolutionists. The early 1920s were still heady days for the prohibition experiment, and the antievolution crusade not only repeated the temperance movement's own progress from voluntarism to coercion but drew its leadership and much of its support from the same source.[51] A similar faith in the power of laws to enforce Christian behavior led many Americans to propose bills against "petting," flirtation, "Hollywood smut," and a variety of other Jazz Age offenses.[52] Although the Kentucky antievolution bill went down on a very narrow vote, the idea spread to North Carolina, Oklahoma, and Bryan's adopted home state of Florida.[53]

In January 1925, antievolution legislation took root in Tennessee. John Washington Butler, a farmer and Primitive Baptist from rural Macon County, rose in the Tennessee House of Representatives to propose an act to "prohibit the teaching of evolution in the public schools of Tennessee." Although Bryan would later privately disagree with the law's criminal penalties for teachers found in violation, the Butler bill clearly expressed the antievolution movement's intentions: It applied to all schools supported "in whole or in part by the public school funds of the state," and it made it a crime there to teach "any theory that denies the story of the Divine creation of man as taught in the Bible, and to teach instead that man has descended from a lower order of animals."

The Tennessee House of Representatives passed the antievolution bill almost casually by a margin of 71 to 5. In the Tennessee Senate, however, the bill quickly became bogged down in controversy. One senator jokingly proposed an amendment "to require teachers to teach that the world is not round," and a more serious body of Nashville ministers sent a petition urging the chamber to vote the Butler bill down.[54] On the other side, Billy Sunday and other evangelists began preaching in support of the bill to hundreds of thousands of enthusiastic Tennesseans in Memphis and other cities. In the senate, supporters distributed to the legislators copies of William Jennings Bryan's most recent antievolution speech, delivered in Nashville the previous year, and the speaker of the senate left the podium to defend the bill

[51]Frank R. Kent, "Evolution War Similar to Wet and Dry Fight," *Baltimore Sun,* 14 July 1925, 1; Larson, *Trial and Error,* 35–36.

[52]Gatewood, *Preachers,* 24–25.

[53]Larson, *Trial and Error,* 47–48; Gatewood, *Preachers,* 106–8.

[54]*Nashville Tennessean,* 14 Mar. 1925, 8.

as a last stand for Christianity, civilization, and motherhood.[55] By a vote of 24 to 6, the senate approved the bill and sent it to Governor Austin Peay. On March 23, 1925, the governor duly signed the Butler bill into law on the general assumption that nobody would be fool enough to enforce a law whose major intent was to reassure voters that their legislators believed in Genesis.

What allowed this to happen? Some critics blamed the law on the ignorance of rural legislators, exemplified by Butler himself, who had passed through only four years of public schooling and who lived in a county burdened with an illiteracy rate of 22 percent for whites and 31 percent for African Americans.[56] Support for the bill was indeed strongest in the rural districts, but legislative delegations from more urban counties also generally supported the bill by large majorities.[57] A better explanation for why the Butler bill passed comes from simple politics. Surely, many legislators believed deeply in the bill, but perhaps a larger number responded more directly to its tremendous popularity. In the weeks leading up to the senate vote, sermons, newspaper columns, and letters to the senators all emphasized the bill's strong support among Tennessee residents of every class and geographic location. The antievolution crusaders had done their work well.

At the same time, the Butler bill's natural opponents remained largely silent. Unlike their counterparts in Kentucky and North Carolina, faculty and students at the University of Tennessee did not raise a protest. The university had only recently become a state-supported institution, and its president was afraid that speaking out against the antievolution law would jeopardize further legislative appropriations. An insecure, mediocre faculty followed his example. The university's caution paid off when the same legislature extended an unprecedented million-dollar appropriation later in the session.[58] Many newspaper editors and prominent attorneys were likewise unwilling to oppose publicly a bill that they privately considered dangerous. The lonely dissent from Vanderbilt University in Nashville carried little

[55] W. B. Marr to William Jennings Bryan, 6 July 1925, in Bryan and Bryan, *Memoirs,* 481; *Nashville Tennessean,* 14 Mar. 1925, 8.

[56] "No Monkeying with Evolution in Tennessee," *Literary Digest,* 18 Apr. 1925, 30.

[57] Kenneth K. Bailey, "The Enactment of Tennessee's Antievolution Law," *Journal of Southern History* 16 (Nov. 1950): 488–89.

[58] James Riley Montgomery, Stanley J. Folmsbee, and Lee Seifert Greene, *To Foster Knowledge: A History of the University of Tennessee, 1794–1970* (Knoxville: University of Tennessee Press, 1984), 185–89.

weight with legislators. Indeed, raucous protests by Vanderbilt students sitting in the senate galleries seemed only to bolster support for the bill.[59] "In Tennessee," concluded Joseph Wood Krutch, a native who had become a nationally recognized journalist, "bigotry is militant and sincere; intelligence is timid and hypocritical."[60]

In the absence of significant opposition, the antievolution law promised political benefits to its supporters. Governor Peay, in particular, had been trying to steer through the legislature a general education bill to lengthen the school term and provide unprecedented support for the state's feeble public education system. His decision to sign the Butler bill into law was motivated in part by his need to secure support from "the church people" for the general education bill.[61] Despite misgivings, Peay comforted himself with the idea that the Butler law was merely symbolic, "a distinct protest against an irreligious tendency to exalt so-called science, and deny the Bible in some schools and quarters." Peay concluded in his message to the legislature, "Nobody believes that it is going to be an active statute."[62] The Butler law thus allowed educational reformers such as Peay to modernize the education system in Tennessee while allaying popular fears of social change. Rather than threatening Tennessee's traditional folkways, the expanded public school system was to become another instrument for conveying traditional morality.[63] Conscience and convenience thus combined to bring overwhelming support to Tennessee's antievolution law.

Governor Peay and many Tennessee legislators clearly hoped that passing the Butler bill would extinguish the evolutionary agitation in the state, and lawmakers were surely encouraged that many Tennesseans wrote letters to newspapers supporting the antievolution law. Mrs. E. P. Blair, for example, noted in the *Nashville Tennessean* that she and other mothers had long been distressed by children learning in school that evolutionary science had proven the Bible wrong. "What are mothers to do," Blair asked, "when unwise education makes boys lose confidence in the home, the bible, the government

[59]Dixon Merritt, "The Theatrical Performance at Dayton," *Outlook,* 15 July 1925, 391; Joseph Wood Krutch, "Tennessee: Where Cowards Rule," *Nation,* 15 July 1925, 88–89.

[60]Krutch, "Tennessee: Where Cowards Rule," 88.

[61]Andrew David Holt, *The Struggle for a State System of Public Schools in Tennessee, 1903–1936,* Contributions to Education, no. 753 (New York: Teachers College, Columbia University, 1938), 345–56.

[62]Austin Peay, quoted in *Nashville Tennessean,* 24 Mar. 1925, 1.

[63]Keith, *Country People in the New South,* 198–99, 208.

and all law?" The Butler Act, she hoped, would prevent this "unwise education" from "acting as a wedge" between children and mothers, and between Americans and their "moral and spiritual" values.[64]

Despite such support, Peay's signature seemed to ignite the flames of a much hotter controversy. Mrs. Blair's words were soon crowded out by letters denouncing the Butler law even in Tennessee newspapers. Observers outside the South were particularly uncharitable. Newspapers everywhere printed cartoons comparing the Tennessee legislators unfavorably with their monkey "relatives," and an editorialist in the *Chicago Tribune* foresaw laws mandating the teaching of biblically accurate "flat earth" theories and a value of 3 for pi spreading out from Tennessee across what he called the "illiteracy belt."[65]

MAKING A TEST CASE

To the men and women in the New York office of the American Civil Liberties Union (ACLU), the Butler Act was no joke. On the contrary, the act seemed to echo too closely the laws that had prompted Roger Baldwin to found the ACLU in the first place. During the Great War, President Woodrow Wilson's Justice Department had used the Espionage Act and the Sedition Act as tools for crushing "disloyalty" to the war effort. During and after the war, localities also passed laws demanding loyalty oaths among teachers and laws forbidding workers from forming labor unions.[66] Galvanized by these threats, Baldwin founded what became the ACLU, an organization dedicated to protecting individual civil liberties and the rights of labor against the rule of the majority.[67] Reading news reports of the Butler bill's progress, Baldwin concluded that the law violated both freedom of speech and the rights of labor for teachers and that it embodied ugly trends already in existence and promised worse for the future. The ACLU sought to launch a test case against the "monkey law" and advertised in Tennessee newspapers for a willing plaintiff.

The ACLU's advertisement produced a response only in the unlikely village of Dayton, Tennessee. Perhaps justifying Joseph Wood Krutch's accusations of timidity, opponents to the Butler law in large

[64] Mrs. E. P. Blair, letter to the editor, *Nashville Tennessean,* 16 Mar. 1925, 4.

[65] Editorial, *Chicago Tribune* [n.d.], reprinted in *Nashville Tennessean,* 20 Mar. 1925, 4.

[66] David M. Kennedy, *Over Here: The First World War and American Society* (New York: Oxford University Press, 1980), 45–92.

[67] Larson, *Summer for the Gods,* 61–67.

cities such as Memphis, Nashville, and even Knoxville, the home of the University of Tennessee, kept quiet. But a small group of men meeting in Robinson's Drugstore in Dayton hatched a plot to bring the test case—and, they hoped, a great deal of positive publicity—to their small town in eastern Tennessee. All they needed was a defendant, and so on May 5, 1925, the Dayton "boosters" asked a young general science teacher named John Thomas Scopes if he was willing to stand for a friendly trial. Like the others, Scopes had no idea what he was getting himself into, but he joined the scheme with little hesitation.

Twenty-four years old at the time of the trial and a native of Kentucky, Scopes was typically described as "quiet" and "popular," but he had inherited a strain of unorthodoxy from his father, an immigrant labor organizer, and he was convinced that the Butler law was a threat to freedom.[68] Better yet, Scopes had little to lose: Any social disapproval that might have followed his action would have little impact on a young, single man only recently arrived in town and unlikely to stay for long. Although it is not clear that Scopes had ever taught about evolution, he was willing to admit that he had for the purposes of the case. With pleasant feelings all around—a sense that the trial was going to be more a public debate than a criminal proceeding—Scopes "confessed" to the local constable that he had taught a class about evolution from George W. Hunter's *A Civic Biology,* which was, after all, the officially adopted biology textbook for the public schools of Tennessee. The constable duly arrested the "Darwin Bootlegger" under the Butler law. Meanwhile, the boosters contacted the ACLU and the newspapers.[69] The superintendent of schools captured the excitement that immediately coursed through all the local participants: "Something has happened that's going to put Dayton on the map!"[70]

The outlines of that map, however, were still blurry. Whereas the ACLU wanted a narrow legal challenge to the law, Daytonians were hunting for publicity. The point of the test case grew still more confused when William Jennings Bryan and Clarence Darrow signed on for prosecution and the defense, respectively. Bryan joined the trial first, under prodding from William Bell Riley and others in the WCFA. Bryan was spurred on not only by his antievolutionist philosophy but also by his democratic majoritarianism—his conviction that the large

[68]John T. Scopes and James Presley, *Center of the Storm: Memoirs of John T. Scopes* (New York: Holt, Rinehart and Winston, 1967), 5–12.

[69]*Memphis Commercial Appeal,* 7 May 1925, 1.

[70]Quotation and particulars of the arrest from Larson, *Summer for the Gods,* 88–96.

John Thomas Scopes
Twenty-four years old at the time of the trial, Scopes was a well-regarded general science teacher at the high school. He did not testify during the trial but spoke after the sentencing to protest what he considered to be an "unjust law."
© Bettmann/CORBIS.

Opposite: *Dayton "Conspirators" during the Trial*
Some of the "boosters" responsible for bringing the test case of the Butler law to Dayton sit around a table at Robinson's Drugstore, scene of the original plot. From left to right are George W. Rappleyea, school superintendent Walter White, Clay Green, and the drugstore's owner, Fred E. Robinson.
© Underwood & Underwood/CORBIS.

majority of Tennesseans who opposed Darwinism had a right to protect their children from hearing about it in the schools. Occasionally, Bryan would describe the contest in even broader terms. On the eve of the trial, he announced that the case came down to only one real question: "Is there a God?"[71] Bryan's presence complicated matters for the ACLU.

The situation deteriorated further when Clarence Darrow, largely in response to Bryan's involvement, offered his services for the defense. The ACLU had already negotiated with several prominent attorneys to represent Scopes, including a future chief justice of the Supreme Court, but Scopes decided instead to engage the controversial Darrow and his associates. "It was going to be a down-in-the-mud fight," Scopes explained, "and I felt the situation demanded an Indian

[71]"Issue Remains Clouded on Eve of Scopes Trial," *Baltimore Evening Sun,* 9 July 1925, 1.

fighter rather than someone who had graduated from the proper military academy."[72] The "Indian fighter" Darrow, however, brought his own baggage to the case. His notoriety as a radical and an agnostic scared off the ACLU's more mainstream attorneys, and his prejudices shifted the defense's priorities. Darrow saw the trial less as a test case than as a public forum for attacking religion with the arguments he and a generation of village skeptics had learned at the feet of Robert G. Ingersoll, the great nineteenth-century agnostic. Throughout the trial and the appeal, therefore, the ACLU would engage in a series of comic maneuvers to elbow Darrow aside, but the man would not be moved. Bryan offered too inviting a target, and the Scopes trial too grand a stage. This was, in fact, the only case in Darrow's long career in which he offered his services for free. Bryan's and Darrow's participation promised to put Dayton even more prominently on the map, but not for the reasons the ACLU intended.[73]

[72] Scopes and Presley, *Center of the Storm,* 70.
[73] Larson, *Summer for the Gods,* 98–103.

OPENING DAY: THE ATTORNEYS AND THEIR STRATEGIES

As the opening day of the Scopes trial drew near, spectators and journalists began to drive over recently paved country roads toward Dayton. In cars marked "Evolution Special" and "Monkeyland Bound," they climbed through the ancient hills of the Cumberland Plateau, past small farms devoted to corn, sweet potatoes, and strawberries, and past barn door signs asking, "Where Will You Spend Eternity?"[74] At the end of their journey, they found Dayton, a tidy valley village of about twenty-two hundred inhabitants that H. L. Mencken grudgingly admitted was "full of charm and even beauty."[75]

Editorialists throughout Tennessee had been fretting that Dayton's boosters were planning to make a circus of the trial, but except for one short-lived movement to erect a stadium or tent for the court proceedings, Daytonians retained a sense of sobriety. Unfortunately, many visitors brought their circus with them. The number of tourists arriving in Dayton was disappointingly small, but an alarming percentage of them seemed to be street performers and traveling evangelists from various exotic denominations. The less prepared set up soapboxes on the sidewalk for singing and preaching. The more enterprising T. T. Martin mounted promotional banners regarding *Hell and the High Schools* and sold antievolution literature from a large table near the courthouse. "From the beginning to the end of the test case," Scopes later recalled, "Ringling Brothers or Barnum and Bailey would have been pressed hard to produce more acts and sideshows and freaks than Dayton had."[76]

These performers were only warm-ups to the main attraction. On the terrifically hot morning of Friday, July 10, 1925, Scopes and his defense team squeezed into the Rhea County courtroom past approximately one thousand spectators and reporters. Scopes's big-city lawyers were a mixed bunch. Clarence Darrow was now sixty-eight years old, and the previous thirty years spent as America's foremost defense attorney seemed etched into the deep lines of his face. Darrow's grandfatherly appearance, noted one reporter, concealed a sharp, cynical mind and "a grim, sardonic humor."[77] Along

[74]Car signs from *Nashville Tennessean,* 26 June 1925, 2; other descriptions from *Baltimore Sun,* 9 July 1925, 1.

[75]H. L. Mencken, "Mencken Finds Daytonians Full of Sickening Doubts about Value of Publicity," *Baltimore Evening Sun,* 9 July 1925, 1.

[76]Scopes and Presley, *Center of the Storm,* 77.

[77]*Baltimore Sun,* 14 July 1925, 1.

with Darrow came his associate Dudley Field Malone—the "slick city fellow"—a wealthy divorce attorney from New York who would impress many in Dayton with his powerful voice, his Irish wit, and his refusal to take off his natty wool suit coat despite the wilting heat; Arthur Garfield Hays, another rich radical attorney from New York, who was the only lawyer directly associated with the ACLU to begin with and who, like Darrow, had learned a deep distrust of majority rule as a result of defending unpopular cases; and John Randolph Neal, the bright but sloppy former University of Tennessee law professor who was serving as local counsel.[78] Watching them pass by from the press area was the bulky, tanned John Washington Butler, author of the infamous law and now a paid reporter for a national news syndicate.

Suddenly, applause rose and crested over the "sweating, mopping, fanning throng": William Jennings Bryan had appeared at the door.[79] "He is an old man now but that great body of his still is sturdy as an oak," marveled a reporter. "That barrel chest, the sheer bulk of the man make most of those in the courtroom seem puny and undernourished."[80] The rest of the prosecution team bobbed in his wake. Tom Stewart, the sober young attorney general for this circuit, was to spend much of the trial attempting to steer arguments back to narrow matters of the law, but he also proudly proclaimed that he shared Bryan's fundamentalist faith. Years later, Stewart would represent Tennessee in the U.S. Senate.[81] The other lead attorney, old "General" Ben G. McKenzie, was a retired attorney general from Dayton possessed of a folksy manner, a "rough and tumble wit," and a readiness to bait the defense attorneys as "outsiders" and "agnostics."[82] The Hicks brothers, Herbert and Sue, were young Dayton city attorneys who had agreed to prosecute their friend John Scopes in the first place, and like the other local attorney on the case, Wallace Haggard, they generally remained in the background. Finally came the leading attorneys' sons, J. G. "Gordon" McKenzie and William Jennings Bryan Jr., who had left behind a legal practice in California to assist his father. The prosecutors were so numerous that the defense was to accuse them half-kiddingly of stealing their chairs.

[78]Descriptions from *Baltimore Sun,* 14 July 1925, 1–2, and Larson, *Summer for the Gods,* 68–71, 79–80, 101–3.

[79]*Nashville Tennessean,* 11 July 1925, 1.

[80]*Baltimore Sun,* 14 July 1925, 1.

[81]Larson, *Summer for the Gods,* 107.

[82]Descriptions here and in next paragraph from *Baltimore Sun,* 14 July 1925, 1–2; Larson, *Summer for the Gods,* 132; and *New York Times,* 11 July 1925, 1.

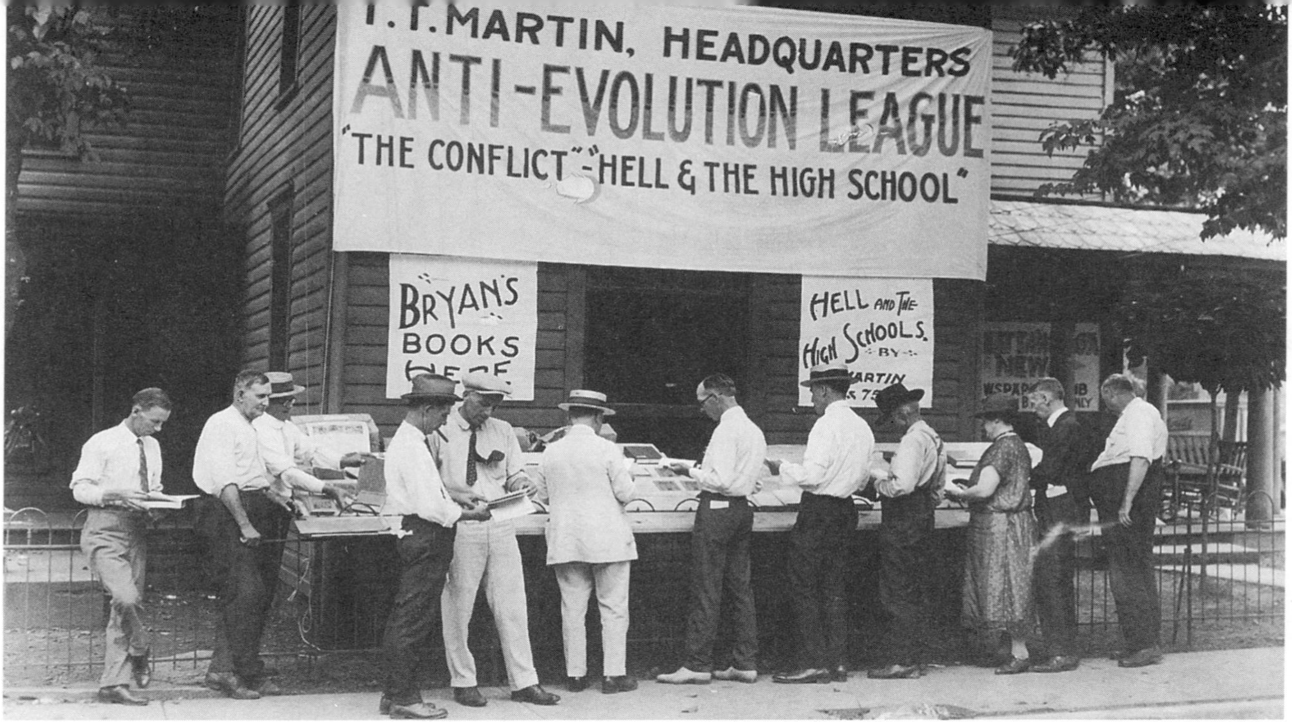

Anti-Evolution League Sales Stand outside the Dayton Courthouse
The evangelist T. T. Martin was one of many itinerant ministers who traveled to Dayton for the trial. Martin used the opportunity to sell copies of his antievolution book, *Hell and the High Schools,* which drew a connection between Darwinism and the "revolt of youth" during the 1920s.

Dayton Crowd Gathered to Hear a Traveling Evangelist
Itinerant preachers who had descended on Dayton for the trial became a common sight on the sidewalks and courthouse greens. The meagerness of the crowds disappointed the Dayton "boosters," who had hoped the trial would bring a tourism windfall to their town.

While Bryan strolled up to greet Scopes's defenders and the presiding judge, John T. Raulston, photographers and "motion-picture men" scrambled up on top of tables and chairs to preserve the moment from

Clarence Darrow and William Jennings Bryan
In previous decades, Darrow (left) and Bryan had been allies in fighting for social justice, but by the time of the Scopes trial, their differences over religion and majority rule had created tension between them. The palm-leaf fan Bryan holds became closely identified with him during the trial.

every possible angle. Throughout the trial, public relations were to have nearly equal billing with legal procedure.

The mundane activities of the first day—certifying the indictment and selecting the jury—gave little hint of the prosecution's and the defense's strategies for the trial. Although Bryan in previous weeks had often proclaimed that the trial would be a war between religion and evolution, by the time the gavel came down on July 10, the prosecution had trimmed its ambitions.[83] Finding reputable experts to testify on the fallaciousness of evolution had proved nearly impossible, so the prosecutors now planned to argue the case as only a narrow legal matter: The state had passed a valid law controlling the school curriculum, and John Thomas Scopes had admitted that he had broken

[83]*New York Times,* 11 July 1925, 1.

this law.[84] Open-and-shut. Bryan chafed at the restricted boundaries, but his alternatives were few.

The defense, on the other hand, faced a more complicated task in seeking to challenge the law itself. As Scopes's attorneys recognized (even if Scopes did not), a mere acquittal would have been disastrous. The ACLU needed Scopes to lose in order to be able to appeal the case to a higher court. Only there, at the level of the state or federal Supreme Court, could the ACLU actually get the Butler law overturned. At the same time, the defense saw the lower-court trial as an opportunity to establish its position that the law violated both the state and federal constitutions. Even if a majority of Tennesseans supported the Butler law, it posited, the court should throw it out. Further, Darrow and his allies perceived the trial as a chance to explain why the Butler law was also unwise, because it contradicted the scientific community's consensus on evolution and it infringed on academic and scientific freedom. More broadly, the defense felt that it should argue that evolutionary theory was compatible with belief in the Bible, though not with the fundamentalist interpretation of it. Darrow, in particular, hoped to use the courtroom as a forum for publicizing the dangers of fundamentalism. The trial, in other words, could have an educational as well as a legal purpose.[85] Confronting such a profusion of strategic alternatives, the defense pursued them all.

DAYS TWO THROUGH FOUR: RELIGIOUS FREEDOM VS. LEGISLATIVE AUTHORITY

After a weekend's respite, Scopes's team began its occupation of the outer walls of the defense strategy. On, Monday, July 13, John Randolph Neal presented Judge Raulston with a motion to quash Scopes's indictment on the grounds that the law under which he had been arrested was unconstitutional. Over the following days, the defense presented a host of minor arguments with regard to the form and clarity of the law, but the heart of its constitutional argument was the contention that the Butler law violated the separation of church and state. To our eyes, this argument might appear to be the defense's strongest point, but in 1925 the separation of church and state was still an inchoate, and vigorously contested, constitutional doctrine.

[84]Larson, *Trial and Error,* 63–64.

[85]Arthur Garfield Hays, "The Strategy of the Scopes Defense," *Nation,* 5 Aug. 1925, 157–58.

In the First Amendment to the U.S. Constitution, James Madison inserted what came to be known as the establishment clause: "Congress shall make no law respecting an establishment of religion, or prohibiting the free exercise thereof." Fundamentally, Madison and most of his colleagues feared the mutual corruption that could follow even from the government's nonpreferential involvement with the churches. Legislation regarding religion not only would improperly inject private religious issues into public life, but it also would inevitably subject religion and personal conscience to government interference.[86] The Founders, therefore, forbade all federal religious legislation as much to protect the integrity of the church as to maintain the peacefulness of civic life. Madison was confident that religion was strong enough to survive without the support of the federal government.

As of 1925, however, the defense was unable to appeal meaningfully to the First Amendment, for it applied only to federal legislation and not to state laws. "*Congress* shall make no laws," the amendment dictated; states were still free, as one historian has noted, to conduct an inquisition, outlaw unpopular religions, or establish a particular church.[87] Not until twenty years after the Scopes trial would the U.S. Supreme Court begin to apply the First Amendment's strictures against religious legislation to the states. Only the incorporation of the First Amendment into the Fourteenth Amendment's guarantees of "liberty" and "due process" in the late 1940s allowed the Court to pass judgment on state-based sectarian laws.[88]

In the meantime, Scopes's team had to appeal primarily to the Tennessee Constitution's separation of church and state. The state's establishment clause was modeled on the First Amendment, but the local meaning of "separation" differed significantly. In Tennessee, as in so many other states at the time, the "wall" of separation between church and state was more like a door.

On the second day of the trial, Darrow rose heavily to his feet, greeted the court cordially, and launched into a frontal assault on the constitutionality of what he called "this foolish, mischievous, and wicked act."[89] The Butler Act, he argued, was in clear violation of the principle of the separation of church and state. By enshrining the fun-

[86]Leonard Levy, *The Establishment Clause: Religion and the First Amendment,* 2nd ed., rev. (Chapel Hill: University of North Carolina Press, 1994), 63–69.

[87]Ibid., 225.

[88]*Everson v. Board of Education,* 330 U.S. 1 (1947); *Illinois ex. rel. McCollum v. Board of Education,* 333 U.S. 203 (1948); Levy, *Establishment Clause,* 149.

[89]*World's Most Famous Court Trial,* 74.

damentalist interpretation of the Bible in the law, the act violated both the establishment clause's broad restriction against *any* religious legislation and its more restricted meaning of not giving preference to any one sect. Brooding, hunching, and stalking the courtroom, Darrow mocked the idea that the Butler law was anything but an attempt by the state to force the fundamentalist Bible on the people. "It makes the Bible the yard stick to measure every man's intellect," Darrow complained. "Every bit of knowledge that the mind has must be submitted to a religious test."[90]

This implementation of fundamentalist doctrine was already unconstitutional, Darrow argued, and he hinted darkly that the Butler law was merely a first step in the fundamentalists' attempt to establish fully a state religion that would crush all dissent inside and outside the classroom. Darrow said:

> Ignorance and fanaticism is ever busy and needs feeding. Always it is feeding and gloating for more. Today it is the public school teachers, tomorrow the private. . . . After a while, your Honor, it is the setting of man against man and creed against creed until with flying banners and beating drums we are marching backward to the glorious ages of the sixteenth century, when bigots lighted fagots to burn the men who dared to bring any intelligence and enlightenment and culture to the human mind.[91]

In spite of themselves, the courtroom spectators burst into applause, but few observers believed that Darrow's oratory had actually made an impact on the court. "The net effect of Clarence Darrow's great speech yesterday," H. L. Mencken wrote, "seems to be precisely the same as if he had bawled it up a rainspout in the interior of Afghanistan."[92]

The truth was that Tennessee, like a great many states at the time, still had an establishment of religion in fact and in law. Since 1915, for example, the state had required a daily reading of ten Bible verses in the public schools. Judge Raulston had a minister open each day's trial session with a prayer. As the attorney general argued during the trial, "The laws of the land recognize the Bible; the laws of the land recognize the law of God and Christianity as a part of the common-law."[93] Tennesseans generally interpreted the strictures against religious establishment to mean that the state could give no particular

[90]Ibid., 84.
[91]Ibid., 87.
[92]H. L. Mencken, "Darrow's Speech Great but Futile," *Baltimore Evening Sun,* 14 July 1925, 1.
[93]*World's Most Famous Court Trial,* 66.

preference to one Protestant sect or denomination over another. Few had contemplated that the state should erect what Thomas Jefferson had called a high "wall of separation" between the state and *all* religion.

In arguing that the Butler law's invocation of the Bible constituted an unlawful "preference" to a particular religion, the defense ran headfirst into the local prosecution's more or less unreflective belief in Protestant supremacy. Attorney General Stewart took the universal acceptance of Christianity so much for granted that he was, at first, completely flummoxed by Darrow's suggestion that the state was giving a preference to the King James Bible over, say, the Koran. Soon enough, Stewart regrouped under questioning over the Butler law from Dudley Field Malone.

Malone: Does not it prefer the Bible to the Koran?
Stewart: We are not living in a heathen country.
Malone: Will you answer my question? Does not it prefer the Bible to the Koran?
Stewart: We are not living in a heathen country, so how could it prefer the Bible to the Koran?[94]

In Stewart's eyes, legislation on behalf of the Bible did not constitute a preference because no other religions worthy of the name competed against Christianity in America. Only preferences for one Christian or Protestant denomination over another would constitute a preference. At the same time, Stewart unconsciously identified Protestant fundamentalism with religion as a whole: That which threatened the fundamentalist interpretation of the Bible menaced all religious beliefs.

The prosecution went further in undermining the defense's constitutional bulwarks. In a brilliant inversion, prosecutors argued that religious liberty was actually more threatened by evolutionary teaching than by the Butler law. Bryan had joined the antievolution movement in part because parents kept complaining to him that "state schools were being used to undermine the religious faith of their children."[95] Teaching evolution, Bryan believed, was an attack on children's religious beliefs. Meanwhile, the separation of church and state left the faithful defenseless against the evolutionary assault, for the schools were not supposed to support religion. "These people in the state—Christian people—have tied their hands by their constitution," Bryan

[94] Ibid.
[95] Bryan and Bryan, *Memoirs,* 459.

lamented in his major speech during the trial.[96] Should they be compelled to allow educators to cast aspersions on the Bible? If the state cannot *advance* religion, he argued, then it also should not be allowed to *attack* religion. The only solution, embodied in the Butler law, was to exclude antireligious evolutionary teaching altogether. In 1952, the U.S. Supreme Court would hold that the "State has no legitimate interest in protecting any or all religions from views distasteful to them,"[97] but in 1925 Bryan's argument appealed strongly to a sense of fair play and a general impulse to protect the faith of young schoolchildren.

Scopes's defense opened up another line of attack. The Butler law, Neal maintained, violated Scopes's rights under the Tennessee Constitution "to worship Almighty God according to the dictates of [his] conscience," without the state or other human authority attempting to "control or interfere with the rights of conscience."[98] Neal admitted that the Tennessee legislature had a right to supervise and control the public schools, but he insisted that its exercise of these powers was limited by the provisions of the state constitution—especially the provisions for religious liberty and free speech. The court should, therefore, throw the Butler law out as unconstitutional.

Such an argument, replied the prosecution, was a red herring. The Butler law interfered with neither Scopes's freedom of speech nor his right to worship freely. As Bryan had already proclaimed before the trial, the teacher had no particular rights of free speech in the classroom: "The teacher is an employee and receives a salary; employees take direction from their employers, and the teacher is no exception." If Scopes did not wish to accept these terms of employment, he could simply take another job—possibly, Bryan suggested, at a private "atheist school."[99] What would happen, asked prosecutor Sue K. Hicks on the second day of the trial, if the schools no longer had the right to tell their teachers what to teach? "Suppose a teacher wanted to teach architecture in a school when he has been employed to teach mathematics," Hicks said. ". . . Under their argument they say that they cannot control him and make him teach that arithmetic in that school."[100] Such a situation, the prosecutors maintained, underlined the absurdity of the defense's free speech argument. Further, the Butler law did not interfere with Scopes's right to believe and worship as he wished. "He

[96] *World's Most Famous Court Trial,* 172.

[97] *Joseph Burstyn, Inc., v. Wilson* 343 U.S. 495 (1952).

[98] *World's Most Famous Court Trial,* 51–52.

[99] William Jennings Bryan, "The Tennessee Case," news release dated 2 June 1925, quoted in Levine, *Defender of the Faith,* 331–32.

[100] *World's Most Famous Court Trial,* 60.

can preach as he wants to on the streets—his religious rights—but cannot preach them in school," Hicks explained.[101] Outside the classroom, Scopes was a free citizen, but inside the classroom, he was a creature of the state. Scopes's teaching was, therefore, a matter for the legislative majority and not for the courts.

Such arguments for Tennessee's right to legislate actually resonated with many "progressives" who otherwise decried the Butler law. The editors of the *New Republic,* in particular, embraced the right of democratic majorities to pass laws without interference from the courts. The U.S. Supreme Court, they observed, was notorious for using its power of judicial review to strike down "progressive" state legislation, such as minimum wage laws. The editors opposed enlarging the conservative Court's authority over the states even for such a good cause as the Scopes case.[102] "The power now exercised by American courts and particularly by the Supreme Court to prohibit legislative experiments," wrote one editor in the *New Republic,* ". . . will in the long run provoke more labor and anxiety for American progressives than all the anti-evolution statutes that are likely to be passed."[103] The people, acting through their democratically elected representatives, should have the right to determine their own destiny, and no court should be allowed or encouraged to interfere with "the right of Tennessee to pass a foolish law."[104] In asking Judge Raulston to find the Butler law unconstitutional, the defense seemed to be seeking a short-term legal victory at the expense of democratic principles.

The defense thus enacted the same turn against majoritarianism that many other reformers had taken during the Great War and the 1920s. Popular repression, lynchings, and other eruptions of patriotic hysteria had soured many intellectuals on the democratic experiment. The eagerness with which elected officials passed such measures as the Butler Act further curdled their faith in voting majorities. Bryan and Darrow embodied this shift: Bryan, the voice of the old democracy, still had faith that a majority of citizens, properly informed, could govern themselves. Majorities were imperfect, but "the people" were the only real repositories of moral and political

[101] Ibid.

[102] See, for example, Nancy Woloch, *Muller v. Oregon: A Brief History with Documents* (New York: Bedford Books/St. Martin's Press, 1996). For an updating of this dynamic, see Gerald N. Rosenberg, *The Hollow Hope: Can Courts Bring About Social Change?* (Chicago: University of Chicago Press, 1991).

[103] "The Baiting of Judge Raulston," *New Republic,* 29 July 1925, 249.

[104] "The Conduct of the Scopes Trial," *New Republic,* 19 Aug. 1925, 332.

virtue, and in time they would correct their own mistakes. By contrast, Darrow (and the ACLU) exemplified a new strain of liberalism that appealed to the courts to make decisions based on individual rights that no majority could violate. In this view, majorities were more likely to be the enemy of liberty than its friend. The Butler law and similar acts seemed to justify the reformist intellectuals' loss of faith in democracy—at least until the romanticism of the New Deal again softened the reformers' view of the common people.

Back in Dayton, Judge Raulston quickly blew down the defense's constitutional wall. On Wednesday, July 15, he rejected the motion to quash the indictment with a judgment that echoed the prosecution's arguments. In a "high, monotonous, slightly nasal voice," with a police officer fanning him against the heat, Raulston addressed the silent courtroom.[105] "I fail to see," he said, "how this act in any wise interferes or in the least restrains any person from worshiping God in the manner that best pleaseth him." Scopes was still welcome to worship and believe as he wished; the law touched only on his contractual obligation to teach as the state dictated.[106] In conclusion, Raulston agreed with the prosecution's contention that the Butler law was a proper exercise of the legislature's power. The legislature holds the power to make uniform rules for the public schools, he said, and hence it "has the power to prescribe a course of study as well as the books to be used."[107]

For the defense, this was a crushing, but not unexpected, decision. "Constitutional guarantees of this freedom or that are feeble reeds on which to lean," observed the *Nation,* "and they are wont to fail a minority when it needs them most."[108] The trial would go on.

DAYS FIVE AND SIX: EXPERTS AND OUTSIDERS

Having lost the constitutional argument, the defense shifted to its broader strategy of publicizing the intellectual shortcomings of the Butler law and its supporters. This was perhaps not the strongest approach legally, but the law was not the defense's sole focus. "The real struggle here," noted one reporter, "is for publicity, not for justice."[109] On the pretext of demonstrating that the Butler law was too

[105] *Baltimore Sun,* 16 July 1925, 2.
[106] *World's Most Famous Court Trial,* 102–3.
[107] Ibid., 108.
[108] *Nation,* 5 Aug. 1925, 156.
[109] *Baltimore Sun,* 12 July 1925, 6.

Scopes and His Attorneys
From left to right: John Randolph Neal, Arthur Garfield Hays, Dudley Field Malone, John T. Scopes, and Clarence Darrow. Note the placard advertising "Deck Carter—Bible Champion of the World" behind them.
© Hulton-Deutsch Collection/CORBIS.

ambiguous to apply to Scopes, the defense proposed bringing in scientific and theological experts to testify that evolution and Christianity were perfectly compatible. The prosecution, which had utterly failed to scare up any experts of its own, fought hard to bar expert testimony. It sought to prevent the defense from "making a school house or a teachers' institute out of this court."[110] This wrangling over expert testimony not only exposed the deep divisions between fundamentalism and liberal Christianity but also laid bare the expanding gulf

[110] *World's Most Famous Court Trial,* 165.

between an older democratic ethos and the rising authority of experts in American culture.

On the fifth day of the trial, Clarence Darrow began to lay out the plea for allowing experts to testify:

> We expect to show by men of science and learning—both scientists and real scholars of the Bible . . . first what evolution is, and, secondly, that any interpretation of the Bible that intelligent men could possibly make is not in conflict with any story of creation, while the Bible, in many ways, is in conflict with every known science.

Evolution and the Bible were not simple matters, and the jurors needed help in understanding just how the "divine story of creation" in the Bible fitted with modern science and theology.[111] Nearly a dozen scientists and theologians had journeyed to Dayton to share their expertise with the court, and Darrow wanted to give them all a chance on the stand.

In the courtroom as well as the classroom, the defense claimed, expertise was needed to reach the truth. Unlike the prosecution, which in the defense's opinion sought only to protect the prejudices of the jury or the citizens of Tennessee, the defense asserted that it was searching for the truth about evolution and religion. Only the professional scientists' hard-earned knowledge would bring the court—and high school students in Tennessee—closer to this ideal. In the minds of many, the prosecution's attempt to bar expert testimony was the same as the Tennessee legislature's attempt to hobble science in the schools through the Butler law. The *Chicago Tribune* opined that scientific truth should not be "compelled to conform to what a majority of the people think is true."[112] Experts, and not voters, would determine the truth of scientific matters.

In the broader culture, if not in the courtroom, the defense attorneys' appeal to scientific expertise found a ready reception. The fruits of scientific progress by the 1920s were too obvious to ignore: electricity, automobiles, a deeper understanding of biological and physical laws of nature. But the regard for science in the 1920s went beyond Americans' appreciation for individual discoveries and inventions. In a decade of questioning old taboos, scientists had become models of antiauthoritarianism and symbols of progress. Sigmund Freud became an unlikely cultural hero for replacing sin with mental sickness and

[111] Ibid., 147.

[112] *Chicago Tribune,* quoted in "Thought Free, or in Chains?" *School and Society,* 11 July 1925, 45.

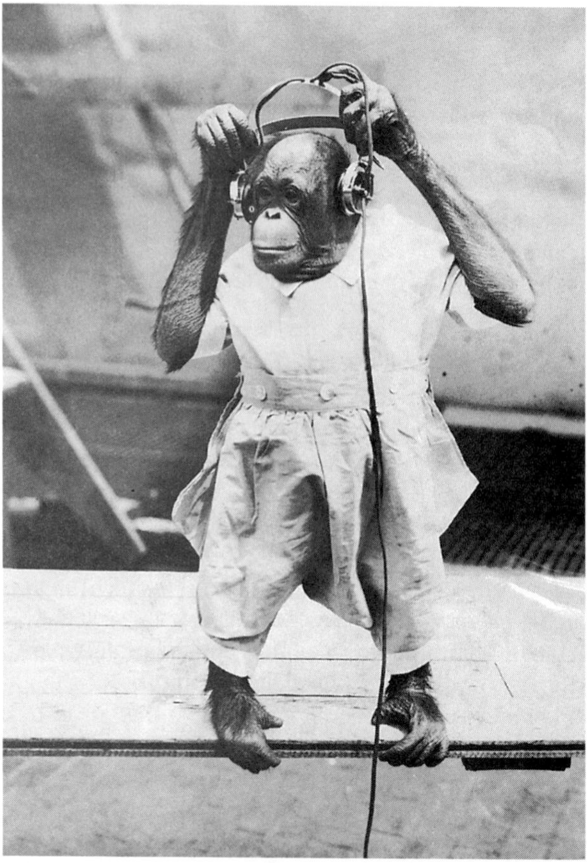

Getting Data on His Family Tree
The monkey motif became very popular during the trial. Duke, a chimpanzee, listens with headphones to a radio broadcast of the Scopes trial. A Chicago newspaper had set up the nation's first radio "network" to carry the proceedings live to the nation.

attacking a supposedly repressive society with scientific psychiatry. Galileo under house arrest became a stock image for writers seeking to criticize society's resistance to social and intellectual change.[113] "The difference between the theological mind and the scientific

[113]On the "military metaphor," see Moore, *Post-Darwinian Controversies,* 20–49; the influential John William Draper, *History of the Conflict between Religion and Science*

mind," defense attorney Dudley Field Malone noted during his major speech on the fifth day, "is that the theological mind is closed."[114] Modern progress would depend on the openness of the scientific mind. Malone's criticism of the theological mind also fitted into the broader process of secularization in America, as scientific authority fought to replace religious authority in matters ranging from medicine and criminology to morality.

At the same time, scientists seemed to offer a perpetuation of the older religious virtues, a sense of sacrifice and discipline, and a disinterested pursuit of the truth. The lives of Galileo, Darwin, and even a fairly young Albert Einstein seemed to exemplify the scientists' high moral calling.[115] Coincidentally, the year of the Scopes trial also saw the publication of Sinclair Lewis's *Arrowsmith,* a best-selling novel about an idealistic young physician and the noble calling of scientific research. The Scopes trial was only the most public engagement in science's winning battle for cultural authority in the 1920s.

The Scopes prosecution, however, was not so ready to roll over for the final victory of Darwinian science. Through the first four days of the trial, William Jennings Bryan had largely remained silent, glowering at the defense attorneys as they repeatedly blamed him for the Butler law. But on day five, Bryan rose to oppose the scientific testimony, and along the way, he defended the Tennessee majority's right to protect its religious faith against an invasion of experts from the North.

No jury needed experts to tell them how to apply the Butler law, Bryan argued. In violation of the letter and spirit of the law, Scopes had taught that "man descended from a lower order of animals"—it was plainly written in the textbook he used—and that was enough to convict him without getting caught up in scientific subtleties about the meaning of "evolution."[116] Although Bryan was proud of his own academic degrees and a strong supporter of an older, empiricist approach to science, he mocked the notion that the plain people of the jury had anything to learn from evolutionary scientists. Few scientists, he noted correctly, were in full agreement on the mechanisms of

(New York: D. Appleton and Company, 1875); and Donald Fleming, *John William Draper and the Religion of Science* (Philadelphia: University of Pennsylvania Press, 1950).

[114] *World's Most Famous Court Trial,* 184.

[115] David Hollinger, "Justification by Verification: The Scientific Challenge to the Moral Authority of Christianity in Modern America," in *Religion and Twentieth-Century American Intellectual Life,* ed. Michael J. Lacey (New York: Wilson Center and Cambridge University Press, 1989), 121–23.

[116] *World's Most Famous Court Trial,* 171.

evolution, and he emphasized other gaps in evolutionary science. "There is not a scientist in all the world who can trace one single species to any other," he said. "And yet they call us ignoramuses and bigots because we do not throw away our Bible."[117] Bryan proclaimed further that most scientists were not to be trusted, because they had embraced Darwin's own agnosticism. "More than half do not believe there is a God or personal immortality," he noted, "and they want to teach that to these children."[118] Did such experts have the right to come down and instruct a jury or Tennessee's children contrary to the wishes of the vast majority of Tennesseans?

Bryan played even more to democratic sympathies as he attempted to bar the testimony of modernist theologians, who sought to reconcile evolution and Christianity. The defense's talk about the experts' qualifications and years of biblical study contradicted Bryan's populist approach to Christianity. "The one beauty about the Word of God," Bryan maintained, "is, it does not take an expert to understand it." All that was really necessary for comprehension was a relationship with God. "More of the jurors are experts on what the Bible is," Bryan concluded, "than any Bible expert who does not subscribe to the true spiritual influences or spiritual discernments of what our Bible says."[119] Later in the day, Attorney General Tom Stewart was more succinct: "The people of Tennessee have a right to interpret the Bible as they understand it."[120] Antievolution literature was full of defensive references to the "sneers" and "contempt" of the "high-brows, the intellectuals," so the prosecution had no difficulty placing the "common people" above the professors.[121] Finally, Bryan invoked the right of a Tennessee majority to determine its own fate. "An expert," he told the court, "cannot be permitted to come in here and try to defeat the enforcement of a law by testifying that it [is] a bad law. . . . The place to prove that, or teach that, was to the legislature."[122]

As Bryan implied, the Butler law's southern supporters felt they were under siege by "outsiders"—by what one prosecutor referred to as "foreign attorneys." The defense attorneys hailed not only from the North but from the large cities that were the symbols of social change in the 1920s—the hotbeds of "free love," communism, syndicalism,

[117]Ibid., 177.
[118]Ibid., 178.
[119]Ibid., 181.
[120]*Baltimore Sun,* 12 July 1925, 6.
[121]Martin, *Hell and the High Schools,* is perhaps the best example.
[122]*World's Most Famous Court Trial,* 171.

"psycho-analysis," and other Jazz Age offenses. They came down to a state that was far more homogeneous. White Tennesseans, at any rate, supported conservative Protestantism by an overwhelming majority, shared a common heritage and history, and prided themselves on maintaining a culture that was more religious, moral, and rural than that of the North. The large legislative majorities that supported the Butler law were an expression of this sense of unity. If a small group of Tennesseans had traveled to New York "and tried to convince the people that a law they had passed ought not to be enforced," Bryan pondered, ". . . don't you think it would be resented as an impertinence?"[123] One Nashville newspaper suggested that the defense "should politely be invited to go back to New York with its bag, baggage and money."[124]

In his major argument on day five, Stewart made clear that this resentment of outsiders went deeper than a fondness for majority rule or mere local chauvinism. Bothered for days by Darrow's attacks on prayer and religion, Stewart finally let loose with a powerful defense of his right to maintain belief in the Bible:

> Why, if the court please, is this invasion here? Why, if the court please, have we not the right to interpret our Bible as we see fit? . . . They say it is a battle between religion and science, and in the name of God, I stand with religion because I want to know beyond this world that there may be an eternal happiness for me and for all. Tell me that I would not stand with it. Tell me that I would believe I was a common worm and would writhe in the dust and go no further when my breath had left my body!

If the outside experts' science struck "at that upon which man's eternal hope is founded," Stewart concluded, then he and his fellow Tennesseans would do without it.[125]

The prosecution had made its point. On day six, Judge Raulston ruled in favor of the prosecution and barred the defense's scientists and theologians from testifying formally. Even some of the prosecution's supporters, such as John Washington Butler himself, were disappointed at not being able to obtain "right smart of an education" from the learned experts.[126] But in the absence of expert testimony, the trial itself seemed at an end. "All that remains of the great cause of

[123] Ibid., 171–72.
[124] *Nashville Tennessean,* 17 June 1925, 1.
[125] *World's Most Famous Court Trial,* 197.
[126] *New York Times,* 18 July 1925, 1.

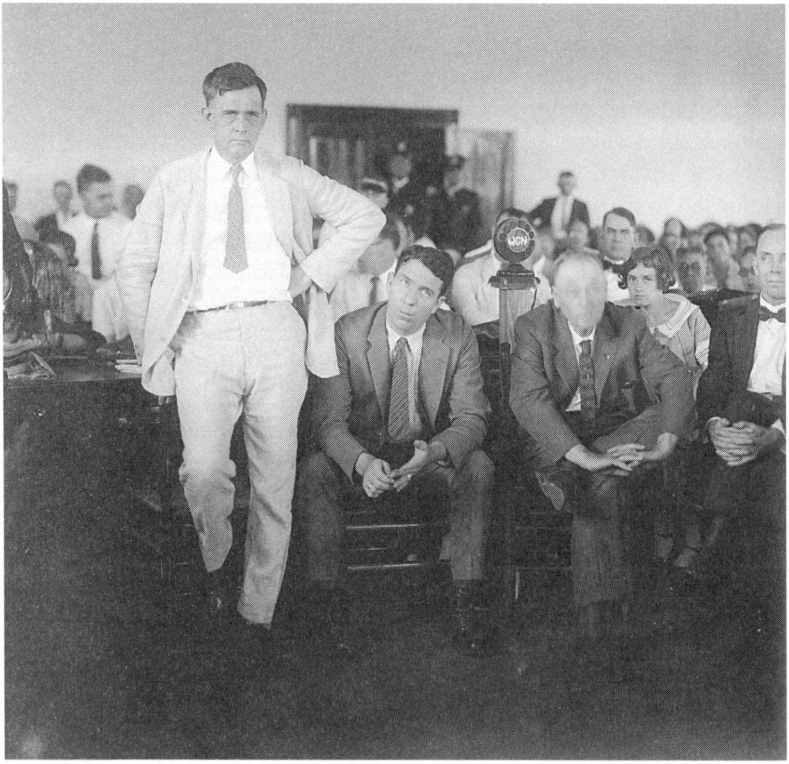

Attorney General Tom Stewart during the Trial
Stewart, the able young leader of the prosecution, stands in front of the silent Wallace Haggard (left) and the local champion, Ben McKenzie.
© Bettmann/CORBIS.

the State of Tennessee against the infidel Scopes," noted H. L. Mencken, "is the formal business of bumping off the defendant."[127]

AND ON THE SEVENTH DAY, BRYAN TOOK THE STAND

Mencken spoke too soon. Judge Raulston had indeed closed off most possible avenues for Darrow and his team. During the final weekend of the trial, many observers, including Mencken, departed Dayton for

[127]H. L. Mencken, "Battle Now Over, Mencken Sees; Genesis Triumphant and Ready for New Jousts," *Baltimore Evening Sun,* 18 July 1925, 1.

cooler climes. But on day seven, the defense sprang its last surprise: It would place fundamentalism itself on trial by calling William Jennings Bryan to testify as an "expert witness" on the Bible.

Much to the dismay of his fellow prosecutors, Bryan accepted the extraordinary challenge. He could have refused, but several forces pushed him into taking the witness stand. Bryan had from the beginning proclaimed that this was to be a "duel to the death" between science and Christianity, and perhaps he felt almost as disappointed as the defense when the trial was narrowed down to more technical legal matters. The defense had done what it could to make Bryan feel guilty about denying experts the opportunity to testify. Dudley Field Malone complained that the prosecutors could hardly call the trial a duel when "our defendant shall be strapped to a board and . . . they alone shall carry the sword."[128] By now, Bryan saw testifying as a necessity both for public relations and for his own pride. He wanted "to keep these gentlemen from saying I was afraid to meet them and let them question me."[129] In agreeing to testify, Bryan fully expected that he would in turn be allowed to call the defense attorneys to the stand and therefore be able to expose their role in what he called "a gigantic conspiracy among the atheists and agnostics against the Christian religion."[130] Bryan's role as "defender of the faith" compelled him to accept the challenge.

Because Judge Raulston feared that the courtroom floor could no longer support so many people, he moved the trial outside to the sunny courthouse lawn for the afternoon of Bryan's testimony. There, before a crowd of three thousand, with soda vendors weaving in and out of the masses, Bryan writhed under Darrow's attack.

Bryan was in a difficult position. He did not particularly like the Tennessee law, with its awkward phrasing and criminal penalties, but he felt bound to defend it. He was, moreover, very concerned that Darrow would trick him into a damaging admission that the Bible must be interpreted rather than taken as the literal truth. To avoid making such a slip, Bryan fell into a stubborn reassertion that he believed in the Bible "as it is written."

The attorney from Chicago had planned the examination carefully. Darrow stayed away both from the question of human evolution and from the more sensitive points of the New Testament—the virgin birth, Jesus' miracles, or the Messiah's resurrection. Instead, Darrow

[128] *World's Most Famous Court Trial,* 186, 187; see also *New York Times,* 18 July 1925, 2.

[129] *World's Most Famous Court Trial,* 300.

[130] *Baltimore Sun,* 20 July 1925, 1.

tried to undermine Bryan's biblical literalism by quizzing him on what one historian has called "the more extravagant miracles" of the Old Testament.[131] Could a whale or "big fish" really have swallowed Jonah whole and then "spewed him upon the land" three days later? Is it possible that Joshua could command the sun to stand still? Could all the animals and all the races of the world have spread across the earth only since Noah saved them on his ark?[132] Darrow and his skeptical allies had been asking such questions for decades.

Sometimes Bryan insisted that the literal language of the Bible was exactly correct, but sometimes, as with Joshua and the sun, Bryan admitted that the Almighty "may have used language that could be understood at that time instead of using language that could not be understood until Darrow was born."[133] The defense sensed an even greater triumph when Bryan agreed, under Darrow's relentless questioning, that the six days of creation in Genesis might not be six days of twenty-four hours. Actually, Bryan's theory that the "days" of Genesis might have been "ages" of thousands or even millions of years apiece was fully within the mainstream of fundamentalist thought. Many other fundamentalists accounted for the age of the earth by positing that a chronological "gap" of thousands or even millions of years existed between the creation of the earth and the appearance of Adam and Eve. Only a handful of believers, mostly Seventh-day Adventists, officially believed that God had created the earth in six days of twenty-four hours.[134] Still, as the defense's Arthur Garfield Hays observed, Bryan's willingness to depart from the literal words of Genesis bolstered the defense's contention that evolutionary theory was compatible with a liberal reading of the Bible: "If Mr. Bryan, who is a student of the Bible, will state that everything in the Bible need not be interpreted literally, that each man must judge for himself . . . [then] we are not bound by a literal interpretation of the Bible."[135]

More damaging than Bryan's "admission" that parts of the Bible must not be accepted literally were his repeated confessions of ignorance about wide swaths of scientific and theological knowledge. Although Bryan wrote a weekly newspaper column about the Bible and religion and had lectured extensively for decades on theological subjects, under questioning he betrayed what charitably can be

[131] Larson, *Summer for the Gods,* 188.
[132] *World's Most Famous Court Trial,* 285–91.
[133] Ibid., 286.
[134] Numbers, *Darwinism Comes to America,* 80–81.
[135] *World's Most Famous Court Trial,* 300.

called a deep lack of curiosity. He had never been interested in the age of civilizations that claimed to stretch back, unbroken, to before the Flood; had never been interested in how long humans had been on earth; had never taken care to learn about the origins of other religions; and had never considered how the story of the Tower of Babel corresponded to modern scholarship on linguistics. Haven't you given these issues any thought at all? Darrow asked.

Bryan: I do not think about things I don't think about.
Darrow: Do you think about things you do think about?
Bryan: Well, sometimes.

The crowd laughed. When Bryan did venture a scientific assertion, as when he claimed his views on the Flood were supported by a scientist named George McCready Price, Darrow said, "He has quoted a man that every scientist in this country knows is a mountebank and a pretender and not a geologist at all."[136] With harsh efficiency, Darrow exposed Bryan's numerous intellectual weaknesses.

Although the debate had its comic moments, during these two hours in the hot sun, Darrow and Bryan also let their bitterness boil over repeatedly. "The world shall know," Bryan stood and proclaimed at one point, "that these gentlemen have no other purpose than ridiculing every Christian who believes in the Bible." Darrow angrily retorted, "We have the purpose of preventing bigots and ignoramuses from controlling the education of the United States and you know it."[137] By the end, both men were shouting, red-faced with rage. Finally, after Darrow had hurled hundreds of questions at the struggling witness, Judge Raulston abruptly adjourned for the day. Bryan slumped in his chair, exhausted, while Darrow accepted congratulations from a score of young men and women who crowded around him.[138]

The defense had done its work well. The spectators, reported the *New York Times,* gave "no pity for [Bryan's] admissions of ignorance of things boys and girls learn in high school."[139] Newspapers across the nation printed verbatim accounts of the cross-examination, and many editorialists agreed that "it has brought about a striking revelation of the fundamentalist mind in all its shallow depth and narrow

[136]Ibid., 297; on Price, see Numbers, *Creationists,* 72–101.
[137]*World's Most Famous Court Trial,* 299.
[138]*Baltimore Evening Sun,* 21 July 1925, 2.
[139]*New York Times,* 21 July 1925, 2.

arrogance."[140] Darrow, in fact, might have done his job too well, as the questioning brought out some latent pity for Bryan's predicament. "Darrow's cross-examination of Bryan was a thing of immense cruelty," wrote one author in *Outlook*. "It could not have been designed save to destroy the last remaining shreds of public confidence in the Great Commoner."[141]

The cross-examination also virtually ended the trial. Before the next day of argumentation, Tom Stewart informed Bryan that he would not allow this farce to continue. The jury had not even been present for the cross-examination, so Bryan's testimony had served no immediate legal purpose. On Tuesday, July 21, the judge expunged Bryan's testimony and heeded the prosecution's new unwillingness to place members of the defense team on the stand. With all of his weapons either banned or already used, Darrow asked the jury to find Scopes guilty so the defense could get on with the business of appealing the case to a higher court. In only nine minutes—the time it took jurors to push through the crowd to the deliberation room and back—Dayton and the world had a verdict: guilty as charged.[142]

AFTERMATH: FROM SCOPES TO CREATIONISM

Although many of Scopes's supporters proclaimed that the trial had damaged fundamentalism by exposing Bryan's ignorance, the "Great Commoner" and his followers also claimed victory—they had, after all, won the case. Indeed, the antievolution crusade would survive the battle at Dayton by many decades, and along the way prove more successful and more adaptable than the majority of historians suspected.

In the first days after the trial, Bryan engaged in a flurry of activity—readying a major antievolution speech for public printing, traveling through the region to deliver portions of the talk, and making plans for an expansion of the antievolution crusade—hardly the actions of a broken man. But then, on July 25, while Bryan took an afternoon nap in Dayton, his Creator carried him off to eternal rest. Unquestionably, the strain of the trial had weakened Bryan. Although some supporters believed that death had come because "the agnostics and atheists unmercifully nailed our Great Commoner to a cross of calumny and vituperation," he most likely died of complications aris-

[140] *Baltimore Sun*, 22 July 1925, 10.
[141] George F. Milton, "A Dayton Postscript," *Outlook*, 19 Aug. 1925, 550.
[142] *World's Most Famous Court Trial*, 305–19.

ing from diabetes. Overeating, not browbeating, had done Bryan in.[143] To antievolutionists, it seemed somehow fitting that Bryan had been "called home" at the height of his crusade for the Lord. To his opponents, especially those reformers who had once been his allies, Bryan's death was simply another part of the tragedy of his final years, when he had exchanged fighting on behalf of democracy and the common man for "selling real estate and attempting to keep science out of the schools." The *Nation* noted, "The lapse of time leaves heroes stranded."[144]

Even with their champion in the ground, antievolutionists pushed forward. At some of the massive rallies held by the Bible Crusaders, Bryan Leaguers, and WCFA, the stage was filled with an enormous, flag-draped portrait of the martyred Bryan. Some antievolutionists discussed the possibility of securing an antievolution amendment to the U.S. Constitution, but the best they could do at the federal level was to try unsuccessfully to cut funding for the Smithsonian Institution's ethnological research into "the origin of man" and to attempt, with an equal lack of success, to halt federal aid going to colleges and universities that taught evolution.[145] At the state level, most legislatures in the South met only every other year, and passions cooled slightly over the rest of 1925 and all of 1926. Nevertheless, North Carolina and Kentucky narrowly defeated antievolution laws in this period, Mississippi enacted a ban on evolution in 1926, and the governor of Texas, Miriam "Ma" Ferguson, ordered her State Textbook Board to take a razor to the chapters in state texts that treated the descent of humans.[146]

The high point for antievolution came in 1927, when nineteen state legislatures from California to Florida considered banning Darwin from the schools. The Scopes trial had aroused enough interest, however, that all of these proposals met with significant opposition. "There will be no more anti-evolution legislation by default, as was virtually the case in Tennessee," observed one journalist.[147] Indeed, enough legislators in these states either opposed the legislation on principle or feared meeting the ridicule that

[143]Peter Turney Hiett, letter to the editor, *Nashville Tennessean,* 1 Aug. 1925, 4; Paolo E. Coletta, *William Jennings Bryan* (Lincoln: University of Nebraska Press, 1969), 3:271–77.

[144]"William Jennings Bryan," *Nation,* 5 Aug. 1925, 154.

[145]*Baltimore Sun,* 20 July 1925, 2; *Baltimore Sun,* 23 July 1925, 10.

[146]Harbor Allen, "The Anti-Evolution Campaign in America," *Current History,* Sept. 1926, 893–94.

[147]*Baltimore Evening Sun,* 23 July 1925, 2.

had been heaped on Tennessee, and they sent all of the laws down to defeat. Rhode Island lawmakers added insult to injury by referring an antievolution bill to the Committee on Wildlife and Game.[148] Only Arkansas, in 1928, passed an antievolution law by popular ballot, with 108,991 citizens voting in favor of the ban and 63,406 opposed. By 1930, the drive for state legislation against evolution had stalled.

Antievolutionists recognized quickly that state laws were not their only weapons. On the county level, hundreds of boards of education, in the South especially, took formal and informal steps to ban evolution and to bar the hiring of evolutionists and "non-believers."[149] Although Georgia had no antievolution laws on the books, a former high official of the Ku Klux Klan in that state launched a "Supreme Kingdom" campaign to ferret out teachers who might be sympathetic to Darwinism. Following "Ma" Ferguson's lead in Texas, a handful of states and countless localities purchased special textbook editions that had been cleansed of evolutionary references.

The antievolution campaign was perhaps most successful in its efforts to change science textbooks, none of which was particularly good on evolution in the first place. In the wake of the trial, George W. Hunter voluntarily revised *A Civic Biology,* the text Scopes had used in Dayton, to give less offense to antievolutionists. He dropped a paragraph under the heading "The Doctrine of Evolution" and the evolutionary tree that Bryan had mocked, and throughout the text he changed the word *evolution* to *development.* Hunter was too late, however, to prevent Tennessee from dropping *A Civic Biology* as its official biology textbook.[150] Determined to avoid such a fate, other publishers similarly gutted their texts of references to evolution, often interspersing religious quotations throughout to ease fundamentalist fears. Many publishers offered two versions of their science textbooks, one that mentioned evolution and one carefully edited, according to a biologist, to eliminate anything "which a Baptist Sunday School teacher could not reconcile with Genesis."[151]

[148]Maynard Shipley, "Growth of the Anti-Evolution Movement," *Current History,* May 1930, 331–32. See also Ferenc M. Szasz, "The Scopes Trial in Perspective," *Tennessee Historical Quarterly* 30 (Fall 1971): 292–93.

[149]Gatewood, *Preachers,* 149–50.

[150]*Nashville Tennessean,* 17 July 1925, 7.

[151]*Quarterly Review of Biology* (Sept. 1929), quoted in Shipley, "Growth of the Anti-Evolution Movement," 332.

The quiet muffling of evolution prompted surprisingly little concern in the biology profession. Except for Alfred C. Kinsey, a young professor of zoology at Indiana University (later to gain fame as a scientist of sexual behavior), few professional biologists at this time were writing textbooks for secondary students, and so the biology profession proceeded blissfully unaware of the state of evolutionary teaching in the nation's high schools.[152] The self-censorship of textbooks, along with state and local antievolution laws, meant that American schools taught less evolution in 1960 than they had in 1920. Had Bryan lived, the antievolution crusade surely would have accomplished even more.

In Tennessee, Bryan's triumph remained intact. Scopes's defenders got the guilty verdict they needed to appeal the case to a higher court, but they fared no better in the higher court than they had under Judge Raulston. When the Tennessee Supreme Court on January 15, 1927, handed down its decision on the appeal, it completely shut the door on the defense by upholding the constitutionality of the Butler law, even as it threw out Scopes's conviction. Darrow no longer had a conviction to appeal, and the Tennessee Supreme Court extracted from the prosecution an agreement not to pursue the Scopes case any further. "No more baffling legal wet blanket could have been contrived to smother the famous case," observed one reporter.[153] The Butler Act remained on the books, largely unchallenged, until the legislature repealed it in 1967.

As the Butler law's eventual repeal suggests, the teaching of evolution eventually experienced a resurgence beginning in the 1960s. By then, evolutionary theory had been placed on a more solid foundation with the "evolutionary synthesis"—a combination of paleontology and population genetics that seemed to support many of Darwin's original insights. This evolutionary synthesis began to find its way into the public school curriculum as the U.S. government in the late 1950s embarked on a crash program of science education to compete with the Soviet Union.

By this time, evolutionists and their supporters, especially in the North, thought they no longer had to fear a fundamentalist attack. Stung by national and even international ridicule during the Scopes trial, fundamentalism had retreated from its engagement with the broader culture. Although crusading evangelicals remained a potent force at the local level, especially in the South, they had largely

[152]Grabiner and Miller, "Effects of the Scopes Trial," 833–36.
[153]"The End of the Scopes Case," *Literary Digest,* 5 Feb. 1927, 14.

disappeared from the national scene. But as they had moved into what historian George Marsden has called "academic exile" from the intellectual life of the nation, conservative evangelicals had begun to build alternative institutions to nurture the spark they had struck at Dayton.[154] For example, shortly after the Scopes trial, a wealthy sympathizer pledged $25,000 to create a fundamentalist college in Dayton, Tennessee, and a few years later, the first students arrived to take courses at Bryan College.[155] Calvin College in Michigan, the Moody Bible Institute in Chicago, and a network of related colleges and Bible institutes also schooled the rising generations in conservative theology and missionary work, even as the institutions came to have less and less contact with mainstream academic thought.

Over the decades after the Scopes trial, cooperation among conservative evangelicals continued to grow out of their participation in interdenominational fellowships, Christian youth organizations, and other activist organizations, as well as from the fundamentalists' early and enthusiastic adoption of radio. And yet most of this activity took place away from the public gaze. By 1955, antievolution and the fundamentalist movement seemed so safely a part of the past that the authors of *Inherit the Wind* used the dramatic framework of the Scopes trial to warn against the dangers not of Bryanism, but of McCarthyism.

But antievolutionism was still there, locked on its target. As fundamentalism grew more powerful institutionally, antievolutionism grew more narrow in its interpretation of natural history. This trend climaxed in 1961, when John C. Whitcomb and Henry M. Morris's seminal tract, *The Genesis Flood,* discarded Bryan's position that the "days" of Genesis might have lasted for centuries in favor of a belief that God accomplished creation in six literal days of twenty-four hours apiece.[156] Antievolutionism, now going by the name creationism, had also grown more sophisticated in presentation. Creationist works such as *The Genesis Flood* bristled with footnotes and references.

In response to the new science curricula and the new creationist impulse, evolutionists and antievolutionists in the late 1960s began to

[154]Marsden, *Understanding Fundamentalism and Evangelicalism,* 149. See also Conkin, *When All the Gods Trembled,* 107, and especially Joel Carpenter, *Revive Us Again: The Reawakening of American Fundamentalism* (New York: Oxford University Press, 1997).

[155]*Nashville Tennessean,* 19 July 1925, 1.

[156]James C. Whitcomb, Jr., and Henry M. Morris, *The Genesis Flood: The Biblical Record and Its Scientific Implications* (Philadelphia: Presbyterian and Reformed Publishing Co., 1961).

clash once again in the nation's court system. By then, however, the U.S. Supreme Court was in the habit of applying the First Amendment doctrine of church-state separation directly to the states. In its 1968 *Epperson et al. v. Arkansas* decision, the Supreme Court struck down Arkansas's antievolution law—and by extension all bans on the teaching of evolution—as a violation of the First Amendment. In response, creationists turned to the underdog's strategy of demanding equal time in the classroom for creationism. With conscious irony, some even invoked Dudley Field Malone's plea during the Scopes trial. "Let them both be taught," Malone had said. "Let them both live."[157]

The Court has to date, however, resisted such appeals, holding in a 1987 decision that creationism is, in fact, a religion and not a science, and thus does not belong in a science classroom even on an equal time basis.[158] Antievolutionists responded in part by changing their focus from state laws to local schools and school boards. Oddly, for a movement that harks back to a tradition of absolute truth, some antievolution leaders have adopted from philosophers and historians the sophisticated argument that scientific "truth" is more a social construction than an objective, eternal entity. In other words, science is not so very different from religion and does not deserve its privileged position in society and the law.[159] Antievolutionism has definitely changed since 1925, but the sentiment has never died.

How could it? The forces that gave birth to the antievolution reaction—biblical modernism, a materialistic culture, a seeming decline in public morality—did not simply disappear after 1925, nor did conservative Christians suddenly make their peace with modern American society. A few years after the Scopes trial, journalist and philosopher Walter Lippmann wrote an inquiry into the Dayton proceedings and concluded that America in the 1920s was struggling over what to do with its belief in God now that the "acids of modernity" had eaten away at the Christian foundations of faith in a kinglike higher being. The Scopes trial was a conflict, Lippmann believed, between secular Americans, who had learned to substitute free inquiry for belief, and religious Americans, whose calls for religious orthodoxy

[157] *World's Most Famous Court Trial,* 187.

[158] *Edwards, et al. v. Aguillard, et al.* 482 U.S. 578 (1987).

[159] Thomas S. Kuhn, *The Structure of Scientific Revolutions* (Chicago: University of Chicago Press, 1962); Gary Gutting, *Michael Foucault's Archaeology of Scientific Reason* (Cambridge: Cambridge University Press, 1989); Bruno Latour and Steve Woolgar, *Laboratory Life: The Social Construction of Scientific Facts* ([1979] Princeton: Princeton University Press, 1986). Modern creationist expressions include Phillip E. Johnson, *Darwin on Trial* (Washington, D.C.: Regnery Gateway, 1991).

had grown louder as their faith grew more threatened. In the end, Lippmann, whose personal sentiments rested squarely on the side of Scopes and his defenders, found that he could not fully condemn the antievolutionists' position, for they were defending not so much specific stories in the Bible as the possibility that God could communicate at all with humans through the Bible or other means of revelation. "It is of no consequence in itself whether the earth is flat or round," Lippmann wrote. "But it is of transcendent importance whether man can commune with God and obey His directions, or whether he must trust his own conscience and reason to find his way through the jungle of life." In such a conflict, Lippmann recognized, the evolutionists' calls for "tolerance" and "open-mindedness" were in fact tantamount to asking fundamentalists to surrender their belief in revelation and an "eternal plan of salvation." No wonder antievolutionists in 1925, and for the rest of the century, chose not "to smile and to commit suicide."[160]

SOUTH VS. NORTH OR COUNTRY VS. CITY? REGION AND RURALISM IN THE ANTIEVOLUTION CONFLICT

It is no mere coincidence that the states that experienced significant antievolution controversies in the 1920s (and beyond)—Tennessee, Arkansas, Mississippi, Louisiana, Oklahoma, and others—share a geographic bond. As the Scopes trial made clear, the Mason-Dixon Line was still very much a real border between the North and the South. The differing demographics of the sections only intensified their mutual disdain, for the South was far more rural, and the North was following the cultural lead of its dynamic cities. At the Scopes trial, the simmering hostility between North and South, city and country, came to a rolling boil.

Sectional differences notwithstanding, fundamentalism was at its genesis a peculiarly American movement. American fundamentalists shared an evangelical heritage with many English and European Protestants, but the Europeans never developed their own militant crusade against modernism and Darwinism. Indeed, when one prominent American fundamentalist traveled to England in the 1920s hoping to spark an antievolution crusade, he met only with ridicule and

[160]Walter Lippmann, *American Inquisitors: A Commentary on Dayton and Chicago* (New York: Macmillan, 1928), 63–64, 66.

apathy.[161] What accounts for the difference? Perhaps most important, the United States had no tradition of an established state church—no central hierarchy existed to moderate American Protestantism. Instead, revivalism dominated American evangelical religion and nurtured powerful strains of biblical literalism, primitivism, and activism.[162] In the absence of a state church, American evangelicals had also been able to achieve dominance in the culture in a way that English evangelicals had not. Revivalist Protestants set the tone for American culture in the nineteenth century. They led the movements for reform, shaped the discussion of public and private issues, and identified their religious beliefs with the character of the nation. Darwinism and its relatives, therefore, struck the Americans with much greater force. When secularism and modernism gained influence in the early twentieth century, English evangelicals complained little because they had always been a minority anyway, but American evangelicals reacted with the anger of a group that had lost its once-unquestioned authority.

Although fundamentalism originated with conservative theologians in the American North, only in the South did it truly flourish. Isolation and poverty fed it. Over half of all white church members in the South belonged to one of the three explicitly southern denominations, such as the Southern Baptists. Most others belonged to locally independent congregations with no connections outside the county, let alone the region.[163] Thus, the vast majority of southern churches never felt the winds of modernism blowing in from Europe and the North. Recall that most of the Scopes jurors were unaware even of the evolution conflict until the test case came to Tennessee. Compounding this isolation was the grinding poverty of the post–Civil War South. Little money was available for training ministers even at the rare theological seminaries that managed to survive for more than a few years, and the South in general did very little to support public education for black or white students. "Both leadership and response," notes one historian of southern religion, "carried the stamp of intellectual backwardness."[164]

In spite of, or perhaps because of, this isolation, white southerners around the 1920s seemed to take religion far more seriously than their

[161]Numbers, *Creationists*, 141–42.

[162]Marsden, "Fundamentalism as an American Phenomenon," 225–28. See also Nathan O. Hatch, *The Democratization of American Christianity* (New Haven, Conn.: Yale University Press, 1989).

[163]Kenneth K. Bailey, "Southern White Protestantism at the Turn of the Century," *American Historical Review* 68 (Apr. 1963): 618.

[164]Ibid., 622.

northern brethren. "The whole region is saturated with religion," marveled reporter Frank Kent in the *New Republic.* "Religion takes the place of golf, bridge, music, art, literature, theatres, dancing, tennis, clubs. It is the fundamental communal factor."[165] Ministers and congregants alike were often unaware of the struggles that were to shake the northern churches, but when pushed, they volunteered in great numbers to fight for the old-time religion.

Inevitably, the North-South differences became conflated with the growing conflict between urban and rural, for the South remained overwhelmingly rural in the 1920s, while the North was clearly being carried along by the dynamism of its cities. In the Jazz Age, the city—especially northern cities such as Chicago and New York—represented an entire constellation of offenses against traditional, rural America. There, native-stock Americans seemed to mingle promiscuously with immigrants and African Americans; Catholics were as strong as Protestants, if not stronger; "foreign radicals" made common cause with intellectuals to attack American institutions; and the new "mongrel culture" of jazz, speakeasies, and movies seemed to be taking over. As early as his first campaign for president in 1896, Bryan had argued that America's economic and moral strength lay in its farms and villages, and he implied that the nation might be better off if someone burned the cities to the ground. The rural sense of cultural resentment had only grown stronger by the 1920s, and the antievolution crusade drew much of its strength from this anger. The majority of white southerners seemed to pride themselves on their separateness from the urban North.

Faced with almost universal ridicule in the northern press, many Tennesseans circled the wagons. The editor of the *Nashville Tennessean,* James I. Finney, maintained, "Thousands of intelligent Tennesseans who realized the futility and unwisdom of the [Butler] law were either silenced or became its defenders when the Civil Liberties Union entered the combat." As long as "outsiders" continued to equate Tennesseans' religiosity with "mental weakness," he noted, they would never repeal the Butler law.[166] The resentment persisted. The Scopes trial helped prompt a group of southern intellectuals, including novelist Robert Penn Warren, to publish *I'll Take My Stand,* a landmark defense of southern culture against a North that seemed overly intellectual, secular, materialistic, and expansionist. Tennessee

[165] Frank R. Kent, "On the Dayton Firing Line," *New Republic,* 29 July 1925, 259.
[166] "Why the 'Monkey Law' Still Stands," *Literary Digest,* 29 Aug. 1931, 18.

and the South would defend their own against an aggressive national culture.

The truly novel element during the Scopes trial, however, was the pride so many city dwellers expressed in their urbanity and the ridicule they reserved for Bryan and his followers as rural people. Gone was the old impulse to pay obeisance to the nobility of the soil and the sturdy virtues of small-town life. In its place lurked the urge to mock small-town America, especially its southern version, as a cultural Sahara—an urge given physical form, it sometimes seemed, in the person of H. L. Mencken. So constant was the reporter's slighting of southern "yokels" during the Scopes trial that Bryan repeatedly felt compelled to rise and defend the Tennesseans' honor and intellect. The split was apparent even in areas remote from the conflict in Dayton. The *New Yorker,* which commenced publication for the "caviar sophisticate" in 1925, also expressed this new confidence in the importance of cosmopolitan city life. The magazine's disdain for the "little old lady in Dubuque" was only a more genteel expression of Mencken's contempt for the cultural values of the village and farm. If the Scopes trial was an attempt by rural America to halt its slide toward irrelevance, as many commentators suggested, it was equally an expression of the urban North's attempts to construct an image of itself as the opposite of the rural South.

When the first antievolution crusade finally sputtered out in 1930, it was not because the Scopes trial had exposed its weaknesses, but because it had reached the geographical limits of its influence.[167] By 1930, all of the southern states and localities that were going to pass antievolution statutes had done so. It also was clear that the antievolution movement was going to have no success at all in the northern states. Although antievolutionists dominated the South and evolutionists the North, both sides now recognized that they were not going to be able to breach the Mason-Dixon wall.

THE ROLE OF THE SCHOOLS: ACADEMIC FREEDOM VS. MAJORITY RULE

Clarence Darrow: Did Prof. Scopes teach you anything about evolution during that time?

Harry Shelton (age 17): He taught that all forms of life begin with the cell.

[167] Larson, *Summer for the Gods,* 230.

. . .

Darrow: You didn't leave church when he told you all forms of life began with a single cell?
Shelton: No, sir.
Darrow: That is all.[168]

Clarence Darrow was invariably gentle when questioning John Scopes's former students—all of them were reluctant to testify against the popular instructor—but Darrow could not resist using their testimony to take a dig at the prosecution. Contrary to the antievolutionists' charges, not a single student testified that learning about evolution had hurt him or shaken his faith. Such a result, the defense suggested, showed that free inquiry in the schools was always a force for good and not for evil; students did not need to be protected from learning. Amid the constitutional and legal sparring of the Scopes trial, the question of education's purpose continually surfaced. Did the schools exist to pass on the values of the local majority, as the Butler law implied, or did they exist to transmit to students the professional educators' regard for science and independent inquiry? Who ruled the schools?

Scopes's supporters saw the case as part of a larger trend toward the suppression of freedom in the schools. The enthusiasms of wartime and the proliferation of schools had inspired such organizations as the American Legion and the Ku Klux Klan to sponsor legislation dictating who could teach and what could be taught. The antievolution legislation in Tennessee was only the southern nephew of measures such as New York's Lusk laws, which required "certificates of loyalty" from public school teachers and helped launch an orgy of investigations against pedagogues suspected of radicalism or pacifism. In both North and South, laws for "loyalty" and "orthodoxy" in the schools multiplied in the postwar years.[169]

Paradoxically, these efforts at repression played a large role in developing the opposing ideal of academic freedom—the ideal that guided the defense's conception of education. Academic freedom was of recent vintage in America, and at first it applied primarily to colleges and universities. In 1915, in the midst of the Great War, the

[168] *World's Most Famous Court Trial,* 129.

[169] Howard K. Beale, *Are American Teachers Free? An Analysis of Restraints upon the Freedom of Teaching in American Schools* (New York: Charles Scribner's Sons, 1936), 61–62; William Gellermann, *The American Legion as Educator,* Contributions to Education, no. 743 (New York: Teachers College, Columbia University, 1938); ACLU, *Gag on Teaching; Baltimore Evening Sun,* 21 July 1925, 19.

American Association of University Professors (AAUP) had issued the "General Declaration of Principles," which defended professors' freedom of inquiry, freedom of teaching, and freedom of opinion outside the college. Professional scholars should be free of outside pressures for loyalty and orthodoxy and left to pursue their inquiries wherever they led. Rather than face trials by "loyalty committees" or governing boards composed of nonacademics, scholars should be responsible only to their professional peers. "Academic freedom" would shelter scholars from the Lusk laws and their brethren.[170]

Although academic freedom seemed to bathe in the reflected glow of rights such as freedom of speech and freedom of the press, it was not clearly a constitutional right. Recognizing this, proponents outlined a series of practical justifications for academic freedom. First, scientific inquiry and progress depended on the "unlimited freedom to pursue inquiry." "Such freedom," argued the AAUP, "is the breath in the nostrils of all scientific activity." Second, educational success depended on the teacher's independence. Students would not respect a teacher who seemed to be part of "a repressed and intimidated class" or whose opinions seemed to be hedged about with caution. Finally, the scholar's role as a disinterested contributor to public discussion depended on his or her independence from political coercion.[171]

Scopes's defenders, inside the court and out, applied this ideal of academic freedom directly to Tennessee high schools. The American Federation of Teachers deplored "the continuance in our national life of the spirit of unenlightened legislative dictatorship." This legislative meddling directly interfered with the preconditions of education. "Without freedom in the intellectual life," the organization explained, "and without the inspiration of uncensored discovery and discussion, there could ultimately be no scholarship, no schools at all and no education."[172] The high schools, no less than the universities, depended on academic freedom.

Not only did the Butler law inhibit teachers' liberty and professional responsibility, argued proponents of academic freedom, but it also betrayed a fundamental misunderstanding of the educational process. It was proper for the legislature to prescribe the curriculum, explained R. S. Woodworth of Columbia University, for that meant

[170]American Association of University Professors, *Report of the Committee on Academic Freedom and Tenure* (n.p., 1915).

[171]Ibid.

[172]"The Tennessee Anti-Evolution Law," *School and Society,* 18 July 1925, 75.

only that the government was determining "what questions shall be taken up in the school." But when the Tennessee statute presumed "to put into the mouth of its teachers the answers which they must give"—when the Butler law mandated that science classes reach a particular religious conclusion—the government was interfering with that "free sifting and winnowing of ideas" essential for training students and for discovering the truth.[173] If education meant something more than rote memorization—if it aimed to inspire curiosity, critical thinking, and intellectual growth in students, as the growing ranks of "progressive" educators proclaimed—the Butler law pointed Tennessee's schools in exactly the wrong direction. As a practical matter, the defense in the Scopes trial called for Tennessee schools to teach both evolution and biblical creation, but this demand was more a strategic move by the underdog than an intellectual position. At heart, Scopes's supporters believed that progressive learning would grow out of scientific inquiry and not from theological inculcation.

Contrary to the legislators' belief, the defense held, no harm would come to students from participating in the free market of ideas. Dudley Field Malone, on Scopes's behalf, pleaded:

> The least that this generation can do is to give the next generation all the facts, all the available data, all the theories, all the information that learning, that study, that observation has produced—give it to the children in the hope of heaven that they will make a better world of this than we have been able to make it. . . . For God's sake let the children have their minds kept open—close no doors to their knowledge; shut no door from them.[174]

Secure in his faith that the children of the 1920s were already "pretty wise," Malone felt that the schools should provoke and not protect them. Malone's vision of education fitted well with the changing role of education in the urban, industrial North. An industrial, differentiated economy, with its demands for constant progress and for workers who could keep up with change, needed schools to teach students the process of learning for themselves, not cut-and-dried answers someone else had dictated. The faith that Malone and his allies placed in the eventual triumph of truth in this academic free market rivaled only the faith that the fundamentalists placed in the Bible.

Against these assertions of academic freedom, Bryan counterposed the principle of majority rule. The content of education, Bryan sug-

[173] R. S. Woodworth, "The Scopes Case and the 'Constitutional Rights' of the Teacher," *School and Society,* 29 Aug. 1925, 274.

[174] *World's Most Famous Court Trial,* 187.

gested, was to be determined only by "the people, speaking through their legislatures."[175] Not only did parents have a higher obligation to their own children than a teacher did, but parents paid the taxes that supported the schools. "The hand that writes the paycheck," Bryan was fond of saying, "rules the school."

The alternatives to majority rule, Bryan argued, were rule by teachers or rule by scientists. In the first case, Bryan emphasized the teacher's status as an employee. "A man cannot demand a salary for saying what his employers do not want said," Bryan argued. For example, no instructor could teach in the United States that monarchy is the only decent form of government or that the patriots ought to have lost the American Revolution. Similarly, a teacher of biology must respect the community's wishes. Leaving the curriculum up to teachers also raised the threat of educational anarchy, for what could compel a man or woman to teach one particular subject and not another? What was to prevent a thousand instructors from teaching a thousand barely related subjects? At the dawn of the twenty-first century, in fact, antievolutionists have raised these questions from a different angle: Does academic freedom protect a high school biology teacher who wants to ignore the official evolutionary biology curriculum in favor of instructing students in creationism?

Scopes's defenders argued that the teachers' professionalism stood in the way of any imagined dangers. As Woodworth argued, any person employed to teach a subject had "a duty, and a correlative right," to teach it "according to the state of knowledge in that subject." Hired to teach science, Scopes had to teach science. But as a trained science instructor, Scopes also had the professional duty and the right to teach the theory of evolution accepted by the vast majority of the scientific profession.[176] Scopes might have been an employee of the Rhea County School District, but his professional training tied him to a national network of teachers, and only they had the right to impose academic obligations and arbitrate academic failings. In other words, only scientists had the right to determine the content of John Scopes's curriculum.

However, rule by scientists—by what supporters of academic freedom might have called the "community of the competent"—raised the opposite threat of dictatorship. Bryan calculated that the United States contained only about eleven thousand scientists, or one scientist for

[175]Here and below, William Jennings Bryan, "Who Shall Control?" in Bryan and Bryan, *Memoirs,* 526.

[176]Woodworth, "The Scopes Case," 274.

every ten thousand people—"a pretty little oligarchy to put in control of the education of all the children."[177] What right did such a small group have to contravene the wishes of millions of parents? Every instinct Bryan had developed through years of fighting for "the people" against the nation's ruling elite rebelled against the idea of leaving educational decisions in the hands of a tiny band of professors—especially when half of them no longer believed in God. Facing such choices, Bryan and Tennessee would take their chances with the majority.

Nevertheless, majority rule also posed a threat that Bryan chose not to notice. In 1925, the "Great Commoner" was confident that majority rule would always be consistent with his own Christian outlook. In the South especially, a large majority of parents agreed with Bryan's religious positions. But what if a majority of citizens in a school district were Catholic or pagan or even agnostic? Similarly, what if the national majority were changing, becoming less rural and Protestant and more urban and diverse? Bryan ignored such questions. He maintained his characteristic optimism by continuing to believe that this cherished "majority" was and always would be white, Protestant, and rural—Bryan people.[178]

Bryan and other supporters of the Butler law could dismiss the authority of professional scientists in part because they believed that education should serve a broader purpose than mere intellectual improvement. Such a purpose had once guided the nation. As John Gould Fletcher, a sympathetic southern intellectual, noted with approval, "The object of public education in the American colonies and the later states up to 1865, was to produce good men." The erosion of this ideal, Fletcher suggested, was responsible for much of the cultural unrest among Jazz Age youths, for an education that focused on the intellect to the exclusion of morals had made the public school graduate of the northern cities "a behaviorist, an experimental scientist in sex and firearms, a militant atheist, a reader of detective fiction, and a good salesman."[179] Similarly, Bryan intimated that academic learning without regard for character or Christianity had been one of the central causes of the Great War. Many Americans wondered why they should value knowledge if it resulted in such disasters. "In my

[177]Bryan, "Who Shall Control?" 526.

[178]Levine, *Defender of the Faith,* 359–60.

[179]John Gould Fletcher, "Education, Past and Present," in Twelve Southerners, *I'll Take My Stand: The South and the Agrarian Tradition* (New York: Harper & Brothers, 1930), 95.

judgment," asserted Tennessee governor Austin Peay, "any state had better dispense with its schools than with its Bible." He added, "We are keeping both," but his sympathies were clear.[180] The Butler law was an expression of the local majority's desire to reassert the moral purpose of the public schools.

Despite posturing over the issue, the academic freedom to teach evolution was something of a moot point. A handful of commentators otherwise sympathetic to Scopes denied that evolution was a high school subject in the first place. The scant pages and thin explanations devoted to the subject in Dayton's official science textbook partially bore this observation out. Further, academic freedom seemed especially tailored to fit university professors. The high school teacher, argued H. L. Mencken, was not involved in a search for enlightenment and so did not deserve to wear the cloak of academic freedom. "He is a workingman, not a thinker,"[181] Mencken wrote. Indeed, one prominent defender of academic freedom noted that the vast majority of high school teachers actually suffered very little under educational repression, for they generally shared "the views and prejudices and ideals of the community out of which they have sprung and in the midst of which they teach." Under the Lusk laws, for example, New York teachers often banded together to call for the dismissal of "disloyal" teachers.[182] Only better training would create teachers who had both the desire and the need for freedom.[183]

Tennessee's teachers were perhaps less ready than most for the challenge of academic freedom. The state had historically lagged behind in supporting education. An investigating committee in the 1920s likened Tennessee's educational landscape to "an arid and almost trackless desert, with here and there a struggling oasis."[184] Reforms from the first decades of the twentieth century had done little to improve the degraded status of teachers in the state. The average teacher's salary in Tennessee was just over half the national average. Not surprisingly, the average quality of the teaching force also trailed the nation. On the eve of the Great War, only a quarter of the state's teachers had the equivalent of four years of high school; just over a quarter had never attended high school at all. A teacher

[180] *Nashville Tennessean,* 27 June 1925, 1.
[181] Mencken, "In Tennessee," *Nation,* 1 July 1925, 22.
[182] Beale, *Are American Teachers Free?* 13–14, 26.
[183] Howard K. Beale, *A History of Freedom of Teaching in American Schools* (1941; reprint, New York: Octagon Books, 1966), 235.
[184] *Baltimore Evening Sun,* 1 July 1925, 1.

certification law intended to "weed out" underqualified instructors lost most of its effectiveness when the governor issued three thousand "secondary certificates" to teachers who had failed the state examination.[185] The underdeveloped state of the teaching profession in Tennessee and elsewhere in the South probably made it much easier for antievolutionists there to embrace the idea that teachers were mere employees and not independent professionals. Perhaps John Scopes was ready for the exercise of academic freedom, but the majority of Tennessee's teachers were not.

RACE AND EVOLUTION

Although the prosecution and the defense seemed willing to debate almost anything over the course of the trial, both sides remained oddly silent about the question of evolution and race. In general, racial concerns rarely surfaced explicitly in antievolutionary arguments, and supporters of evolution seldom referred to racial difference.[186] To a large extent, whites on both sides of the question simply accepted white supremacy without question. But in a decade in which New York and other northern cities were experimenting with a "mongrel culture" that mixed, among other things, black and white, and the Ku Klux Klan was burning crosses of intolerance in nearly every state of the Union, the question of race always lurked nearby.

Race relations in 1920s America presented a complex picture. On the one hand, the decade saw a flowering of African American culture—jazz, literature, painting, sculpture—and the development of vibrant urban communities in Harlem and other northern destinations for southern black emigrants. The African American philosopher Alain Locke proclaimed the arrival of "the New Negro" (in a book by that title), who would stake a claim on America through labor and through the artistic achievements of the Harlem Renaissance. Increasing numbers of white Americans, especially cultural radicals such as H. L. Mencken, were willing to honor that claim. On the other hand, such acceptance remained the exception rather than the rule. The Tennessee Constitution, like state constitutions throughout the South, mandated separate schools for black and white students, and the 1920s saw the South export its racial attitudes and racial violence to

[185] Holt, *Struggle for a State System of Public Schools,* 308, 277, 272.
[186] Numbers, *Darwinism Comes to America,* 67.

the rest of the nation. The second Ku Klux Klan, founded in Georgia during the Great War, expanded its arena of hatred to include Jews and Catholics as well as African Americans, and it found much support in the North and West as well as in its southern heartland. The question of race was not the same everywhere in the country, but it was unavoidable.

Although we would like to believe that scientific inquiry rescued the intellectual elite of the 1920s from expressing overt racism, in fact white scientists freely employed both progressive and reactionary racial arguments as proof of evolution. In testimony filed with the court in the Scopes case, Horatio Hackett Newman, a zoologist from the University of Chicago, noted merely that the "high degree of diversity" within the human race contradicted the prosecution's biblical assumptions that all humans were descended from Adam and that species were immutable. Only evolutionary mechanisms operating over a much longer time span, Newman argued, could have produced "so many widely different races."[187] Other supporters of Darwin took a less benign view of racial difference and forced racial diversity to fit into a ladder of racial hierarchy. As "evidence" that humans had evolved, some evolutionists and lay supporters suggested that "the lowest type of humanity, such as the vermin eaters, Fuegians [residents of Tierra de Fuego, off southern South America], or the lower still wife eaters, Australian savages," represented an intermediate stage of evolution between modern Caucasians and their species ancestors.[188]

Caucasian scientists were divided among themselves. Beginning in the late nineteenth century, many had used Darwinian ideas to bolster their arguments about the racial superiority of Anglo-Saxons, and they usually attached to this belief a more or less fully elaborated racial hierarchy of all the peoples of the world, with white Anglo-Saxons at the top and Africans and their descendants at the bottom.[189] The textbook at issue in the Scopes case, George W. Hunter's *A Civic Biology,* reproduced these false distinctions without question. Such beliefs

[187] *World's Most Famous Court Trial,* 272.

[188] *Baltimore Evening Sun,* 13 July 1925, 13. See also "Darwinism Again to the Fore," *Literary Digest,* 24 Sept. 1927, 19.

[189] John S. Haller, *Outcasts from Evolution: Scientific Attitudes of Racial Inferiority, 1859–1900* (Urbana: University of Illinois Press, 1971). See also Constance Areson Clark, "Evolution for John Doe: Pictures, the Public, and the Scopes Trial Debate," *Journal of American History* 87 (Mar. 2001): 1275–1303.

also bolstered the increasingly powerful eugenics movement, led by biologists who wanted to encourage reproduction among the "better people" and discourage reproduction among the "unfit"—often racial and ethnic minorities. *A Civic Biology* discussed the eugenics program very favorably. By the 1920s, however, some biologists and anthropologists were turning toward the position that observable diversity among races grew out of cultural rather than physical or genetic differences. Over the next two decades, crusaders such as Franz Boas would use the tools of science to dismantle the edifice of scientific racism. Although a scientific degree usually meant that its holder disagreed with the Butler Law, it did not determine the scientist's racial outlook.

If the African American subjects of so much speculation were united against scientific racism, they were also significantly divided over fundamentalism and antievolutionism. Some leaders of the largest black denomination, the African Methodist Episcopal Church (AME), embraced theistic evolution enthusiastically, but the house organ, the *A.M.E. Church Review,* eventually came to take a harder antievolution stance.[190] The editors expressed a willingness to overlook William Jennings Bryan's racial prejudices, for these seemed insignificant next to "his stand in defense of the church."[191] The Reverend John W. Norris, an AME minister in Baltimore, offered a proof of Darwinism's fallaciousness that was aimed directly at his African American audience. Slavery was wrong, Norris argued, "because man was never made to be a slave." On the contrary, man was created "to rule all other creatures." Humans, therefore, could not have evolved from animals, for humans could not descend from the creatures they ruled.[192] This argument, as well as Norris's belief that God had also placed life on millions of other planets, was utterly his own, but his general support of antievolutionism certainly echoed that of many African American believers. As with white Methodists, however, members of the AME were generally more interested in religious experi-

[190]Charles H. Wesley, "Does the First Chapter of Genesis Teach Evolution?" *A.M.E. Church Review,* Oct. 1923, 75–77. On the earlier period, see Eric D. Anderson, "Black Responses to Darwinism, 1859–1915," in *Disseminating Darwinism: The Role of Place, Race, Religion, and Gender,* eds. Ronald L. Numbers and John Stenhouse (Cambridge: Cambridge University Press, 1999), 247–66.

[191]"William Jennings Bryan," *A.M.E. Church Review,* Oct. 1925, 331–32.

[192]John W. Norris, "Evolution Not a Fact—The Bible a Fact," *A.M.E. Church Review,* Oct. 1925, 323–25.

ence than religious doctrine, and their hostility toward Darwin seldom impelled them to action.

More secular African Americans were much more likely to see southern racism, rather than righteous religion, as motivating the Scopes prosecution. An editorialist in the *Chicago Defender,* the nation's leading African American newspaper, believed that Tennessee's legislators were suppressing evolution because of the Darwinian implication "that the entire human race . . . started from a common origin." The writer continued, "Admit that premise and they will have to admit that there is no fundamental difference between themselves and the race they pretend to despise."[193] In his book *The Mind of the South,* the white southerner W. J. Cash wrote, "One of the most stressed notions which went around was that evolution made a Negro as good as a white man—that is, threatened White Supremacy."[194] Evolution held destabilizing implications for Anglo-Saxons' place in the world.

The African American intellectual W. E. B. Du Bois agreed with the *Chicago Defender*'s condemnation of Tennessee, but he was unwilling to see antievolutionism as a purely southern matter. "Dayton, Tennessee, is America," asserted Du Bois, "a great, ignorant, simple-minded land."[195] As much as Du Bois condemned Tennessee's folly, he also used his position as chief propagandist for the National Association for the Advancement of Colored People (NAACP) to decry journalists and other northerners who pretended that the problem was unique to the Volunteer State. "The folk who leave white Tennessee in blank and ridiculous ignorance," Du Bois observed, ". . . are the same ones who would leave black Tennessee and black America with just as little education as is consistent with fairly efficient labor and reasonable contentment." He concluded, "The whole modern Nordic civilization . . . has sold its soul to Ignorance."[196] As usual, Du Bois was something of a lonely northern voice in the larger African American community. Just as evolutionary scientists were divided in their opinions about race, so were African Americans divided by religion and region in their opinions about evolutionary science.

[193] *Chicago Defender,* 23 May 1925, 12.
[194] W. J. Cash, *The Mind of the South* (New York: Alfred A. Knopf, 1941), 347.
[195] W. E. B. Du Bois, "Scopes," *Crisis,* Sept. 1925, 218.
[196] Ibid.

WOMEN AND GENDER IN THE SCOPES TRIAL

Outside the ACLU, only one prominent visitor to the trial seemed particularly dissatisfied with the composition of the prosecution and defense teams. Oddly, the discontented spectator was defense attorney Dudley Field Malone's wife, Doris Stevens. She announced to the press:

> I came all the way from New York to find that the defendant was a man, the prosecutor a man, the judge a man, the jury all men, the attorneys on both sides men. . . . One would think there weren't any women in this world, or that they didn't do any thinking.[197]

Contrary to what Stevens believed, however, women played a prominent role in the Scopes trial as activists and as symbols.

Stevens represented a new class of women in the 1920s. The Great War had accelerated the rate of women's entry into the workplace, and although the large majority of workingwomen in the 1920s were ethnic and African American women toiling in the basement of the economy, elite professional women such as Stevens were increasingly visible. Not only did many of these women demand still greater female participation at work and in the public sphere, but some even endorsed the movement among younger women for social and sexual equality. These latter demands especially bolstered the antievolutionists' sense that some force had set the nation on the downward slope to hell. Even the young women of Dayton, including Judge Raulston's daughters, sported the more openly sexual dresses favored by flappers and rolled their stockings in the approved daring manner.

Stevens might not have noticed the presence of women in the contest because women as activists were affiliated almost solely with the antievolution movement. Support for antievolutionism was particularly strong among women. Although the leaders of the movement were all men, one writer estimated that 70 percent of antievolutionists were women.[198] During the debate over the Butler bill, the speaker of the Tennessee House of Representatives claimed that he had been petitioned to support the bill by "the women of the state and the teachers association." A state senator poignantly gestured toward a woman in the gallery "whose son had been made a confirmed infidel by having

[197] *Baltimore Evening Sun,* 17 July 1925, 2.
[198] Rollin Lynde Hartt, "What Lies Beyond Dayton," *Nation,* 22 July 1925, 111.

been taught evolution in a high school."[199] The letters that newspapers received in favor of the Butler law were almost always sent by women, whereas letters against the law tended to come from men. As Mrs. E. P. Blair proclaimed in a poem supporting the Butler law, the anti-evolution struggle was being waged "For country, God, and mother's song."[200]

Antievolutionism fitted well with the maternal ideal. Although antievolution women tended to hold traditional values about a woman's place in the home and society, they claimed the right to participate in this public crusade because evolutionary teaching affected children, and rearing the next generation was a mother's responsibility. Female opponents repeatedly invoked their status as mothers and lamented that evolutionary teaching ripped their children away from them and interfered with their right to bring up children "on the Bible," as one Nashville mother put it.[201] These women supported the Butler law and other similar laws, such as mandatory religious instruction, as a way to make public institutions reinforce rather than refute maternal teachings. As with prohibition, antievolutionism was a female-dominated reform movement that invoked a mother's duty to protect her children and make the state an extension of maternal moral influence.

The defense attorneys did not attack actual antievolution women so much as they committed what one historian has called "symbolic matricide," as they condemned the female-dominated reform tradition.[202] As a practical matter, Malone tried to invert the antievolutionists' argument that schools were interfering with a mother's right to raise her children. "The women of America," Malone intoned, "can take care of the morals of their children without the help of Mr. Bryan or state legislatures."[203] But more broadly, the defense attempted to undermine the notion that children's morals needed so much protection in the first place. Scopes's team thus joined with the cultural rebels of the 1920s in attacking moral ideals represented by their stereotype of

[199]Bailey, "Enactment of Tennessee's Antievolution Law," 478; Royce Jordan, "Tennessee Goes Fundamentalist," *New Republic,* 29 Apr. 1925, 259.

[200]Mrs. E. P. Blair, "The Battle Hymn of Tennessee," *Nashville Tennessean,* 29 June 1925, 2.

[201]*Nashville Tennessean,* 3 July 1925, 4.

[202]Ann Douglas, *Terrible Honesty: Mongrel Manhattan in the 1920s* (New York: Farrar, Straus and Giroux, 1995), 8.

[203]*Nashville Tennessean,* 28 June 1925, 2.

the Victorian matriarch—reform, gentility, and sexual and emotional repression. Often they agreed with Sigmund Freud that young men needed to free themselves from their mothers' Oedipal influence. Contrary to what the Victorians and their reforming descendants believed, young people did not need to be "protected"—not by their mothers, and certainly not by a maternalistic state government. Instead, they needed the truth, raw and unadorned. Malone and his team had faith that the rising generation would be able to find its way in the world without constantly being mothered. Many young people in turn lionized the defense attorneys for proclaiming the freedom and maturity of youths. Perhaps the antievolutionists were right: Science and education did threaten to tear children away from the shelter of maternalism.

PART TWO

The Scopes Trial Day by Day: Transcript and Commentary

A NOTE ON THE TEXT

The original transcript suffered from a number of misspellings and grammatical errors as the court reporter attempted to take down all of the participants' words. I have generally left the text alone, although I have occasionally changed the punctuation to accord more closely with the way participants spoke. For the first time an attorney speaks on a given day, I have added a parenthetical *p* or *d* to signify affiliation with the prosecution or the defense. After each day's testimony, you will find a newspaper or periodical reflection on the day's events, just as newspapers of the time printed opinion pieces alongside straight reporting on the trial.

Official trial transcript originally reprinted in *The World's Most Famous Court Trial: Tennessee Evolution Case* (1925; reprint, Dayton, Tenn.: Rhea County Historical Society, 1978).

1

First Day's Proceedings

Friday, July 10, 1925

After weeks of tremendous anticipation, the first day of the Scopes trial was anticlimactic. The court devoted most of the day to jury selection, during which Clarence Darrow learned that the jury pool was a fairly accurate sampling of Rhea County's churchgoing population. One potential jury member, a minister, drew great applause from the crowd when he loudly proclaimed that he preached against evolution. Darrow excused him from the jury box, but in general the defense attorney found that he had to settle for jurors who at least claimed they would listen to the evidence before convicting Scopes.

Partial Text of the Butler Law

(Transcript)

State Representative John Washington Butler's law seemed at first glance to outlaw the teaching of evolution, but the defense and prosecution would in succeeding days fight mightily over the meaning of "divine creation" and the relevance of the final clause to the rest of the act. See in particular the dispute over expert testimony in part two, chapter 5.

Signed into law in Tennessee on 21 March, 1925.

Section 1. Be it enacted by the general assembly of the state of Tennessee, that it shall be unlawful for any teacher in any of the universities, normals and all other public schools of the state, which are supported in whole or in part by the public school funds of the state, to teach any theory that denies the story of the divine creation of man as taught in the Bible, and to teach instead that man has descended from a lower order of animals.

Clarence Darrow Examines a Potential Juror

(Transcript)

Each side in a trial has the right to challenge a certain number of potential jurors to keep them from sitting on the jury. Darrow's relaxed interrogation of one potential juror, J. R. McKenzie, exemplifies the casual atmosphere of the trial's early days. Interestingly, most of the jurors, like McKenzie, confessed that they had heard little or nothing about evolution until the Scopes case came to light.

Clarence Darrow (d): You have lived here a good many years?
J. R. McKenzie: Yes, sir. I have lived in this county all my life. I haven't been here all my life; I was born in this county and raised here.
Q: You are a United States marshal?
A: Yes, sir, I was, for six or five years during Wilson's administration.
Q: That doesn't prejudice you with me. You aren't a farmer, are you?
A: I own a farm; I am no farmer.
Q: Do you know Mr. Scopes?
A: I do not. I hardly know the man by sight. I have seen him; I have seen him on the streets since I have been here, but as to knowing him, I don't.
Q: I presume that you belong to the church?
A: I do. I am not a good member, not as good as I ought to be.
Q: Of what church?
A: Methodist.
Q: Do you work at it very hard?
A: Well, no, sir; not as hard as I ought to.
Q: You go to church sometimes?
A: Yes, I do.
Q: Your wife probably goes more than you do.

A: More than I do.
Q: Well, now, do you read much?
A: I am not an extensive reader, outside of magazines and newspapers; I am not a book reader.
Q: You are not a book reader?
A: No, sir.
Q: Do you take a number of magazines?
A: No, sir, I can't say that I do; I read a great many magazines, but am not a subscriber.
Q: Have you ever heard evolution argued?
A: Yes, I have read that a good deal, and also in the papers.
Q: Now, Mr. Scopes is charged with violating the law. Have you ever given much, if any, attention to the question of evolution?
A: I never have.
Q: That is one of the things you have not studied?
A: No, sir.
Q: You haven't any opinion about it at the present time?
A: Well, I couldn't say that I have no opinion. I have never—it is a question I have made no study of.
Q: So your opinion would not be worth much?
A: No, I don't think it would be, General.

. . .

Darrow: You haven't heard anybody talk about evolution?
McKenzie: General, it has been talked about, especially in this section, since this case came up. I have heard it talked about pro and con, especially since this case came up in this county.
Q: There has been something about it since this case came up?
A: Seems so, yes, sir.
Q: Do you know whether you have heard anybody talk about it who knew anything about it, that you know of?
A: I don't think I have heard anybody talk about it except just generally. I haven't mixed up with the farmers, and the reason I don't know any more about it than I do is perhaps they didn't know much more about it than I did.
Q: That is probably right. Now, let me ask you a little more.
A: Yes, sir; glad to have it.
Q: You are a church member. Are you much of a Bible student?
A: No, sir.
Q: You don't pretend to be very much posted on the Bible, do you?

A: I do not.
Q: And if it was necessary for you to have kept posted, you would not have permitted it to prejudice you one way or another?
A: I have no prejudice whatever.
Q: I can see no reason why I should not take you for a juror. Of course, they would rather not have you on the other side; we are not prejudiced.
A: That is to be left up to you.
Q: Well, you think you can decide it without prejudice?
A: I wouldn't be willing to go into the jury box unless I could.
Q: But you are willing to go in?
A: I prefer not to go.
Q: We understand that. But you think you could be perfectly fair as a juror?
A: Yes, sir.
Darrow: All right; have a seat.

HENRY M. HYDE

Jury Pious, Dayton Hot

July 11, 1925

Most of the reporters in town were, like Henry M. Hyde, from urban areas far removed from Dayton, Tennessee. Do you think Hyde presented an objective picture of the trial? What do you think his biases were?

In a packed courtroom blazing with heat, the first day of the Scopes case ends with twelve men finally accepted in the jury box. Court adjourns until 9 o'clock Monday morning.

Every man but one of the accepted jurors is asked what church he belongs to. That exception is the first man accepted and it develops later that he is not a church member. The one talesman [member

Henry M. Hyde, "Jury for Scopes Trial Selected; Recess Is Taken," *Baltimore Sun,* 11 July 1925, 1.

of the jury pool] who admitted that he belongs to no church is peremptorily challenged by the State. Six of the jurymen are Baptists, four are Methodists and one is a member of the Christian Church. One of the Methodists admits that he does not work at it very hard. . . .

It is a glaring, steaming day here in the mountains. Until after midnight scores of earnest well-dressed men are milling around under the trees in the courthouse yard arguing fine points of religious doctrine. Out in the woods on the mountains around Dayton the echoes of the wild shrieks and the hysteric moans of the Holy Rollers[1] are just dying away. . . .

[1]Hyde and a number of other reporters had earlier watched a Pentecostal service in which participants spoke in tongues.

2

Second Day's Proceedings

Monday, July 13, 1925

The second day saw the defense attempt to quash the indictment of Scopes—which would have ended the trial before it officially began—on the ground that the law itself was unconstitutional. Clarence Darrow had already decided that the defense would deny William Jennings Bryan the opportunity to make a rousing closing speech in the trial by giving up Scopes's right to a closing argument, so the defense attorneys tried to bring out their full battery during the argument over the indictment and during the later argument over whether to admit expert testimony. In addition to arguing a number of minor points of Tennessee law, defense attorneys Arthur Garfield Hays, Dudley Field Malone, and Darrow maintained that the Butler law was too vague and unreasonable in its appeal to the "story of the divine creation of man as taught in the Bible." After the prosecutors Ben McKenzie and Tom Stewart defended the Butler law as a reasonable use of the legislature's authority, Darrow delivered his major speech of the trial—a defense of religious liberty and the high wall of separation between church and state. Note that the attorneys directed most of their constitutional arguments to the Tennessee Constitution; not for another twenty years would the U.S. Supreme Court begin to apply the protections in the Bill of Rights to the states.

Court Opened with a Prayer by Reverend Moffett of Rhea County

(Transcript)

Judge John T. Raulston had each day's session opened with a prayer by a local minister. Why do you think the defense eventually objected to this practice on the third day of the trial?

Rev. Moffett: Oh God, our Father, Thou who are the creator of the heaven and the earth and the sea and all that is in them. Thou who are the preserver and controller of all things, Thou who wilt bring out all things to Thy glory in the end, we thank Thee this morning that Thou doest not only fill the heavens, but Thou doest also fill the earth. We pray Thy blessings upon this Court this morning.

. . .

Indictment Read

(Transcript)

The grand jurors for the state aforesaid, being duly summoned, elected, empaneled, sworn, and charged to inquire for the body of the county aforesaid, upon their oaths present:

That John Thomas Scopes, heretofore on the 24th day of April, 1925, in the county aforesaid, then and there, unlawfully did willfully teach in the public schools of Rhea County, Tennessee, which said public schools are supported in part and in whole by the public school fund of the state, a certain theory and theories that deny the story of the divine creation of man as taught in the Bible, and did teach instead thereof that man has descended from a lower order of animals, he, the said John Thomas Scopes, being at the time, or prior thereto, the teacher in the public schools of Rhea County, Tennessee, aforesaid, against the peace and dignity of the state.

. . .

Defense and Prosecution Dispute Butler Law's Constitutionality

(Transcript)

The defense and prosecution arguments tended to center on the question of whether the Butler law was a reasonable exercise of the legislature's authority. Note the ways in which the defense focused on the liberty of the individual, while the prosecution emphasized the legislature's duty to direct the state's educational system and its teachers. Why did they take such positions? Which arguments seem strongest to you? What other rhetorical strategies did the attorneys employ? How do you think the sectional differences between North and South affected their arguments?

Arthur Garfield Hays (d): Consider this act under the police powers of the state. The only limitation on the liberty of the individual is in the police power of the state. The preservation of public safety and public morals falls under this head. The determination of what is the proper exercise of the police power is under the jurisdiction and supervision of the court.

Now, as to whether a law is reasonable or unreasonable under the police power of the state, I have taken the liberty of drafting a law, which it seems to me would be constitutional if this law is constitutional. I have entitled this an act prohibiting the teaching of the heliocentric theory in all the universities, normals,[1] and all other public schools of Tennessee. . . .

Section 1—Be it enacted by the general assembly of Tennessee, it shall be unlawful for any teacher in any of the universities, normals and all other public schools in the state to teach any theory that denies the story that the earth is the center of the universe, as taught in the Bible, and to teach instead, that the earth and planets move around the sun.

Section 2—Be it further enacted that any teacher found guilty of a violation of this act shall be guilty of a felony, and upon conviction shall be put to death.

Now, my contention is that an act of this sort is clearly unconstitutional in that it is a restriction upon the liberties of the individual,

[1]A normal school, from the French *école normale,* was a teacher-training institution.

and the only reason your Honor would draw a distinction between the proposed act and the one before us is that it is so well fixed scientifically that the earth and planets move around the sun. I might say that when the Copernican theory was first promulgated, he was under censure of the state. . . . The only distinction you can draw between the statute and what we're discussing is that evolution is as much a scientific fact as the Copernican theory, but the Copernican theory has been fully accepted, as this must be accepted.

My contention is that no law can be constitutional unless it is within the right of the state under the police power, and it would only be within the right of the state capacity if it were reasonable, and it would only be reasonable if intended in some way to promote public morals. And, your Honor, and you, gentlemen of the jury, would have to know what evolution is in order to pass upon it. And I feel that it would be in the interest of justice for your Honor to reserve a decision on this motion until after the case is in; then you can determine more definitely whether this comes within the police power of the state. If it is unreasonable, if it is not necessary, or does not conserve the public morals, it is not within the police power. To my mind, the chief point against the constitutionality of this law is that it extends the police powers of the state unreasonably and is a restriction upon the liberty of the individual.

. . .

Gen. Ben McKenzie (p): Under the laws of the land, the Constitution of Tennessee, no particular religion can be taught in the schools. We cannot teach any religion in the schools, therefore you cannot teach any evolution, or any doctrine that conflicts with the Bible. That sets them up exactly equal. No part of the Constitution has been infringed by this act. Under the law we have the right to regulate these matters. . . . Now, the distinguished gentleman, Mr. Hays, got up some indictment by which he was to hang somebody. That was not at all a similar case to this act; it has no connection with it; no such act as that has ever passed through the fertile brain of a Tennessean. I don't know what they do up in his country. It has been held by the Supreme Court that the Tennessee Legislature has the right to arbitrate and to judge as to how they shall proceed in the operation of the schools. . . .

The questions have all been settled in Tennessee, and favorable to our contention. If these gentlemen have any laws in the great metropolitan city of New York that conflict with it, or in the great white city of the Northwest [i.e., Chicago] that will throw any light on it, we will be glad to hear about it. They have many great lawyers and courts up there.

The United States Supreme Court has also sustained our contention in this matter. As to the scientific proposition, the words employed in the Constitution or a statute are to be taken in their natural and popular sense, unless they are technical legal terms, in which event they are to be taken in their technical sense. This is not a statute that requires outside assistance to define. The smallest boy in our Rhea County schools, 16 years of age, knows as much about it as they would after reading it once or twice.

Dudley Field Malone (d): We object to this argument. . . . We are discussing the constitutionality of this indictment on a motion to quash. And I would like to say here, though I do not mean to interrupt the gentleman, but I cannot consider further allusions to geographical parts of the country as particularly necessary, such as reference to New Yorkers and to citizens of Illinois. We are here, rightfully, as American citizens.

The Court: Col. Malone, you do not know Gen. McKenzie as well as the court does. Everything he says is in a good humor.

Malone: I know there are lots of ways of saying—

The Court: I want you gentlemen from New York or any other foreign state, to always remember that you are our guests, and that we accord you the same privileges and rights and courtesies that we do any other lawyer.

Malone: Your Honor, we want to have it understood we deeply appreciate the hospitality of the court and the people of Tennessee, and the courtesies that are being extended to us at this time, but we want it understood that while we are in this courtroom we are here as lawyers, not as guests.

. . .

Sue K. Hicks (p): Taking up another exception or two, the right of religious worship, "that all men have a natural and indefeasible right to worship Almighty God according to the dictates of their own conscience," that seems to me as perfectly ridiculous to say when a state employs a teacher, and he is employed under men appointed by the legislature by their acts, it is perfectly ridiculous to me to think that when they employ that teacher that he can go in and teach any kind of doctrine he wants to teach, and yet be violating that act of free speech, but they say they cannot do that, it would be violating it, if they did. Suppose a teacher wanted to teach architecture in a school when he has been employed to teach mathematics. Suppose he is employed to teach arithmetic to the class which the uniform textbook commission has adopted, and by the way, the uniform textbook commission, as your Honor knows, has been established by the legislature. Suppose that instead of teaching arithmetic this teacher wants to teach architecture. Under their argument they say that they cannot control him and make him teach that arithmetic in that school. They go on and say that his religious worship is hindered thereby. The teaching in the schools has nothing whatever to do with religious worship.... He can preach as he wants to on the streets—his religious rights—but cannot preach them in school.

. . .

Atty. Gen. Tom Stewart (p): "That all men have a natural and indefeasible right to worship Almighty God according to the dictates of their conscience, that no man can of right be compelled to attend, direct, or support any place of worship, that no human authority in no case whatever can control or interfere with the rights of conscience, that no preference shall ever be given by law to any religious establishment or mode of worship."

If your Honor please, this law is as far removed from that interference with the provision in the constitution as it is from any other that is not even cited. This does not interfere with the religious worship—it does not even approach interference with religious worship. This addresses itself directly to the public school system of the state. This does not prevent any man from worshiping God as his conscience directs and dictates. A man can belong to the Baptist, the Methodist, the Lutheran, the Christian or any other church, but still that would not interfere with any portion by any construction you might place on it.... How could it interfere in any particular with religious worship? You can attend the public schools of this state and go to any church you please. This does not require you to harbor within the four walls of your home any minister of any denomination, even. Or, what is there in this act that says you shall contribute to the maintenance of any particular religious sect or cult? There is nothing in the question, if your Honor please, there is not an infringement of the rights of religious freedom or worship.

Clarence Darrow (d): I suggest you eliminate that part you are on so far. The part we claim is that last clause, "no preference shall ever be given, by law, to any religious establishment or mode of worship."

Stewart: Yes, that "no preference shall ever be given, by law, to any religious establishment or mode of worship." Then, how could that interfere, Mr. Darrow?

Darrow: That is the part we claim is affected.

Stewart: In what wise?

Darrow: Giving preference to the Bible.

Stewart: To the Bible?

Darrow: Yes. Why not the Koran?

. . .

Stewart: If your Honor please, the Saint James version of the Bible is the recognized one in this section of the country. The laws of the land recognize the Bible; the laws of the land recognize the law of God and Christianity as a part of the common-law.

Malone: Mr. Attorney General, may I ask a question?

Stewart: Certainly.

Malone: Does the law of the land or the law of the state of Tennessee recognize the Bible as a part of a course, in biology or science?

Stewart: I do not think the law of the land recognizes them as confusing one another in any particular.

Malone: Why does not this statute impose the duty of teaching the theory of creation, as taught in the Bible, and exclude under penalty of the law any other theory of creation; why does not that impose upon the course of science or specifically the course of biology in this state a particular religious opinion from a particular religious book?

Stewart: It is not a religious question.

. . .

Malone: Does not it prefer the Bible to the Koran?

Stewart: We are not living in a heathen country.

Malone: Will you answer my question? Does not it prefer the Bible to the Koran?

Stewart: We are not living in a heathen country, so how could it prefer the Bible to the Koran? . . . Do you say teaching the Bible in the public school is a religious matter?

Malone: No. I would say to base a theory set forth in any version of the Bible to be taught in the public school is an invasion of the rights of the citizen, whether exercised by the police power or by the legislature.

Stewart: Because it imposes a religious opinion?

Malone: Because it imposes a religious opinion, yes. What I mean is this: if there be in the state of Tennessee a single child or young man or young woman in your school who is a Jew, to impose [on] any course of science a particular view of creation from the Bible is interfering, from our point of view, with his civil rights under our theory of the case. That is our contention.

Stewart: Mr. Malone, could not he go to school on Friday and study what is given him by the public school; then on Sunday study his Bible?

Malone: No, he should be given the same right in his views and his rights should not be interfered with by any other doctrine.

Stewart: It is not an invasion of a man's religious rights. He can go to church on Sunday or any other day that there might be a meeting, and worship according to the dictates of his conscience. It is not an invasion of a man's religious liberty or an invasion of a man's religious right. That question cannot determine this act. It is a question of the exercise of the police power. That is what it is, and nothing else, and if they undertake to pass an act to state you shall not teach a certain Bible or theory of anything in your churches, an invasion of a private or civil act, then, according to my conception of this, it might interfere with this provision of the Constitution. But this is the authority, on the part of the legislature of the state of Tennessee, to direct the expenditure of the school funds of the state, and through this act to require that the money shall not be spent in the teaching of the theories that conflict or contravene the Bible story of man's creation. It is an effort on the part of the legislature to control and direct the expenditure of state funds, which they have the right to do. It is an effort on the part of the legislature to control the public school system, which they have the right to do.

. . .

Stewart (cont.): Now this assignment under freedom of speech. . . . Under that question, I say, Mr. Scopes might have taken his stand on the street corners and expounded until he became hoarse as a result of his effort and we could not interfere with him; but he cannot go into the public schools, or a schoolhouse, which is controlled by the legislature and supported by the public funds of the state and teach this theory. Under the exercise of the police power, we should have a right to object to it. The legislature has a right to control that.

. . .

Now, what is the difference? If the state has a right in the exercise of its police power to say you cannot teach Wentworth's *Arithmetic* or Fry's *Geography,* it has the same right to say you cannot teach any theory that denies the divine creation of man. That is true because the legislature is the judge of what shall be taught in the public schools. . . . They have a right to say and no one else has a right to say, and I say, your Honor, that in the passage of this act the legislature abused no discretion, but used only the reasonable means at hand.

. . .

Darrow's Major Speech in Defense of Religious Liberty

(Transcript)

Darrow began by arguing that the guarantees of religious worship in the Tennessee Constitution protected teachers even against the will of the majority acting through the legislature. Although his ostensible purpose was to underline the unconstitutionality of the Butler Act, Darrow also seized the opportunity to lay out a philosophical defense of religious liberty in a diverse society. What were Darrow's legal objections to the Butler law? Were they consistent with his philosophical objections? Why did Darrow consider the Butler law to be so dangerous?

Darrow: I know my friend, McKenzie, whom I have learned not only to admire, but to love in our short acquaintance, didn't mean anything in referring to us lawyers who come from out of town. For myself, I have been treated with the greatest courtesy by the attorneys and the community.

The Court: No talking, please, in the courtroom.

Darrow: And I shall always remember that this court is the first one that ever gave me a great title of "Colonel" and I hope it will stick to me when I get back north.

The Court: I want you to take it back to your home with you, Colonel.

Darrow: That is what I am trying to do.

But, so far as coming from other cities is concerned, why, your Honor, it is easy here. I came from Chicago, and my friend, Malone, and friend Hays came from New York, and on the other side we have a distinguished and very pleasant gentleman who came from California and another who is prosecuting this case, and who is responsible for this foolish, mischievous, and wicked act, who comes from Florida.[2]

This case we have to argue is a case at law, and hard as it is for me to bring my mind to conceive it, almost impossible as it is to put my mind back into the sixteenth century, I am going to argue as if it was serious, and as if it was a death struggle between two civilizations.

Let us see, now, what there is about it. We have been informed that the legislature has the right to prescribe the course of study in the public schools. Within reason, they no doubt have, no doubt. They could not prescribe it, I am inclined to think, under your Constitution, if it omitted arithmetic and geography and writing, neither under the rest of the Constitution if it shall remain in force in the state, could they prescribe it if the course of study was only to teach religion, because several hundred years ago, when our people believed in freedom, and when no man felt so sure of their own sophistry that they were willing to send a man to jail who did not believe them, the people of Tennessee adopted a constitution, and they made it broad and plain, and said that the people of Tennessee should always enjoy religious freedom in its broadest terms. So I assume that no legislature could fix a course of study which violated that. For instance, suppose the legislature should say, "We think the religious privileges and duties of the citizens of Tennessee are much more important than education; we agree with the distinguished governor of the state, if religion must go, or learning must go, why, let learning go." I do not know how much it would

[2]A dig at William Jennings Bryan Jr., who had taken leave from his law practice in California to aid the prosecution, and at William Jennings Bryan himself, who had recently relocated from Nebraska to Florida.

have to go, but let it go. "And therefore we will establish a course in the public schools of teaching that the Christian religion as unfolded in the Bible is true, and that every other religion, or mode or system of ethics is false, and to carry that out, no person in the public schools shall be permitted to read or hear anything except Genesis, *Pilgrim's Progress,* Baxter's *Saint Rest,* and *In His Image.*" Would that be constitutional? If it is, the Constitution is a lie and a snare and the people have forgot what liberty means.

I remember long ago, Mr. Bancroft[3] wrote this sentence, which is true: "That it is all right to preserve freedom in constitutions, but when the spirit of freedom has fled from the hearts of the people, then its matter is easily sacrificed under law." And so it is. Unless there is left enough of the spirit of freedom in the state of Tennessee, and in the United States, there is not a single line of any constitution that can withstand bigotry and ignorance when it seeks to destroy the rights of the individual; and bigotry and ignorance are ever active. Here, we find today as brazen and as bold an attempt to destroy learning as was ever made in the middle ages, and the only difference is we have not provided that they shall be burned at the stake, but there is time for that, your Honor. We have to approach these things gradually.

Now, let us see what we claim with reference to this law. If this proceeding both in form and substance can prevail in this court, then your Honor, no law—no matter how foolish, wicked, ambiguous, or ancient—but can come back to Tennessee. All the guarantees go for nothing. All of the past has gone, will be forgotten, if this can succeed.

. . .

Darrow (cont.): Now, as to the statute itself. It is full of weird, strange, impossible and imaginary provisions. . . . It says you shan't teach any theory of the origin of man that is contrary to the divine theory contained in the Bible. Now let us pass up the word "divine"! No legislature is strong enough in any state in the Union to characterize and pick any book as being divine. Let us take it as it is. What is the Bible? Your Honor, I have read it myself. I might read it more or less wisely. Others may understand it better. Others may think they understand it better when they do not. But in a general way I know what it is. I know there are millions of people who look

[3]American historian George Bancroft (1800–1891).

on it as a divine book, and I have not the slightest objection to it. I know there are millions of people in the world who derive consolation in their times of trouble and solace in times of distress from the Bible. I would be pretty near the last one in the world to do anything or take any action to take it away. I feel just exactly the same toward the religious creed of every human being who lives. If anybody finds anything in this life that brings them consolation and health and happiness, I think they ought to have it whatever they get. I haven't any fault to find with them at all. But what is it? The Bible is not one book. The Bible is made up of 66 books written over a period of about 1,000 years, some of them very early and some of them comparatively late. It is a book primarily of religion and morals. It is not a book of science. Never was and was never meant to be. Under it there is nothing prescribed that would tell you how to build a railroad or a steamboat or to make anything that would advance civilization. It is not a textbook or a text on chemistry. It is not big enough to be. It is not a book on geology; they knew nothing about geology. It is not a book on biology; they knew nothing about it. It is not a work on evolution; that is a mystery. . . . There are no doubt certain primitive, elemental instincts in the organs of man that remain the same; he finds out what he can and yearns to know more and he supplements his knowledge with hope and faith. That is the province of religion and I haven't the slightest fault to find with it. Not the slightest in the world. . . .

Let's see now. Can your Honor tell what is given as the origin of man as shown in the Bible? Is there any human being who can tell us? There are two conflicting accounts in the first two chapters. There are scattered all through it various acts and ideas, but to pass that up for the sake of argument, no teacher in any school in the state of Tennessee can know that he is violating a law, but must test every one of its doctrines by the Bible, must he not? . . .

[The law] does not specify what you cannot teach, but says you cannot teach anything that conflicts with the Bible. Then just imagine making a criminal code that is so uncertain and impossible that every man must be sure that he has read everything in the Bible and not only read it but understands it, or he might violate the criminal code. Who is the chief mogul that can tell us what the Bible means? He or they should write a book and make it plain and distinct, so we would know. Let us look at it. There are in America at least 500 different sects or churches, all of which quarrel with each other over the importance and nonimportance of certain things or the construction of certain passages. All along the line they do not agree among themselves and cannot agree among themselves. They never have and probably never will. There is a great division between the Catholics and the Protestants. There is such a disagreement that my client, who is a schoolteacher, not only must know the subject he is teaching, but he must know everything about the Bible in reference to evolution. And he must be sure that he expresses his right or else some fellow will come along here, more ignorant perhaps than he and say, "You made a bad guess and I think you have committed a crime." No criminal statute can rest that way.

. . .

Darrow (cont.): If this section of the constitution which guarantees religious liberty in Tennessee cannot be sustained in the spirit, it cannot be sustained in the letter. What does it mean? What does it mean? I know two intelligent people can agree only for a little distance, like a company walking along in a road. They may go together a few blocks and then one branches off. The remainder go together a few more blocks and another branches off and still further someone else branches off, and the human minds are just that way, provided they are free, of course. The fundamentalists may be put in a trap so they cannot think differently if at all, probably not at all, but leave two free minds and they may go together a certain distance but not all the way together. There are no two human machines alike and no two human beings have the same experiences and their ideas of life and philosophy grow out of their construction of the experiences that we meet on our journey through life. It is impossible, if you leave freedom in the world, to mold the opinions of one man upon the opinions of another—only tyranny can do it—and your constitutional provision, providing a freedom of religion, was meant to meet that emergency. . . .

There is nothing else, your Honor, that has caused the difference of opinion, of bitterness, of hatred, of war, of cruelty, that religion has caused. With that, of course, it has given consolation to millions. But it is one of those particular things that should be left solely between the individual and his Maker, or his God, or whatever takes expression with him, and it is no one else's concern. . . .

It was meant by the constitutional convention of Tennessee to leave these questions of religion between man and whatever he worshiped, to leave him free.

. . .

Your life and my life and the life of every American citizen depends after all upon the tolerance and forbearance of his fellowman. If men are not tolerant, if men cannot respect each other's opinions, if men cannot live and let live, then no man's life is safe, no man's life is safe.

Here is a country made up of Englishmen, Irishmen, Scotch, German, Europeans, Asiatics, Africans, men of every sort and men of every creed and men of every scientific belief. Who is going to begin this sorting out and say, "I shall measure you; I know you are a fool, or worse; I know and I have read a creed telling what I know and I will make people go to heaven even if they don't want to go with me, I will make them do it." Where is the man wise enough to do it?

. . .

To strangle puppies is good when they grow up into mad dogs, maybe. I will tell you what is going to happen, and I do not pretend to be a prophet, but I do not need to be a prophet to know. Your Honor knows the fires that have been lighted in America to kindle religious bigotry and hate. . . . If today you can take a thing like evolution and make it a crime to teach it in the public school, tomorrow you can make it a crime to teach it in the private schools, and the next year you can make it a crime to teach it to the hustings or in the church. At the next session you may ban books and the newspapers. Soon you may set Catholic against Protestant and Protestant against Protestant, and try to foist your own religion upon the minds of men. If you can do one you can do the other. Ignorance and fanaticism is ever busy and needs feeding. Always it is feeding and gloating for more. Today it is the public school teachers, tomorrow the private. The next day the preachers and the lecturers, the magazines, the books, the newspapers. After a while, your Honor, it is the setting of man against man and creed against creed until with flying banners and beating drums we are marching backward to the glorious ages of the sixteenth century, when bigots lighted fagots to burn the men who dared to bring any intelligence and enlightenment and culture to the human mind.

(Court adjourned for the day.)

H. L. MENCKEN

Darrow's Speech Great but Futile

July 14, 1925

Henry Louis Mencken (1880–1956), a reporter and free-ranging intellectual from Baltimore, had been gaining fame before the 1920s as a caustic commentator on American social life, but his national reputation blossomed with his reportage from Dayton.

The net effect of Clarence Darrow's great speech yesterday seems to be precisely the same as if he had bawled it up a rainspout in the interior of Afghanistan. That is, locally, upon the process against the infidel Scopes, upon the so-called minds of these fundamentalists of upland Tennessee. You have but a dim notion of it who have only read it. It was not designed for reading, but for hearing. The clangtint [sound or timbre] of it was as important as the logic. It rose like a wind and ended like a flourish of bugles. The very judge on the bench, toward the end of it, began to look uneasy. But the morons in the audience, when it was over, simply hissed it.

During the whole time of its delivery the old mountebank, Bryan, sat tightlipped and unmoved. There is, of course, no reason why it should have shaken him. He has these hill billies locked up in his pen and he knows it. His brand is on them.

H. L. Mencken, "Darrow's Speech Great but Futile," *Baltimore Evening Sun,* 14 July 1925, 1.

3

Third Day's Proceedings

Tuesday, July 14, 1925

Judge John T. Raulston adjourned court early on the third day while he prepared his decision on the constitutionality of the Butler law, to be read the following day. However, in the wake of Clarence Darrow's pointed attacks the previous day on William Jennings Bryan and the Butler law, a tone of hostility crept into the third day's proceedings. This tone was amplified by the defense team's objections to Judge Raulston's practice of opening each court session with a prayer, usually from a fundamentalist-leaning minister, even though this was a fairly common practice in many jurisdictions throughout the nation. After some sniping over the defense team's religion and geographic origins, defense attorney Arthur Garfield Hays presented a petition from a group of more liberal clergy objecting to the prayers. Was it wise of the defense to object to the prayers? Why do you think the prosecution responded so strongly?

Defense Objects to Prayers; Prosecution Defends Practice

(Transcript)

However well supported by modernist ministers, the defense's attack on courtroom prayers was perhaps the single most controversial element of its conduct of the trial, at least in the South.

The Court: Rev. Stribling will you open with prayer?

Clarence Darrow (d): Your Honor, I want to make an objection before the jury comes in.

The Court: What is it, Mr. Darrow?

Darrow : I object to prayer and I object to the jury being present when the court rules on the objection.

. . .

I understand from the court himself that he has sometimes opened the court with prayer and sometimes not, and we took no exceptions on the first day, but seeing this has persisted in every session, and the nature of this case being one where it is claimed by the state that there is a conflict between science and religion, above all other cases there should be no part taken outside of the evidence in this case and no attempt by means of prayer or in any other way to influence the deliberation and consideration of the jury of the facts in this case.

For that reason we object to the opening of the court with prayer. . . . I do not object to the jury or anyone else praying in secret or in private, but I do object to the turning of this courtroom into a meetinghouse in the trial of this case. You have no right to do it.

The Court: You have a right to put your exceptions in the record.

Atty. Gen. Tom Stewart (p): . . . The state makes no contention, as stated by counsel for the defense, that this is a conflict between science and religion insofar as the merits are concerned. It is a case involving the fact as to whether or not a schoolteacher has taught a doctrine prohibited by statute, and we, for the state, think it is quite proper to open the court with prayer if the court sees fit to do it, and such an idea extended by the agnostic counsel for the defense is foreign to the thoughts and ideas of the people who do not know anything about infidelity and care less.

Arthur Garfield Hays (d): May I ask to enter an exception to the statement, "agnostic counsel for the defense"?

Dudley Field Malone (d): I would like to reply to this remark of the attorney general. Whereas I respect my colleague Mr. Darrow's right to believe or not to believe as long as he is as honest in his unbelief as I am in my belief. As one of the members of counsel who is not an agnostic, I would like to state the objection from my point of view. . . . I would like to ask your Honor whether in all the trials over which your Honor has presided, this court has had a clergyman every morning of every day of every trial to open the court with prayer?

Our objection goes to the fact that we believe that this daily opening of the court with prayers, those prayers we have already heard, having been duly argumentative that they helped to increase the atmosphere of hostility to our point of view, which already exists in this community by widespread propaganda.

Stewart: In reply to that there is still no question involved in this lawsuit as to whether or not Scopes taught a doctrine prohibited by the statute, that is that man descended from a lower order of animals. So far as creating an atmosphere of hostility is concerned, I would advise Mr. Malone that this is a God fearing country.

Malone: And it is no more God fearing country than that from which I came.

The Court: Gentlemen, do not turn this into an argument. . . . I believe in prayer myself; I constantly invoke divine guidance myself, when I am on the bench and off the bench; I see no reason why I should not continue to do this. . . . Therefore, I am pleased to overrule the objection of counsel and invite Dr. Stribling to open the court with prayer.

Dr. Stribling: Our Father, to Thee we give all the praise for every good thing in life and we invoke Thy blessings upon us this morning. . . . We pray, our Father, to bless the proceedings of this court, bless the court, the judge, as he presides, and may there be in every heart and in every mind a reverence to the Great Creator of the world.

. . .

Hays: Before your Honor presents a decision or the proceedings go further, may I present a petition to the court? . . . "We, the following named representatives of various well-known religious organizations, churches, and synagogues, do hereby petition your Honor that if you continue your custom of opening the daily sessions of the court of Rhea County with prayer—"

Stewart: Your Honor, just a minute. I submit that is absolutely out of order. . . .

Hays: I insist upon making this motion.

Stewart: I am making my exception to the court, will you please keep your mouth shut?

. . .

The Court: I will hear it. Proceed, Mr. Hays.

Hays: "We, the following representatives of various well-known religious organizations, churches, and synagogues, do hereby petition your Honor that, if you continue your custom of opening the daily sessions of the court of Rhea County with prayer, you select the officiating clergymen from among other than fundamentalist churches in alternation with fundamentalist clergymen.

"We beg you to consider the fact that among the persons intimately connected with, and actively participating in this trial of Mr. John T. Scopes there are many to whom the prayers of the fundamentalists are not spiritually uplifting and are occasionally offensive. Inasmuch as by your own ruling all the people in the courtroom are required to participate in the prayers by rising, it seems to us only just and right that we should occasionally hear a prayer which requires no mental reservations on our part and in which we can conscientiously participate.

"Signed, Rev. Charles Potter, Minister, West Side Unitarian Church, New York; Rabbi Jerome Mark, Temple Beth-El, Knoxville, Tenn.; Rev. Fred W. Hagan, First Congregational Church, Huntington, W. Va.; Rev. D. M. Welch, Minister, Knoxville Unitarian Church."

My motion, your Honor, is, without, of course, giving up our exception to your Honor's ruling, that if the court denies that, this petition be granted and that we have an opportunity to hear prayer by men who think that God has shown his divinity in the wonders of the world, in the book of nature, quite as much as in the book of the revealed word.

The Court: I shall refer that petition to the pastors' association of this town, and I shall ask them—

(Laughter and loud applause, and rapping for order by the policeman.[1])

—I shall ask the pastors' association from now on to name the man who is to conduct prayer. I shall have no voice, make no suggestions as to who they name, but I will invite the man named by the association to conduct prayer each morning.

[1]Court attendees laughed because Dayton's pastors' association was strongly antievolutionist. Interestingly, the association chose the Reverend Charles Potter, a celebrated modernist who had signed the petition of objection, to deliver the next day's prayer.

NASHVILLE TENNESSEAN

Courtroom Prayer Defended

July 21, 1925

As the lead newspaper of the state's capital city, the Nashville Tennessean *became a prime outlet for the debate between evolutionists and antievolutionists, although the paper itself inclined toward support for Bryan. In the following editorial, how did the* Tennessean *present the trial? In what ways did this image differ from the portrait offered by "outsiders" such as Henry Hyde and H. L. Mencken?*

Many of those at Dayton from other states (and especially the imported members of the bar) have forgotten, if they ever knew, that we are a people predominantly of Anglo-Saxon blood; a people who have never failed to receive as a call to arms a challenge of [*sic*] any of the bulwarks of liberty bequeathed to our common country; a people who are sprung from a race of pioneers who relied upon the Bible and the guidance of a Supreme Being to win a new empire from a wilderness, that in the winning those principles enunciated in the Bill of Rights might be practiced undisturbed and held inviolate for posterity.

That counsel for the defense made a grave error when objection was entered to the creditable custom of opening a session of court with prayer is now conceded. . . .

In this hour of our trial it is good to remember that in the last analysis we will not be judged by what has been done at Dayton, but how the people of Tennessee as a whole have conducted themselves under difficult conditions. We have no apologies to offer for our customs that include an appeal to Divine Power and we are content to await the sober judgment of the American people as to who are the provincials, the "yokels" and the "bigots"—the people of Tennessee or the learned counsel for the defense at Dayton.

Editorial, *Nashville Tennessean,* 21 July 1925, 4.

4

Fourth Day's Proceedings

Wednesday, July 15, 1925

Fortunately for all concerned, Judge John T. Raulston declined to quash the indictment of Scopes for violating the Butler law. The trial could go on. The prosecution and defense then both outlined their theories of the case. The prosecutors felt that all they needed to do was prove that Scopes had taught that man descended from a lower order of animal, and this would automatically mean that he had taught contrary to the biblical story of creation. The defense attorneys, according to Dudley Field Malone, maintained that the prosecutors had to prove both elements—that Scopes had taught evolution and that evolution contradicted the divine account in Genesis. Malone promised that the defense's expert witnesses would demonstrate that evolution and Christianity were indeed compatible. The day ended with the examination of witnesses to Scopes's evolutionary teaching, including a pair of his former students, and with some preliminary expert testimony from Dr. Maynard Metcalf of Johns Hopkins University, the only defense expert allowed to take the witness stand during the trial.

Darrow Proud of Agnosticism

(Transcript)

The issue of Clarence Darrow's faith—or lack thereof—surfaced repeatedly during the trial. How do you think Darrow's outlook affected his legal strategy? How do you think it affected popular perceptions of his motives?

Clarence Darrow (d): I don't want the court to think I take any exceptions to Mr. Stewart's statements [on day three]. Of course, the weather is warm, and we may all go a little further at times than we ought, but he is perfectly justified in saying that I am an agnostic, for I am, and I do not consider it an insult, but rather a compliment to be called an agnostic. I do not pretend to know where many ignorant men are sure; that is all agnosticism means. . . . But while I take no offense for anybody to say in any way that I am an agnostic, for I am, I think everybody's religious rights and religious liberties are protected under the Constitution of Tennessee, and if not, they would be protected under the fellowship that we owe to each other, and I do not think that anybody's religious creed should be used for the purpose of prejudicing or influencing any action in this case. . . .

The Court: What do you say, General Stewart?

Atty. Gen. Thomas Stewart (p): I think we are wasting a lot of valuable time, your Honor, in felicitation, and I am ready if these gentlemen will join me, in trying this lawsuit as lawyers. I would like to get done with this thing.

Raulston Rules on Motion to Quash Indictment; Cases Outlined

(Transcript)

Judge Raulston agreed with the prosecution that the Butler law did little to interfere with Tennessee's constitutional guarantees of freedom of religion and speech. Which parts of his argument seem strongest to you? Weakest? The prosecution and defense then outlined their arguments for the rest of the case.

The Court: . . . Now, the court is about to read his opinion on the motion to quash the indictment, but I shall expect absolute order in the courtroom because people are entitled to hear this opinion.

Let us have order. No talking, now; let us have order in the courtroom.

If you gentlemen want to make my picture, make it now. (Laughter in the courtroom.)

(Photographing of the court follows.)

The Court: It will be observed that the first provision in this section of our constitution provides that all men shall have the natural and indefeasible right to worship almighty God according to the dictates of their own consciences. I fail to see how this act in any wise interferes or in the least restrains any person from worshiping God in the manner that best pleaseth him. It gives no preference to any particular religion or mode of worship. Our public schools are not maintained as places of worship, but, on the contrary, were designed, instituted, and maintained for the purpose of mental and moral development and discipline. . . .

I cannot conceive how the teacher's rights under this provision of the constitution would be violated by the act in issue. There is no law in this state of Tennessee that undertakes to compel this defendant, or any other citizen, to accept employment in the public schools. The relations between the teacher and his employer are purely contractual and if his conscience constrains him to teach the evolution theory, he can find opportunities elsewhere in other schools in the state, to follow the dictates of his conscience, and give full expression to his beliefs and convictions upon this and other subjects without any interference from the state of Tennessee or its authorities, so far as the act is concerned. Neither do I see how the act raises any restraint on his right to worship according to the dictates of his conscience. Under the provisions of this act this defendant, or any other person, can entertain any religious belief which most appeals to their conscience. He can attend any church or connect himself with any denomination or contribute to the erection of buildings to be used for public worship as he sees fit. The court is pleased to overrule these grounds.

. . .

The court, having passed on each ground chronologically, and given the reasons therefor, is now pleased to overrule the whole motion, and require the defendant to plead further.

. . .

Defense Pleads Not Guilty; Cases Outlined

(Transcript)

The Court: What is your plea, gentlemen?

John Randolph Neal (d): Not guilty, may it please your Honor.

The Court: Not guilty. Now gentlemen, I shall ask the counsel for both sides to make an opening statement, please, in which you will please briefly outline what your theory is in the case, before I swear the jury.

Stewart: It is the insistence of the state in this case, that the defendant, John Thomas Scopes, has violated the antievolution law, what is known as the antievolution law, by teaching in the public schools of Rhea County the theory tending to show that man and mankind is descended from a lower order of animals. Therefore, he has taught a theory which denies the story of divine creation of man as taught in the Bible.

. . .

Dudley Field Malone (d): In contradiction of the opinion of the legal leader of the prosecution, the attorney general, the defense contends that before you, gentlemen of the jury, can convict the defendant, Scopes, of a violation of this act, the prosecution must prove two things:

First—That Scopes taught a theory that denies the story of the divine creation of man as taught in the Bible, and

Second—That instead and in place of this theory he taught that man is descended from a lower order of animals.

The defense contends that to convict Scopes the prosecution must prove that Scopes not only taught the theory of evolution, but that he also, and at the same time, denied the theory of creation as set forth in the Bible.... We shall show by the testimony of men learned in science and theology that there are millions of people who believe in evolution and in the stories of creation as set forth in the Bible and who find no conflict between the two. The defense maintains that this is a matter of faith and interpretation, which each individual must determine for himself.... While the defense thinks there is a conflict between evolution and the Old Testament, we believe there is no conflict between evolution and Christianity. There may be a conflict between evolution and the peculiar ideas of Christianity which are held by Mr. Bryan as the evangelical leader of the prosecution, but we deny that the evangelical leader of the prosecution is an authorized spokesman for the Christians of the United States. The defense maintains that there is a clear distinction between God, the church, the Bible, Christianity, and Mr. Bryan.

. . .

Malone (cont.): We maintain and we shall prove that Christianity is bound up with no scientific theory, that it has survived 2,000 years in the face of all the discoveries of science and that Christianity will continue to grow in respect and influence if the people recognize that there is no conflict with science and Christianity. We will show that science occupies a field of learning separate and apart from the learning of theology which the clergy expound. . . .

Much of this learning we hope to set before you will not be found in the Bible, but we maintain that all scientific truth cannot be contained in the Bible since so many truths that we all know about have been discovered since the Bible was written. Moses never heard about steam, electricity, the telegraph, the telephone, the radio, the aeroplane, farming machinery, and Moses knew nothing about scientific thought and principles from which these vast accomplishments of the inventive genius of mankind have been produced. . . .

The defense denies that it is part of any movement or conspiracy on the part of scientists to destroy the authority of Christianity or the Bible. . . . The defense maintains that the book of Genesis is in part a hymn, in part an allegory and a work of religious interpretations written by men who believed that the earth was flat and whose authority cannot be accepted to control the teachings of science in our schools.

. . .

Examination of Howard Morgan, One of Scopes's Students

(Transcript)

A crime needs witnesses, and so the state produced several students who testified, at Scopes's urging, that the teacher had indeed taught them evolution from George W. Hunter's book A Civic Biology.

Stewart: How old are you?
Howard Morgan: 14 years.
Q: Did you attend school here at Dayton last year?
A: Yes, sir.
Q: What school?
A: High school.
Q: Central High School?
A: Yes, sir.
Q: Did you study anything under Prof. Scopes?
A: Yes, sir.

. . .

Stewart: I ask you further, Howard, how did he classify man with reference to other animals; what did he say about them?
Morgan: Well, the book and he both classified man along with cats and dogs, cows, horses, monkeys, lions, horses and all that.
Q: What did he say they were?
A: Mammals.
Q: Classified them along with dogs, cats, horses, monkeys and cows?
A: Yes, sir.

. . .

Darrow: Now, Howard, what do you mean by classify?
Morgan: Well, it means classify these animals we mentioned, that men were just the same as them, in other words—
Q: He didn't say a cat was the same as a man?
A: No, sir; he said man had a reasoning power; that these animals didn't have a reasoning power.
Q: There is some doubt about that, but that is what he said, is it?
(Laughter in the court.)
The Court: Order.
Stewart: With some men.
Darrow: A great many. Now, Howard, he said they were all mammals, didn't he?
Morgan: Yes, sir.
Q: Did he tell you what a mammal was, or don't you remember?
A: Well, he just said these animals were mammals and man was a mammal.

. . .

Darrow: Now, he said the earth was once a molten mass of liquid, didn't he?
Morgan: Yes, sir.
Q: By molten, you understand melted?
A: Yes, sir.
Q: Running molten mass of liquid, and that it slowly cooled until a crust was formed on it?
A: Yes, sir.
Q: After that, after it got cooled enough, and the soil came, that plants grew; is that right?
A: Yes, sir; yes, sir.
Q: And that the first life was in the sea? And that it developed into life on the land?
A: Yes, sir.
Q: And finally into the highest organism which is known as man?
A: Yes, sir.
Q: Now, that is about what he taught you? It has not hurt you any, has it?
A: No, sir.
Darrow: That's all.

W. O. McGEEHAN

Trial Shows Wisdom of Youth

October 1925

McGeehan, a reporter from the North, demonstrated a fine eye for the sociology of Dayton. Note as well the author's attempt to place Howard Morgan's testimony in the broader context of the rise of a "youth culture" in the 1920s. Where does the Scopes trial fit with what you know of the struggle over young people in that decade? See also the readings on educational freedom and the New Woman in chapters 3 and 4 of part three.

W. O. McGeehan, "Why Pick on Dayton?" *Harper's Monthly,* Oct. 1925, 625–27.

Everywhere in Dayton there was this touching curiosity. Robinson's drugstore sold out the complete stock of Hunter's *Civic Biology*. The place was swamped with orders for forbidden literature concerning evolution. . . .

There was little Howard Morgan, aged fourteen, a pupil of this heretic from Paducah, Kentucky [i.e., Scopes]. . . . Of course the first witness called had to be a Morgan. Most of the voters of Rhea County are Morgans. The McKenzies are fairly numerous, but the Morgans are the indigenous family.

Under questioning by the Attorney General of Tennessee, little Howard Morgan told how he had been taught the nebular hypothesis after the teaching of that iniquity had been made illegal in Tennessee. Also, he had been taught about mammals. He delivered this damning testimony in low tones because Howard Morgan worshipped John Thomas Scopes. All of the pupils worshipped him.

Under cross-examination by Mr. Clarence Darrow, Howard volunteered the information that he had not known that the whale was a mammal.

"Well, you do know now," said Mr. Darrow. "It has not done you any harm, has it?"

"No, sir," replied Howard Morgan.

"It is for the mother of this boy to say what harm this diabolical business has done him," thundered a member of the prosecution. Mr. Darrow only twiddled his galluses. [suspenders]

That night one of the more enterprising correspondents interviewed the mother of young Howard Morgan. She said that the morals of her boy had been unimpaired by the course in Hunter's *Civic Biology*. He was a good boy and a bright boy. She was proud of him. She wanted him to learn more about evolution and everything else. He was as keen a Bible student as he was a student of biology. This testimony, of course, did not go to the jury. . . .

Tennessee's future is in the hands of such as Howard. All of our states are in the hands of such as these, who are taught at an early age that whales are mammals and whose imaginations are stimulated by such intriguing works as Hunter's *Civic Biology*—which leads me to believe that the future of the whole country is safe and sane.

The world-wide conflict between youth and settled maturity was being waged in Dayton, and youth was winning as youth is winning all over the world. Age remained resentful and bitter.

5

Fifth Day's Proceedings

Thursday, July 16, 1925

Except for Clarence Darrow's lecture on day two, all of the major speeches of the trial were delivered on the fifth day. The central issue was expert testimony: Did the defense have the right to present experts to argue that evolution was compatible with the story of divine creation in the Bible, or did a plain reading of the Butler law make expert witnesses unnecessary? The question resonated well beyond its legal meaning, for arguments about the admissibility of scientific testimony echoed the broader debate over whether Tennessee should bar scientific expertise from the classroom.

For the first time during the trial, William Jennings Bryan spoke, arguing against expert testimony and against the dangers of outside experts subverting the will of a Tennessee majority. Bryan's well-received speech brought forth a counterargument from his former deputy in the State Department, Dudley Field Malone, who delivered at high volume a plea for tolerance and scientific knowledge that even the author of the Butler Act hailed as "the greatest speech of the century."[1] Finally, Attorney General Thomas Stewart rebutted Malone, albeit at a lower volume, with an explanation of the legislature's intent in passing the Butler Act, and an anguished defense of the right to faith in an age of scientific progress. Can you see grounds for compromise between the prosecution and defense positions? Why or why not?

[1]Edward J. Larson, *Summer for the Gods: The Scopes Trial and America's Continuing Debate over Science and Religion* (New York: Basic Books, 1997), 179.

Defense Pleads for Expert Testimony

(Transcript)

In the course of arguing for their scientific and theological experts to be heard, Scopes's defenders reproduced the modernists' objections to a literal interpretation of the Bible. Do you agree that the defense had a right to introduce expert testimony? Did the defense's faith in scientific expertise differ significantly from the prosecution's religious faith? Why or why not?

Clarence Darrow (d): We expect to show by men of science and learning—both scientists and real scholars of the Bible—men who know what they are talking about—who have made some investigation—expect to show first what evolution is, and, secondly, that any interpretation of the Bible that intelligent men could possibly make is not in conflict with any story of creation, while the Bible, in many ways, is in conflict with every known science, and there isn't a human being on earth believes it literally. We expect to show that it isn't in conflict with the theory of evolution. We expect to show what evolution is, and the interpretation of the Bible that prevails with men of intelligence who have studied it. This is an evolutionist who has shown amply that he knows his subject and is competent to speak, and we insist that a jury cannot decide this important question which means the final battle ground between science and religion—according to our friend here—without knowing both what evolution is and the interpretation of the story of creation.

. . .

Atty. Gen. Tom Stewart (p): The state moves to exclude the testimony of the scientists by which the counsel for the defendant claim that they may be able to show that there is no conflict between science and religion, or in question, and the story of divine creation of man, on the grounds that under the wording of the act and interpretation of the act, which we insist interprets itself, this evidence would be entirely incompetent.

The act states that should be unlawful, that this theory that denies the divine story of creation, and to teach instead thereof that man descended from a lower order of animals, with that expression, and they have admitted that Mr. Scopes taught that man descended from a lower order of animals. The act under what we insist is a proper construction thereof, would preclude any evidence from any scientist, any expert, or any person, that there is no conflict between the story of divine creation, as taught in the Bible, and proof that a teacher tells his scholars that man descended from a lower order of animals.

The act says that they shall not teach that man descended from a lower order of animals according to our construction, and for these reasons this testimony would be incompetent.

In other words, the act does say that it shall be a violation of the law to teach such a theory, and, therefore, they cannot come in here and try to prove that what is the law is not the law. That would be the effect of it.

. . .

William Jennings Bryan Jr. (p): If the court please.

The attorney general has requested me on this discussion to divide the time on the expert testimony. It is, I think, apparent to all that we have now reached the heart of this case. Upon your Honor's ruling, as to whether this expert testimony will be admitted largely determines the question of whether this trial from now on, will be an orderly effort to try the case upon the issues raised by the indictment and by the plea, or whether it will degenerate into a joint debate upon the merits or demerits of someone's views upon evolution.

John Randolph Neal (d): We are very anxious to hear every word. Can you speak a little louder?

Bryan Jr.: This expert evidence is being offered for the avowed purpose of showing that the theory of evolution as understood by the witness offering the testimony does not contradict the Biblical account of creation, as understood by the witness. All of which, the state contends, is wholly immaterial, incompetent and inadmissible.

. . .

Now, if the court please, as the state sees this case, the only issue this jury has to pass upon is whether or not what John Scopes taught is a violation of the law. That is the issue, and it is the only issue that the jury is to pass upon, and we maintain that this cannot be the subject of expert testimony. To permit an expert to testify upon this issue would be to [substitute] trial by experts for trial by jury, and to announce to the world your Honor's belief that this jury is too stupid to determine a simple question of fact.

. . .

Arthur Garfield Hays (d): If your Honor please, I am learning every day more about the procedure in the state of Tennessee. First, our opponents object to the jury hearing the law; now, they are objecting to the jury hearing the facts. The jury is to pass on questions that are agitated not only in this country, but, I dare say, in the whole world. . . . Certainly no court has ever held it to be dangerous to admit the opinions of scientific men in testimony. Jurors cannot pass upon debatable scientific questions without hearing the facts from men who know. Is there anything in Anglo-Saxon law that insists that the determination of either court or jury must be made in ignorance? Somebody once said that God has bountifully provided expert witnesses on both sides of every case. But, in this case, I believe all our expert witnesses, all the scientists in the country are only on one side of the question; and they are not here, your Honor, to give opinions; they are here to state facts. . . .

With respect to the remark made by Gen. McKenzie the other day when he said that any Tennessee schoolboy of 16 should understand this law, I wish to say, that if that is so, they forget it by the time they get to the age of Attorney General Stewart, and do not again acquire it by the time they reach the charming age of Gen. McKenzie.

Now, as to evolution, does your Honor know what evolution is? Does anybody know? The title of the act refers to evolution in the schools, but when that is done, you do not know what evolution is. I suppose ultimately, the jury, because under your Constitution they are the judges, ultimately, of the law as well as the facts, and they will have to pass on the evidence, and that is a question that has been observed by scientific men for at least two centuries.

. . .

When these gentlemen tell your honor what their theory of the case is, and then say, "The defense should put in no evidence because this is our theory," they immediately suggest to your Honor that you should hear one side of the case only. Your Honor may know of the occasion some time ago when a man argued a question for the plaintiff before a judge who had a very Irish wit and after he had finished the judge turned to the defendant and said, "I don't care to hear anything from the defendant; to hear both sides has a tendency to confuse the court." (Laughter in the courtroom.) These people cannot bind us by their story of what our case is. Now we start at the beginning with a very simple proposition of evidence. . . . What are the questions of fact? A man is guilty of a violation of the law if he teaches any theory different from the theory taught in the Bible. Has the judge a right to know what the Bible is? Does that law say that anything is contrary to the Bible that does not interpret the Bible literally—every word interpreted literally? Oh, no, the law says that he must teach a theory that denies the story as stated in the Bible. Are we able to say what is stated in the Bible? Or is it a matter of words interpreted literally? Is your Honor going to put into that statute "any theory contrary to creation as stated in the Bible" with the words "literally interpreted word by word"? Because if you are, the statute doesn't say so. Are we entitled to show what the Bible is? Are we entitled to show its meaning? Are we entitled to show what evolution is?

We are entitled to show that, if for no other reason than to determine whether the title is germane to the act. Are we entitled to show that the development of man from a cell does not make him a lower order of animals? I know that every human being develops from a cell in the very beginning of life. I know that in the womb of the mother the very first thing is a cell and that cell grows and it subdivides and it grows into a human being and a human being is born. Does that statement, as the boy stated on the stand, that he was taught that man comes from a cell—is that a theory that man descended from a lower order of animals? I don't know and I dare say your Honor has some doubt about it. Are we entitled to find out whether it is or not in presenting this case to the jury?

Further than that, how well substantiated is the doctrine of evolution? I presented your Honor in opening this case, with what I conceive to be a parallel statute and a great many people smiled. You remember my supposed statute concerning the Copernican theory and my friend, the attorney general, proposed another statute concerning the rights of teachers. I would like to say the only difference between the attorney general and myself is that I believe such statutes are unconstitutional—I believe his was unconstitutional, as well as my own and this. The only difference between the parallel I proposed and the law we are discussing, humorous as my parallel may have been—is that the Copernican theory is accepted by everybody today—we know the earth and the planets revolve about the sun. Now, I claim, and it is the contention of the defense these things we are showing are just as legitimate facts, just as well substantiated as the Copernican theory and if that is so, your Honor, then we say at the very beginning that this law is an unreasonable restraint on the liberty of the citizens and is not within the police power of the state. Apparently, my opponents have the idea that just as long as the question is one of law for the court, then no evidence is required. There was never anything further from the truth.

. . .

Hays (cont.): We men in New York, when we read the opinion of this distinguished lawyer [Bryan] to the effect that this case was a duel to the death, to the effect that this case was a duel to the death without evidence, was evidence to be given? We relied then upon the opinion of that distinguished lawyer and we have spent thousands of dollars bringing witnesses here. And I have heard that men, even though charged with more religion than I am, ordinarily obey the golden rule and there is a proposition of ethics in that. . . .

Your Honor, this is a serious thing. It is an important case. The eyes of the country, in fact of the world, are upon you here. This is not a case where the sole fact at issue is whether or not Mr. Scopes taught Howard Morgan that life was evolved from a single cell.

. . .

"Plain Sense" of Law Makes Experts Unnecessary, Argues Prosecution

(Transcript)

Prosecutors Sue K. Hicks and Ben McKenzie offered two related arguments against admitting expert testimony: First, the second clause of the Butler law—"and to teach instead . . ."—explained the first, thus eliminating ambiguity because the defense freely admitted that Scopes had "taught instead" that man came from lower animals. Second, laws must be interpreted in plain language, so the court needed no experts to tell it what was in the Bible. Though generally confining themselves to a discussion of law, the prosecutors occasionally attacked the defense's own quasi-religious faith in the power of experts.

Sue K. Hicks (p): If your Honor pleases, it is now insisted by the defense that they have the right to inject into this lawsuit a large number of theologians and scientists from different parts of the United States who will come in here and testify that science and the Bible are not in conflict, that the subject that was taught by J. T. Scopes does not conflict with the Bible.

. . .

If your Honor please, the words of the statute itself preclude the introduction of such testimony as they are trying to bring into the case. I call your Honor's attention to the last clause of this act. They are very careful to [omit] that—they are very careful to leave out even any mention of Section 1, and this law reads: "Be it enacted by the general assembly of the state of Tennessee that it shall be unlawful for any teacher in any of the universities, normals or other public schools of the state, which are supported in whole or in part by the public school funds of the state, to teach any theory that denies the story of the divine creation of man as taught in the Bible, and to teach instead"—instead of what?—"instead of the story of divine creation as taught in the Bible that man has descended from a lower order of animals."

Now, this proof is amply shown, that Mr. Scopes taught that man descended from a lower order of animals—

The Court: Do you think that that meets the requirements of the statute?

Hicks: Absolutely. There is no question as to that, your Honor. In other words, instead of the Bible theory of creation, he taught that man descended from the lower order of animals.

. . .

The issue of fact for the jury to determine is whether or not Prof. Scopes taught man descended from the lower order of animals. Now, if your Honor is going to permit them to make a special issue of these experts, if you are going to permit them to come in here as a secondary jury, which they are endeavoring to do, that is an unheard of procedure in the courts of Tennessee. We are not endeavoring to run here a teachers' institute; we do not want to make out of this a high school or college; we do not object for these foreign gentlemen, as they please to call themselves—

The Court: Do not call them that.

Hicks: They call themselves that.

Dudley Field Malone (d): That is all right.

The Court: That is all right.

Hicks: We do not object to them coming into Tennessee and putting up a college; we will give them the ground to put the college on, if they want to educate the people of Tennessee as they say they do. But this is a court of law; it is not a court of instruction for the mass of humanity at large. They, themselves admit that it is their purpose, your Honor, to enlighten the people of Tennessee.

. . .

Now, if your Honor please, I insist this, when the experts come in they have to qualify upon two subjects, as experts upon the Bible and experts upon the particular branch of science, which they are supposed to know about. Now, why should these experts know anything more about the Bible than some of the jurors? There is one on there I will match against any of the theologians they will bring down, on the jury; he knows more of the Bible than all of them do.

Malone: How do you know?

Hicks: What is the interpretation of the Bible? Some of the experts whom they have brought here do not believe in God; the great majority, the leading ones, do not believe in God; they have different ideas—

Malone: If your Honor please, how does he know until he gets them on the stand, what they believe? We object.

The Court: Sustain the objection; you cannot assume what they believe.

Malone: We would prefer for the sake of speed to have discussed only the witnesses whom we have called, and not the ones we may have called, but have not.

The Court: Sustain the objection. You cannot anticipate what they will say.

Hicks: I say this, this witness, when asked the hypothetical question as to whether or not what Prof. Scopes taught denies the story of the divine creation as taught in the Bible, is absolutely usurping the place of the jury. He is taking the place of the jury. He is invading it. Now, all these Tennessee decisions hold it is a kind of evidence that should be received with great caution—it is a matter of speculation—these scientists differ over it—Mr. Darrow said in his speech not long ago, that evolution is a mystery. Therefore, if expert testimony is full of pitfalls or dangers, or uncertainties in any issue, how much more so must it be in this issue; how much more so must it be in this issue in regard to evolution when Mr. Darrow himself says that evolution is a mystery. So, why admit these experts? . . . I do not know how about where these foreign gentlemen come from, but I say this in defense of the state, although I think it is unnecessary: The most ignorant man of Tennessee is a highly educated, polished gentleman compared to the most ignorant man in some of our northern states, because of the fact that the ignorant man of Tennessee is a man without an opportunity, but the men in our northern states, the northern man in some of our larger northern cities have the opportunity without the brain. (Laughter.)

. . .

Gen. Ben McKenzie (p): We have done crossed the Rubicon. Your Honor has held that the act was reasonable. . . . That never left anything on the face of the earth to determine, except as to the guilt or the innocence of the defendant at bar in violating that act. The theory of evolution, as to whether it contradicts the Bible, your Honor has allowed and correctly so, to introduce that Bible on the stand and it has been read to the jury. . . . [I]s there any ambiguity about it, that these distinguished gentlemen through their experts can explain, that is competent in evidence in this case? No, a thousand times no, if it has a single bit of ambiguity bearing on the face of the instrument, there is no remedy for it. . . .

They do not undertake to destroy the Bible, or set up a story in contradiction of it, but attempt to reconcile, that is the point I want your Honor to catch, and I know your Honor does.

The Court: General, let me ask you a question. Is this your position, that the story of the divine creation is so clearly set forth in the Bible, in Genesis, that no reasonable minds could differ as to the method of creation, that is, that man was created, complete by God?

Gen. McKenzie: Yes.

The Court: And in one act, and not by a method of growth or development; is that your position?

Gen. McKenzie: From lower animals—yes, that is exactly right.

The Court: That God created Adam first as a complete man, did not create a single cell of life.

Gen. McKenzie: That is right.

The Court: The cell of life did not develop in time.

Gen. McKenzie: That is right, and man did not descend from a lower order of animals that originated in the sea and then turned from one animal to another and finally man's head shot up.

. . .

Now, if your Honor please, as said a minute ago, they don't want to destroy that account.

The Court: They want to reconcile—

Gen. McKenzie: They are seeking to reconcile it, if your Honor please, and come right along and prove by the mouth of their scientist that when he said God created man in his own image, in his own image created he him out of the dust of the ground and blew into him the breath of life, and he became as a living creature, they want to put words into God's mouth, and have him to say that he issued some sort of protoplasm, or soft dish rag, and put it in the ocean and said, "Old boy, if you wait around about 6,000 years, I will make something out of you." (Laughter.) And they tell me there is no ambiguity about that.

. . .

William Jennings Bryan's First Speech

(Transcript)

After sitting in silence during the first four days of the trial, Bryan spoke at length against admitting expert testimony. He dwelled less on the wording of the law than on the general principle that a small minority of experts—especially experts who lacked Christian faith—did not have the right to tell a large majority of Tennesseans what to believe. Echoing the speeches he had been giving in public in recent years, Bryan mocked the theory of evolution and warned that it threatened belief in the Bible as the revealed word of God. In the end, Bryan argued that one who accepted the word of God was more of an expert on the Bible than any academic investigator who lacked faith. Trace the structure of Bryan's speech. Which of his arguments seems most convincing? What was the nature of Bryan's appeal to the public? Why did he consider the defense's arguments to be dangerous?

William Jennings Bryan (p): If the court please we are now approaching the end of the first week of this trial and I haven't thought it proper until this time to take part in the discussions that have been dealing with phases of this question, or case, where the state laws and the state rules of practice were under discussion and I feel that those who are versed in the law of the state and who are used to the customs of the court might better take the burden of the case, but today we come to the discussion of a very important part of this case, a question so important that upon its decision will determine the length of this trial. If the court holds, as we believe the court should hold, that the testimony that the defense is now offering is not competent and not proper testimony, then I assume we are near the end of this trial and because the question involved is not confined to local questions, but is the broadest that will possibly arise, I have felt justified in submitting my views on the case for the consideration of the court. I have been tempted to speak at former times, but I have been able to withstand the temptation. I have been drawn into the case by, I think, nearly all the lawyers on the other side. The principal attorney has often suggested that I am the archconspirator and that I am responsible for the presence of this case and I have almost been credited with leadership of the ignorance and bigotry which he thinks could alone inspire a law like this. . . .

Mr. Hays says that before he got here he read that I said this was to be a duel to the death, between science—was it?—and revealed religion. I don't know who the other duelist was, but I was representing one of them and because of that they went to the trouble and the expense of several thousand dollars to bring down their witnesses. Well, my friend, if you said that this was important enough to be regarded as a duel between two great ideas or groups I certainly will be given credit for foreseeing what I could not then know, and that is that this question is so important between religion and irreligion that even the invoking of the divine blessing upon it might seem partisan and partial.

. . .

We do not need any expert to tell us what that law means. An expert cannot be permitted to come in here and try to defeat the enforcement of a law by testifying that it isn't a bad law and it isn't—I mean a bad doctrine—no matter how these people phrase the doctrine—no matter how they eulogize it. This is not the place to try to prove that the law ought never to have been passed. The place to prove that, or teach that, was to the legislature. If these people were so anxious to keep the state of Tennessee from disgracing itself, if they were so afraid that by this action taken by the legislature, the state would put itself before the people of the nation as ignorant people and bigoted people—if they had half the affection for Tennessee that you would think they had as they come here to testify, they would have come at a time when their testimony would have been valuable and not at this time to ask you to refuse to enforce a law because they did not think the law ought to have been passed.

And, my friends, if the people of Tennessee were to go into a state like New York—the one from which this impulse comes to resist this law, or go into any state—if they went into any state and tried to convince the people that a law they had passed ought not to be enforced just because the people who went there didn't think it ought to have been passed, don't you think it would be resented as an impertinence? They passed a law up in New York repealing the enforcement of prohibition. Suppose the people of Tennessee had sent attorneys up there to fight that law, or to oppose it after it was passed, and experts to testify how good a thing prohibition is to New York and to the nation, I wonder if there would have been any lack of determination in the papers in speaking out against the offensiveness of such testimony. The people of this state passed this law, the people of this state knew what they were doing when they passed the law, and they knew the dangers of the doctrine—that they did not want it taught to their children, and my friends, it isn't—your Honor, it isn't proper to bring experts in here to try to defeat the purpose of the people of this state by trying to show that this thing that they denounce and outlaw is a beautiful thing that everybody ought to believe in. . . . These people want to come here with experts to make your Honor believe that the law should never have been passed and because in their opinion it ought not to have been passed, it ought not to be enforced. It isn't a place for expert testimony. We have sufficient proof in the book—doesn't the book state the very thing that is objected to, and outlawed in this state? Who has a copy of that book?

The Court: Do you mean the Bible?

Bryan: No, sir; the biology.

(Laughter in the courtroom.)

A Voice: Here it is; Hunter's *Biology*.

Bryan: No, not the Bible, you see in this state they cannot teach the Bible.[2] They can only teach things that declare it to be a lie, according to the learned counsel. These people in the state—Christian people—have tied their hands by their Constitution. They say we all believe in the Bible for it is the overwhelming belief in the state, but we will not teach that Bible which we believe even to our children through teachers that we pay with our money. No, no, it isn't the teaching of the Bible, and we are not asking it. The question is can a minority in this state come in and compel a teacher to teach that the Bible is not true and make the parents of these children pay the expenses of the teacher to tell their children what these people believe is false and dangerous? Has it come to a time when the minority can take charge of a state like Tennessee and compel the majority to pay their teachers while they take religion out of the heart of the children of the parents who pay the teachers?

. . .

So, my friends, if that were true, if man and monkey were in the same class, called primates, it would mean they did not come up from the same order. It might mean that instead of one being the ancestor of the other they were all cousins. But it does not mean that they did not come from the lower animals, if this is the only place they could come from, and the Christian believes man came from above, but the evolutionist believes he must have come from below.

(Laughter in the courtroom.)

And that is from a lower order of animals.

Your Honor, I want to show you that we have evidence enough here, we do not need any experts to come in here and tell us about this thing. Here we have Mr. Hunter. Mr. Hunter is the author of this biology and this is the man who wrote the book Mr. Scopes

[2]Bryan exaggerated slightly. Tennessee law had for the previous decade provided for daily Bible readings in the public schools.

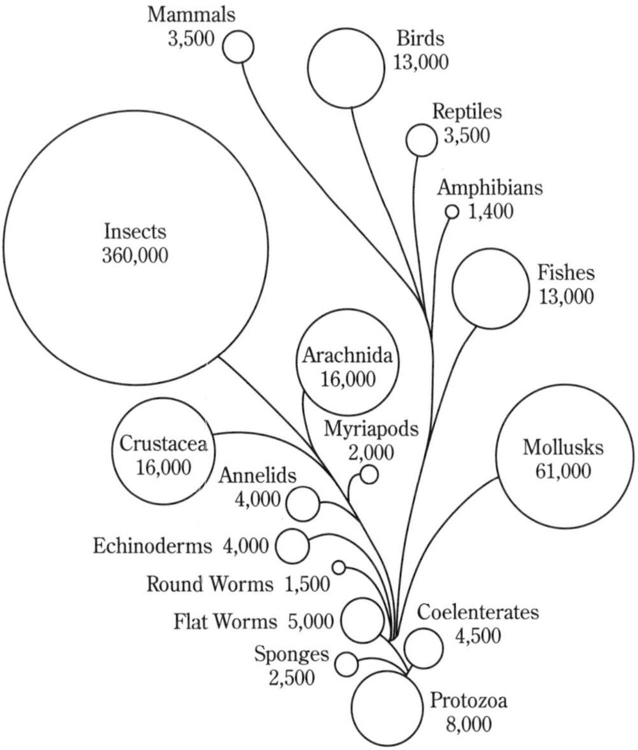

Evolutionary tree from Hunter, *A Civic Biology.* William Jennings Bryan complained that such illustrations did not differentiate sufficiently between humans and other creatures.

was teaching. And here we have the diagram. Has the court seen this diagram?

The Court: No, sir, I have not.

Bryan: Well, you must see it (handing book to the court).

(Laughter in the courtroom.)

On page 194—I take it for granted that counsel for the defense have examined it carefully?

Darrow: We have examined it.

Bryan: On page 194, we have a diagram [shown above], and this diagram purports to give someone's family tree. Not only his ancestors but his collateral relatives. We are told just how many animal species there are, 518,900. And in this diagram, beginning with protozoa we have the animals classified. We have circles differing in size according to the number of species in them and we have the guess that they give.

Of course, it is only a guess, and I don't suppose it is carried to a one or even to ten. I see they are round numbers, and I don't think all of these animals breed in round numbers, and so I think it must be a generalization of them.

(Laughter in the courtroom.)

The Court: Let us have order.

Bryan: 8,000 protozoa, 3,500 sponges. I am satisfied from some I have seen there must be more than 35,000 sponges.

(Laughter in the courtroom.)

And then we run down to the insects, 360,000 insects. Two-thirds of all the species of all the animal world are insects. And sometimes, in the summer time we feel that we become intimately acquainted with them. A large percentage of the species are mollusks and fishes. Now, we are getting up near our kinfolks, 13,000 fishes. Then there are the amphibia. I don't know whether they have not yet decided to come out, or have almost decided to go back.

(Laughter in the courtroom.)

But they seem to be somewhat at home in both elements. And then we have the reptiles, 3,500; and then we have 13,000 birds. Strange that this should be exactly the same as the number of fishes, round numbers. And then we have mammals, 3,500, and there is a little circle and man is in the circle, find him, find man.

There is that book! There is the book they were teaching your children that man was a mammal and so indistinguishable among the mammals that they leave him there with thirty-four hundred and ninety-nine other mammals.

(Laughter and applause.)

Including elephants?

Talk about putting Daniel in the lion's den! How dare those scientists put man in a little ring like that with lions and tigers and everything that is bad! Not only the evolution is possible, but the scientists possibly think of shutting man up in a little circle like that with all these animals, that have an odor, that extends beyond the circumference of this circle, my friends.

(Extended laughter.)

He tells the children to copy this, copy this diagram. In the notebook, children are to copy this diagram and take it home in their notebooks. To show their parents that you cannot find man. That is the great game to put in the public schools to find man among animals, if you can.

Tell me that the parents of this day have not any right to declare that children are not to be taught this doctrine? Shall not be taken down from the high plane upon which God put man? Shall be detached from the throne of God and be compelled to link their ancestors with the jungle, tell that to these children? Why, my friend, if they believe it, they go back to scoff at the religion of their parents! And the parents have a right to say that no teacher paid by their money shall rob their children of faith in God and send them back to their homes, skeptical, infidels, or agnostics, or atheists.

This doctrine that they want taught, this doctrine that they would force upon the schools, where they will not let the Bible be read!

. . .

Bryan (cont.): Now, my friends, I want you to know that they not only have no proof, but they cannot find the beginning. I suppose this distinguished scholar [Dr. Maynard Metcalf, who testified on day four] who came here shamed them all by his number of degrees—he did not shame me, for I have more than he has, but I can understand how my friends felt when he unrolled degree after degree. Did he tell you where life began? Did he tell you that back of all these that there was a God? Not a word about it. Did he tell you how life began? Not a word; and not one of them can tell you how life began. The atheists say it came some way without a God; the agnostics say it came in some way they know not whether with a God or not. And the Christian evolutionists say we come away back there somewhere, but they do not know how far back—they do not give you the beginning—not that gentleman that tried to qualify as an expert; he did not tell you how life began. He did not tell you whether it began with God or how. No, they take all life as a mystery that nobody can explain, and they want you to let them commence there and ask no questions. They want to come in with their little padded up evolution that commences with nothing and ends nowhere. They do not dare to tell you that it ended with God. They come here with this bunch of stuff that they call evolution, that they tell you that everybody believes in, but do not know that everybody knows as a fact, and nobody can tell how it came, and they do not explain the great riddle of the universe—they do not deal with the problems of life—they do not teach the great science of how to live—and yet they would undermine the faith of these little children in that God who stands back of everything and whose promise we have that we shall live with him forever by and by. They shut God out of the world. They do not talk about God. Darwin says the beginning of all things is a mystery unsolvable by us. He does not pretend to say how these things started.

The Court: Well, if the theory is, Col. Bryan, that God did not create the cell, then it could not be reconcilable with the Bible?

Bryan: Of course, it could not be reconcilable with the Bible.

The Court: Before it could be reconcilable with the Bible it would have to be admitted that God created the cell?

Bryan: There would be no contention about that, but our contention is, even if they put God back there, it does not make it harmonious with the Bible. The court is right that unless they put God back there, it must dispute the Bible. . . . They did not tell us where in this long period of time, between the cell at the bottom of the sea and man, where man became endowed with the hope of immortality. They did not, if you please, and most of them do not go to the place to hunt for it, because more than half of the scientists of this country—Prof. James H. [Leuba], one of them, and he bases it on thousands of letters they sent to him—says more than half do not believe there is a God or personal immortality, and they want to teach that to these children, and take that from them, to take from them their belief in a God who stands ready to welcome his children.[3]

And your Honor asked me whether it has anything to do with the principle of the virgin birth. Yes, because this principle of evolution disputes the miracle; there is no place for the miracle in this train of evolution, and the Old Testament and the New are filled with miracles, and if this doctrine is true, this logic eliminates every mystery in the Old Testament and the New, and eliminates everything supernatural, and that means they eliminate the virgin birth—that means that they eliminate the resurrection of the body—that means that they eliminate the doctrine of atonement and they believe man has been rising all the time, that man never fell, that when the Savior came there was not any reason for His coming, there was no reason why He should not go as soon as He

[3]James H. Leuba, *The Belief in God and Immortality: A Psychological, Anthropological and Statistical Study* (Boston: Sherman, French & Co., 1916), found that only a minority of elite scientists subscribed to an orthodox religious faith.

could, that He was born of Joseph or some other co-respondent, and that He lies in his grave, and when the Christians of this state have tied their hands and said we will not take advantage of our power to teach religion to our children, by teachers paid by us, these people come in from the outside of the state and force upon the people of this state and upon the children of the taxpayers of this state a doctrine that refutes not only their belief in God, but their belief in a Savior and belief in heaven, and takes from them every moral standard that the Bible gives us.

. . .

Now, your Honor, when it comes to Bible experts, do they think that they can bring them in here to instruct the members of the jury, eleven of whom are members of the church? I submit that of the eleven members of the jury, more of the jurors are experts on what the Bible is than any Bible expert who does not subscribe to the true spiritual influences or spiritual discernments of what our Bible says—

Voice in audience: Amen!

Bryan (cont.): — and the man may discuss the Bible all he wants to, but he does not find out anything about the Bible until he accepts God and the Christ of whom He tells.

Darrow: I hope the reporters got the amens in the record. I want somewhere, at some point, to find some court where a picture of this will be painted. (Laughter.)

Bryan: Your Honor, we first pointed out that we do not need any experts in science. . . . And, when it comes to Bible experts, every member of the jury is as good an expert on the Bible as any man that they could bring, or that we could bring. The one beauty about the word of God is, it does not take an expert to understand it. They have translated that Bible into five hundred languages, they have carried it into nations where but a few can read a word, or write, to people who never saw a book, who never read, and yet can understand that Bible, and they can accept the salvation that that Bible offers, and they can know more about that book by accepting Jesus and feeling in their hearts the sense of their sins forgiven than all of the skeptical outside Bible experts that could come in here to talk to the people of Tennessee about the construction that they place upon the Bible, that is foreign to the construction that the people here place upon it. Therefore, your Honor, we believe that this evidence is not competent. . . . Then why should we prolong this case?

We can bring our experts here for the Christians; for every one they can bring who does not believe in Christianity, we can bring more than one who believes in the Bible and rejects evolution, and our witnesses will be just as good experts as theirs on a question of that kind. We could have a thousand or a million witnesses, but this case as to whether evolution is true or not, is not going to be tried here, within this city; if it is carried to the state's courts, it will not be tried there, and if it is taken to the great court at Washington, it will not be tried there. No, my friends, no court of the law, and no jury, great or small, is going to destroy the issue between the believer and the unbeliever. The Bible is the word of God; the Bible is the only expression of man's hope of salvation. The Bible, the record of the Song of God, the Savior of the world, born of the virgin Mary, crucified and risen again. That Bible is not going to be driven out of this court by experts who come hundreds of miles to testify that they can reconcile evolution, with its ancestor in the jungle, with man made by God in his image, and put here for purposes as a part of the divine plan. No, we are not going to settle that question here, and I think we ought to confine ourselves to the law and to the evidence that can be admitted in accordance with the law. Your court is an office of this state, and we who represent the state as counsel are officers of the state, and we cannot humiliate the great state of Tennessee by admitting for a moment that people can come from anywhere and protest against the enforcement of this state's laws on the ground that it does not conform with their ideas, or because it banishes from our schools a thing that they believe in and think ought to be taught in spite of the protest of those who employ the teacher and pay him his salary.

The facts are simple, the case is plain, and if those gentlemen want to enter upon a larger field of educational work on the subject of evolution, let us get through with this case and then convene a mock court for it will deserve the title of mock court if its purpose is to banish from the hearts of the people the word of God as revealed! (Great applause.)

. . .

Dudley Field Malone Replies to Bryan

(Transcript)

In a speech louder than Bryan's—H. L. Mencken said listeners outside the courthouse stopped up the loudspeakers because they could hear Malone's unamplified voice perfectly well—and as carefully wrought, Malone drew a sharp line of separation between science and religion and argued that the court and the nation's youths had nothing to fear from scientific truth. Do you think Malone accurately answered all of Bryan's objections? What was Malone's view of science? What do you think was his view of social changes in the 1920s?

Malone (d): If the court please, it does seem to me that we have gone far afield in this discussion. However, probably this is the time to discuss everything that bears on the issues that have been raised in this case, because after all, whether Mr. Bryan knows it or not, he is a mammal, he is an animal and he is a man. But, your Honor, I would like to advert to the law, and to remind the court that the heart of the matter is the question of whether there is liability under this law.

I have been puzzled and interested at one and the same time at the psychology of the prosecution and I find it difficult to distinguish between Mr. Bryan, the lawyer in this case; Mr. Bryan, the propagandist outside of this case; and the Mr. Bryan who made a speech against science and for religion just now—Mr. Bryan my old chief and friend.[4] I know Mr. Bryan. I don't know Mr. Bryan as well as Mr. Bryan knows Mr. Bryan, but I know this, that he does believe—and Mr. Bryan, your Honor, is not the only one who believes in the Bible. As a matter of fact there has been much criticism, by indirection and implication, of this text, or synopsis, if you please, that does not agree with their ideas. If we depended on the agreement of theologians, we would all be infidels. . . .

Are we to hold mankind to a literal understanding of the claim that the world is 6,000 years old, because of the limited vision of men who believed the world was flat, and that the earth was the center of the universe, and that man is the center of the earth? . . .

[4]Malone worked under Bryan when Bryan was secretary of state for President Woodrow Wilson.

Are we to have our children know nothing about science except what the church says they shall know? I have never seen harm in learning and understanding, in humility and open-mindedness, and I have never seen clearer the need of that learning than when I see the attitude of the prosecution, who attack and refuse to accept the information and intelligence, which expert witnesses will give them.

Mr. Bryan may be satisfactory to thousands of people. It is in so many ways that he is satisfactory to me; his enthusiasm, his vigor, his courage, his fighting ability these long years for the things he thought were right. And many a time I have fought with him, and for him; and when I did not think he was right, I fought just as hard against him. This is not a conflict of personages; it is a conflict of ideas, and I think this case has been developed by men of two frames of mind. Your Honor, there is a difference between theological and scientific men. Theology deals with something that is established and revealed; it seeks to gather material, which they claim should not be changed. It is the word of God and that cannot be changed; it is literal, it is not to be interpreted. That is the theological mind. It deals with theology. The scientific is a modern thing, your Honor.... The difference between the theological mind and the scientific mind is that the theological mind is closed, because that is what is revealed and is settled. But the scientist says no, the Bible is the book of revealed religion, with rules of conduct, and with aspirations—that is the Bible. The scientist says, take the Bible as guide, as an inspiration, as a set of philosophies and preachments in the world of theology.

And what does this law do? We have been told here that this was not a religious question. I defy anybody, after Mr. Bryan's speech, to believe that this was not a religious question. Mr. Bryan brought all of the foreigners into this case. Mr. Bryan had offered his services from Miami, Fla.; he does not belong in Tennessee. If it be wrong for American citizens from other parts of this country to come to Tennessee to discuss issues which we believe, then Mr. Bryan has no right here, either. But it was only when Mr. Darrow and I had heard that Mr. Bryan had offered his name and his reputation to the prosecution of this young teacher, that we said, Well, we will offer our services to the defense.

. . .

Malone (cont.): We maintain our right to present our own defense, and present our own theory of our defense and to present our own theory of this law, because we maintain, your Honor, that if everything that the state has said in its testimony be true—and we admit it is true—that under this law the defendant Scopes has not violated that statute. Haven't we the right to prove it by our witnesses if that is our theory, if that is so? . . . [W]e maintain that we have a right to introduce evidence by these witnesses that the theory of the defendant is not in conflict with the theory of creation in the Bible. And, moreover, your Honor, we maintain we have the right to call witnesses to show that there is more than one theory of the creation in the Bible.

Mr. Bryan is not the only one who has spoken for the Bible; Judge McKenzie is not the only defender of the word of God. There are other people in this country who have given their whole lives to God. Mr. Bryan, to my knowledge, with a very passionate spirit and enthusiasm, has given most of his life to politics. . . . But is that any reason that I should fall down when Bryan speaks of theology? Is he the last word on the subject of theology?

Well do I remember in my history the story of the burning of the great library at Alexandria, and just before it was burned to the ground that the heathen, the Mohamedians [*sic*] and the Egyptians, went to the hostile general and said, "Your Honor, do not destroy this great library, because it contains all the truth that has been gathered," and the Mohamedian general said, "But the Koran contains all the truth. If the library contains the truth that the Koran contains we do not need the library, and if the library does not contain the truth that the Koran contains then we must destroy the library anyway."[5]

But these gentlemen say the Bible contains the truth—if the world of science can produce any truth or facts not in the Bible as we understand it, then destroy science, but keep our Bible. And we say, "Keep your Bible." Keep it as your consolation, keep it as your guide, but keep it where it belongs, in the world of your own conscience, in the world of your individual judgment, in the world of the Protestant conscience that I heard so much about when I was a boy, keep your Bible in the world of theology where it belongs and do not try to tell an intelligent world and the intelligence of this country that these books written by men who knew none of the accepted

[5]Malone's history is slightly incorrect. The library was destroyed in A.D. 391, about 180 years before Mohammed was born.

fundamental facts of science can be put into a course of science, because what are they doing here? This law says what? It says that no theory of creation can be taught in a course of science, except one which conforms with the theory of divine creation as set forth in the Bible. In other words, it says that only the Bible shall be taken as an authority on the subject of evolution in a course on biology.

. . .

What I don't understand is this, your Honor, the prosecution inside and outside of the court has been ready to try the case and this is the case. What is the issue that has gained the attention, not only of the American people, but people everywhere? Is it a mere technical question as to whether the defendant Scopes taught the paragraph in the book of science? You think, your Honor, that the News Association in London, which sent you that very complimentary telegram you were good enough to show me in this case, because the issue is whether John Scopes taught a couple of paragraphs out of his book? Oh, no, the issue is as broad as Mr. Bryan himself has made it. The issue is as broad as Mr. Bryan has published it and why the fear? If the issue is as broad as they make it, why the fear of meeting the issue? Why, where issues are drawn by evidence, where the truth and nothing but the truth are scrutinized and where statements can be answered by expert witnesses on the other side—what is this psychology of fear? I don't understand it. My old chief—I never saw him back away from a great issue before. I feel that the prosecution here is filled with a needless fear. I believe that if they withdraw their objection and hear the evidence of our experts their minds would not only be improved but their souls would be purified.

I believe and we believe that men who are God-fearing, who are giving their lives to study and observation, to the teaching of the young—are the teachers and scientists of this country in a combination to destroy the morals of the children to whom they have dedicated their lives? Are preachers the only ones in America who care about our youth? Is the church the only source of morality in this country? And I would like to say something for the children of the country. We have no fears about the young people of America. They are a pretty smart generation. Any teacher who teaches the boys or the girls today an incredible theory—we need not worry about those children of this generation paying much attention to it. The children of this generation are pretty wise. People, as a matter of fact I feel that the children of this generation are probably much wiser than many of their elders. The least that this generation can do, your Honor, is to give the next generation all the facts, all the available data, all the theories, all the information that learning, that study, that observation has produced—give it to the children in the hope of heaven that they will make a better world of this than we have been able to make it. We have just had a war with twenty million dead. Civilization is not so proud of the work of the adults. Civilization need not be so proud of what the grown-ups have done. For God's sake let the children have their minds kept open—close no doors to their knowledge; shut no door from them. Make the distinction between theology and science. Let them have both. Let them both be taught. Let them both live. . . .

We want everything we have to say on religion and on science told and we are ready to submit our theories to the direct and cross-examination of the prosecution. We have come in here ready for a battle. We have come in here for this duel.

I don't know anything about dueling, your Honor. It is against the law of God. It is against the church. It is against the law of Tennessee, but does the opposition mean by duel that our defendant shall be strapped to a board and that they alone shall carry the sword? Is our only weapon the witnesses who shall testify to the accuracy of our theory—is our weapon to be taken from us, so that the duel will be entirely one-sided? That isn't my idea of a duel. Moreover it isn't going to be a duel.

There is never a duel with the truth. The truth always wins and we are not afraid of it. The truth is no coward. The truth does not need the law. The truth does not need the forces of government. The truth does not need Mr. Bryan. The truth is imperishable, eternal, and immortal and needs no human agency to support it. We are ready to tell the truth as we understand it and we do not fear all the truth that they can present as facts. We are ready. We are ready. We feel we stand with progress. We feel we stand with science. We feel we stand with intelligence. We feel we stand with fundamental freedom in America. We are not afraid. Where is the fear? We meet it! Where is the fear? We defy it! We ask your honor to admit the evidence as a matter of correct law, as a matter of sound procedure and as a matter of justice to the defense in this case. (Profound and continued applause.)

(The bailiff raps for order.)

. . .

Attorney General Stewart Answers Malone

(Transcript)

Attorney General Stewart spent most of the trial desperately trying to steer the court back toward a simple consideration of the law, but he grew furious with the defense's attempts to introduce expert testimony. Contradicting many commentators' portraits of the Butler law's supporters as "rural ignoramuses," the urbane, well-educated Stewart proudly asserted his religious faith and defended his right, and the right of all Tennesseans, to believe in the Bible despite the encroachments of science. Why did Stewart become so passionate about the question of expert testimony? Do you think his rebuttal was effective? Why or why not?

Stewart: Under a correct construction of this act, if the court please, when this teacher teaches to the children of the high schools of Rhea County, that they are descended from a lower order of animals, he has done all that is necessary to violate this act. He has at the same time taught a theory that denies the divine story of the creation of man. . . .

What will these scientists testify? They will say, no, this was simply the method by which God created man. I don't care. This act says you cannot testify concerning that, because it denies the literal story that the Bible teaches, and that is what we are restricted to. That is what the legislature had in mind.

Why did they pass that act? They passed it because they wanted to prohibit teaching in the public schools of the state of Tennessee a theory that taught that man was descended from a lower order of animals. Why did they want to pass an act which would deny the right of science to teach this in the schools? Because it denies the story of divine creation. . . . This act in so many words says that when you teach that man descended from a lower order of animals you have taught a theory that denies God's Bible, that is what they are driving at.

And to bring experts here to testify upon a construction of the Bible, is (pounding with his hand on the shorthand reporter's table) I submit, respectfully, to your Honor, that would be a prostitution upon the courts of the state of Tennessee.

. . .

What is this thing that comes here to strike within the bounds of this jurisdiction, and to tell the people of this commonwealth that they are doing wrong to prohibit the teaching of this theory in the public schools? From whence does this opposition originate? Who conceived the idea that Tennessee did not know what she was doing? They say it is sponsored by a lot of religious bigots. Mr. Darrow said that, substantially that. . . .

If we, if the court please, who live in this sovereign jurisdiction prefer to worship God according to the dictates of our own consciences, and we give everyone that right to do so, and your Honor, I would criticize no man for his individual view of things, but, why, if the court please, is this invasion here? Why, if the court please, have we not the right to interpret our Bible as we see fit? Why have we not the right to bar the door to science when it comes within the four walls of God's church upon this earth? Have we not the right? Who says that we have not? Show me the man who will challenge it. We have the right to pursue knowledge—we have the right to participate in scientific investigation, but, if the court please, when science strikes at that upon which man's eternal hope is founded, then I say the foundation of man's civilization is about to crumble.

They say this is a battle between religion and science. If it is, I want to serve notice now, in the name of the great God, that I am on the side of religion. They say it is a battle between religion and science, and in the name of God, I stand with religion because I want to know beyond this world that there may be an eternal happiness for me and for all. Tell me that I would not stand with it. Tell me that I would believe I was a common worm and would writhe in the dust and go no further when my breath had left my body!

There should not be any clash between science and religion. I am sorry that there is, but who brought it on? How did it occur? It occurred from teaching that infidelity, that agnosticism, that which breeds in the soul of the child infidelity, atheism, and drives him from the Bible that his father and mother raised him by—which, as Mr. Bryan has so eloquently said, drives man's sole hope of happiness and of religion and of freedom of thought, and worship, and Almighty God, from him. I say, bar the door, and not allow science to enter. That would deprive us of all the hope we have in the future to come.

And I say it without any bitterness. I am not trying to say it in the spirit of bitterness to a man over there, it is my view, I am sincere about it. Mr. Darrow says he is an agnostic. He is the greatest criminal lawyer in America today. His courtesy is noticeable—his ability is known—and it is a shame, in my mind, in the sight of a great God, that a mentality like his has strayed so far from the natural goal that it should follow—great God, the good that a man of his ability could have done if he had aligned himself with the forces of right instead of aligning himself with that which strikes its fangs at the very bosom of Christianity.

Yes, discard that theory of the Bible—throw it away, and let scientific development progress beyond man's origin. And the next thing you know, there will be a legal battle staged within the corners of this state, that challenges even permitting anyone to believe that Jesus Christ was divinely born—that Jesus Christ was born of a virgin—challenge that and the next step will be a battle staged denying the right to teach that there was a resurrection, until finally that precious book and its glorious teachings upon which this civilization has been built will be taken from us.

. . .

Stewart (cont.): Yes, we have all studied the history of this country.

We are taught that George Washington, on one occasion, before a battle he fought, led his army in prayer, and on another occasion that he secreted himself in a hiding place and prayed in private to the great God for victory. We are told that the great general of the southern Confederacy, Robert E. Lee, prayed to God before each battle, and yet here we have a test by science that challenges the right to open the court with a prayer to God. I ask you again, who is it, and what is it, that comes here to attack this law and to say to this people that even though we are but a handful, you are a bunch of fools—who is it, I say—I do not know just who they might be, but they are in strange company. They come and say, "Ye shall not open your court with prayer, we protest"—they say we shall not teach our Bible to our children, because it conflicts with scientific investigation. I say scientific investigation is nothing but a theory and will never be anything but a theory. Show me some reasonable cause to believe it is not. They cannot do it.

Hays: Give us a chance.

Stewart: A chance to what?

Hays: To prove it, to show you what it is.

Stewart: If your Honor please, that charge strikes at the very vitals of civilization and of Christianity and is not entitled to a chance (applause and laughter throughout house) to prove by the word or mouth of man that man originated in the bottom of the sea. It is as absurd and as ridiculous as to say that a man might be half monkey, half man. Who ever saw one—at what stage in development did he shed his tail—where did he acquire his immortality—at what stage in his development did he cross the line from monkeyhood to manhood? Yes, I confess, your Honor, their purpose might be to show that to me, but not because they descended from a lower order of animals

Now, if your Honor please, this has been an unusual discussion. We have all gone beyond the pale of the law in saying these things. . . . I submit, your Honor, that under a correct construction of this statute that this scientific evidence would be inadmissible, and I ask your Honor, and I say to your Honor, to let us not make a blunder in the annals of the tribunals in Tennessee, by permitting such as this. It would be a never-ending controversy, it would be a babble of song. . . .

JOSEPH WOOD KRUTCH

Fairness Lies on the Defense's Side

July 29, 1925

Though a native Tennessean, Krutch was fairly typical of a press corps that heavily favored the defense team. Although his effusions over Malone's speech were fairly temperate compared to other journalists' reports, Krutch also did not bother to mention Stewart's able reply. Do you see other hints of unfairness in Krutch's account?

. . . At last the moment came and [William Jennings Bryan] arose to make his plea for the exclusion of all testimony from either scientists or theologians. He began with the now famous references to his long list of honorary degrees, but he must have been subconsciously aware of the fact that though any college can grant honorary degrees it is

Joseph Wood Krutch, "Darrow vs. Bryan," *Nation,* 29 July 1925, 136–37.

beyond human power to confer any honorary learning, for he soon turned to develop his chief plea—a plea for ignorance as uncorrupted as possible by any knowledge. There is, he said, no such thing as a Bible expert; learning is useless and only faith can count. . . . Even the most ignorant man in all the throng was, I believe, a little ashamed, and all eyes turned to Dudley Malone, who had been chosen to answer him of the silver tongue.

Of Malone's speech I have no space to give an account but it was, like the speech of Darrow, undoubtedly great when considered as a part of the drama which the defense was staging. With all the vocal art and the genuine passion for which the occasion called it pleaded for fair play, it stated the simple case for light against darkness, and, reaching its height, it taunted Bryan in stinging words with his cowardice in declaring before the world that the trial at Dayton was a duel to death between science and religion and then refusing to fight the contest which he himself had so loudly proclaimed. Nor was there the slightest doubt who, for the moment, had won. A dormant sense of fair play had turned even the fundamentalists for an instant against their leader, and the applause which broke forth, twice as great in volume and duration as that which had greeted Mr. Bryan, showed conclusively that in this particular duel Mr. Bryan had lost even in the midst of his own camp.

6

Sixth Day's Proceedings

Friday, July 17, 1925

The court met only briefly on Friday morning. After the major arguments of day five, Judge John T. Raulston ruled against allowing expert testimony on the meaning of evolution and its compatibility with the story of creation in the Bible. The defense's frustration over Judge Raulston's ruling, which echoed all of the prosecution's arguments against expert testimony, eventually boiled over. Clarence Darrow deliberately offended the judge, who on the following Monday issued a citation for contempt of court to the Chicago attorney.

Raulston Rejects Expert Testimony; Darrow Offends

(Transcript)

In the end, Judge Raulston agreed with the prosecution that the second clause of the Butler law explained the first, and thus the court needed no experts to explain the story of the divine creation.

The Court: The state says that it is both proven and admitted that this defendant did teach in Rhea County, within the limits of the statute, that man descended from a lower order of animals . . . and that no amount of expert testimony can aid and enlighten the court and jury upon the real issues, or affect the final results. . . .

In the final analysis this court after a most earnest and careful consideration, has reached the conclusions that under the provisions of the act involved in this case, it is made unlawful thereby to teach in the public schools of the state of Tennessee the theory that man descended from a lower order of animals. If the court is correct in this, then the evidence of experts would shed no light on the issues.

Therefore, the court is content to sustain the motion of the attorney general to exclude the expert testimony.

. . .

Clarence Darrow (d): I do not understand why every request of the state and every suggestion of the prosecution should meet with an endless waste of time, and a bare suggestion of anything that is perfectly competent on our part should be immediately overruled.

The Court: I hope you do not mean to reflect upon the court.

Darrow: Well, your Honor has the right to hope.

The Court: I have the right to do something else, perhaps.

Darrow: All right; all right.

NEW REPUBLIC

Courts Should Not Rule over Legislature

July 8, 1925

The New Republic *surprised many readers by its careful refusal to support the Scopes defense despite its condemnation of the Butler law. How did the editors reconcile these positions? Do they seem closer to Bryan's position or to Darrow's? Why? Do these arguments still make sense today?*

The circus conception of the controversy seems to be about as congenial to Mr. Scopes's defenders as it is to those who invoke against him the majesty of the law. Behind the whole performance some Barnum is at work.[1] . . . If ever a great issue was cheapened by descent to the ridiculous, the issue of freedom of inquiry and freedom of teaching is

[1]A reference to Phineas Taylor (P. T.) Barnum (1810–1891), the great promoter and circus master.

"Tennessee and the Constitution," *New Republic,* 8 July 1925, 167–68.

cheapened by the clap-trap of the histrionics masquerading as a legal trial in Tennessee.

It is hard to decide whether to lament or to rejoice that out of the monkey-play some good may come. It may be good to get a fundamental issue on the front page of the newspaper even though it gets there as a clown. Farce in the news columns may be recompensed by serious discussion on the editorial page. The longer the trial lasts, the more will public attention be given to the menace of a temporary political majority trying to tell us what to know and what to think.

Yet it remains to be regretted that an issue of such import should be entangled with burlesque and that the fate of freedom of inquiry should seem to any one to be tied up with the outcome of the prosecution of Mr. Scopes. If the jury or the court should let Mr. Scopes go free, toleration will not thereby be established. If the jury convicts and the highest court in the land holds that Tennessee has not violated the Fourteenth Amendment, the fate of freedom of inquiry will still rest where always it must rest. Courts can no more make us wise and tolerant and eager for the truth than they can make us kind or generous. No community can become enlightened by having enlightenment judicially thrust upon it. The crime against intelligence which the legislature of Tennessee has committed will remain no less a crime against intelligence whether it is declared constitutional or unconstitutional. This crime will become the crime of the people of Tennessee if they condone it by failing to force the obnoxious statute off the books.

7

Seventh Day's Proceedings

Monday, July 20, 1925

Although Judge John T. Raulston on this day moved the trial to an outdoor platform to accommodate the crowd, many observers had left town over the weekend. Judge Raulston's rejection of the defense's constitutional arguments on day four of the trial, and his unwillingness to allow the jury to hear expert testimony on evolution and the Bible, seemed to have stripped the defense of all its possible weapons. But after some preliminary skirmishing over Governor Austin Peay's statement that the Butler Act would never be enforced and over whether to take down a large sign admonishing, "Read Your Bible," Darrow dug deep into his arsenal and called William Jennings Bryan to the stand as an expert on the Bible. Incredibly, Bryan accepted the challenge, and for two hours in the hot sun, the two men sparred over the literal veracity of the Bible. Bryan sought to defend biblical revelation, while Darrow plainly sought to discredit Bryan—and, by extension, fundamentalism—as intellectually inconsistent and willfully ignorant.

Darrow Objects to "Read Your Bible" Banner

(Transcript)

With the court moved outdoors, the jurors sat facing a large religious sign. In a continuation of his objection to the opening prayers, Darrow requested that the sign be removed so as not to prejudice the jury. Once again, Darrow's strategy provoked deep resentment.

Clarence Darrow (d): Your Honor, before you send for the jury, I think it my duty to make this motion. Off to the left of where the jury sits a little bit and about ten feet in front of them is a large sign about ten feet long reading, "Read Your Bible," and a hand pointing to it. The word "Bible" is in large letters, perhaps a foot and a half long. . . . I move that it be removed.

The Court: Yes.

Gen. Ben McKenzie (p): If your Honor please, why should it be removed? It is their defense and stated before the court, that they do not deny the Bible, that they expected to introduce proof to make it harmonize. Why should we remove the sign cautioning the people to read the word of God just to satisfy the others in the case?

The Court: Of course, you know I stand for the Bible, but your son has suggested that we agree to take it down.

Gen. McKenzie: I do not agree with my son.

Dudley Field Malone (d): The house is divided against itself.

Darrow: The purpose, I do not know why it was put there, but I suggest that it be removed.

The Court: I do not suppose it was put there to influence the trial.

Atty. Gen. Tom Stewart (p): Do I understand you to ask it to be removed?

Darrow: Yes.

The Court: What do you say about it being removed?

Stewart: I do not care for it being removed, I will be frank.

J. G. McKenzie (p): If your Honor please, I believe in the Bible as strong as anybody else here but if that sign is objectionable to the attorneys for the defense, and they do not want to be repeatedly reminded of the fact that they should read their Bible, I think this court ought to remove it.

Malone: May your Honor please—

Arthur Garfield Hays (d): May we make our record—

Malone (cont.): —I do not think that is the statement of the position of the attorneys for the defense. We are trying a case here which we believe has very definite issues, aspects. We believe even though the court has moved downstairs for safety and comfort, that everything which might possibly prejudice the jury along religious lines, for or against the defense, should be removed from in front of the jury. The opinions of the members of the counsel for the defense, our religious beliefs, or Mr. Darrow's nonbelief, are none of the business of counsel for the prosecution. We do not wish that referred to again. The counsel for the defense are not on trial here. Mr. Scopes here is on trial and we are merely asking this court to remove anything of a prejudicial nature that we may try these issues and the court will be taken out of a prejudicial atmosphere. (Applause.)

J. G. McKenzie: If the court please, in reply to the statement of Mr. Malone, I want to withdraw my suggestion in regard to removing the sign, "Read Your Bible," for this reason: I have never seen the time in the history of this country when any man should be afraid to be reminded of the fact that he should read his Bible, and if they should represent a force that is aligned with the devil and his satellites—

Malone: Your Honor, I object to that kind of language.

J. G. McKenzie (cont.): Finally I say when that time comes that then is time for us to tear up all of the Bibles, throw them in the fire and let the country go to hell!

Hays: May I ask that our exception to those remarks be put on the record and I should like to move the court to expunge the last remarks.

The Court: Yes, expunge that part of Mr. McKenzie's statement from the record, where he said, if you were satellites of the devil. Anybody else want to be heard?

Malone: Yes, I think it is all right for the individual members of the prosecution to make up their minds as to what forces we represent. I have a right to assume I have as much chance of heaven as they have, to reach it by my own goal, and my understanding of the Bible and of Christianity, and I will be a pretty poor Christian when I get any biblical or Christian or religious views from any member of the prosecution that I have yet heard from during this trial. (Applause and laughter, with Court Officer Kelso Rice rapping for order.)

William Jennings Bryan (p): If the court please—

The Court: Col. Bryan, I will hear you.

Officer Rice: People, this is no circus! There are no monkeys up here! This is a lawsuit! Let us have order!

Bryan: May it please the court. . . . I cannot see that there is any inconsistency, even subtechnically, between taking that "Bible" up there off for the defense, if the defense insists that there is nothing in evolution that is contrary to it. (Applause.) If their arguments are sound and sincere, that the Bible can be construed so as to recognize evolution, I cannot see why "Read Your Bible" would necessarily mean partiality toward our side. . . . But if leaving that up there during the trial makes our brother to offend, I would take it down during the trial.

. . .

Darrow: This sign is not here for no purpose and it can have no effect but to influence this case, and I read the Bible myself—more or less—and it is pretty good reading in places. But this case has been made a case where it is to be the Bible or evolution, and we have been informed by Mr. Bryan, who, himself, a profound Bible student and has an essay every Sunday as to what it means[1]—we have been informed that a Tennessee jury who are not especially educated are better judges of the Bible than all of the scholars in the world, and when they see that sign, it means to them their construction of the Bible. It is pretty obvious it is not fair, your Honor, and we object to it.

. . .

The Court: The issues in this case, as they have been finally determined by this court, is whether or not it is unlawful to teach that man descended from a lower order of animals. I do not understand that issue involved the Bible. If the Bible is involved, I believe in it and am always on its side, but it is not for me to decide in this case. If the presence of the sign irritates anyone, or if anyone thinks it might influence the jury in any way, I have no purpose except to give both sides a fair trial in this case. Feeling that way about it, I will let the sign come down. (The sign was thereupon removed from the courthouse wall.)

. . .

[1]Darrow is referring to Bryan's syndicated newspaper column on the Bible.

Darrow Questions William Jennings Bryan on the Stand

(Transcript)

In an unprecedented maneuver, a prosecuting attorney agreed to take the stand as a witness—albeit a hostile one—for the defense. Why do you think Bryan accepted the invitation to testify? Was it a wise decision? What was Darrow's purpose throughout the questioning? Why did Bryan answer as he did?

Hays: The defense desires to call Mr. Bryan as a witness, and, of course, [if] the only question here is whether Mr. Scopes taught what these children said he taught, we recognize what Mr. Bryan says as a witness would not be very valuable. We think there are other questions involved and we should want to take Mr. Bryan's testimony for the purposes of our record, even if your Honor thinks it is not admissible in general, so we wish to call him now.[2]

The Court: Do you think you have a right to his testimony or evidence like you did these others?

Gen. McKenzie: I don't think it is necessary to call him, calling a lawyer who represents a client.

The Court: If you ask him about any confidential matter, I will protect him, of course.

Darrow: I do not intend to do that.

The Court: On scientific matters, Col. Bryan can speak for himself.

Bryan: If your honor, please, I insist that Mr. Darrow can be put on the stand, and Mr. Malone and Mr. Hays.

The Court: Call anybody you desire. Ask them any questions you wish.

Bryan: Then, we will call all three of them.

Darrow: Not at once?

Bryan: Where do you want me to sit?

The Court: Mr. Bryan, you are not objecting to going on the stand?

Bryan: Not at all.

The Court: Do you want Mr. Bryan sworn?

[2]The jury was excused from hearing Bryan's testimony, but Judge Raulston allowed this and other testimony to be recorded to help form the basis for the appeal the defense expected to make to a higher court.

Darrow: No.

Bryan: I can make affirmation; I can say, "So help me God, I will tell the truth."

Darrow: No, I take it you will tell the truth, Mr. Bryan.

You have given considerable study to the Bible, haven't you, Mr. Bryan?

Bryan: Yes, sir, I have tried to.

Q: Well, we all know you have. We are not going to dispute that at all. But you have written and published articles almost weekly, and sometimes have made interpretations of various things?

A: I would not say interpretations, Mr. Darrow, but comments on the lesson.

Q: If you comment to any extent these comments have been interpretations?

A: I presume that my discussion might be to some extent interpretations, but they have not been primarily intended as interpretations.

Q: But you have studied that question, of course?

A: Of what?

Q: Interpretation of the Bible.

A: On this particular question?

Q: Yes, sir.

A: Yes, sir.

Q: Then you have made a general study of it?

A: Yes, I have; I have studied the Bible for about fifty years, or sometime more than that, but, of course, I have studied it more as I have become older than when I was but a boy.

Q: Do you claim that everything in the Bible should be literally interpreted?

A: I believe everything in the Bible should be accepted as it is given there; some of the Bible is given illustratively. For instance: "Ye are the salt of the earth." I would not insist that man was actually salt, or that he had flesh of salt, but it is used in the sense of salt as saving God's people.

Did the Whale Swallow Jonah?

(Transcript)

Darrow commenced his questioning with a miracle from the biblical Book of Jonah (1:17). Why do you think Darrow began here rather than with questions about Genesis or evolution? Did Bryan's answers have relevance to his position on evolution?

Darrow: But when you read that Jonah swallowed the whale—or that the whale swallowed Jonah—excuse me please—how do you literally interpret that?

Bryan: When I read that a big fish swallowed Jonah—it does not say whale.

Q: Doesn't it? Are you sure?

A: That is my recollection of it. A big fish, and I believe it, and I believe in a God who can make a whale and can make a man and make both do what he pleases.

. . .

Darrow: Now, you say, the big fish swallowed Jonah, and he there remained how long—three days—and then he spewed him upon the land. You believe that the big fish was made to swallow Jonah?

Bryan: I am not prepared to say that; the Bible merely says it was done.

Q: You don't know whether it was the ordinary run of fish, or made for that purpose?

A: You may guess; you evolutionists guess.

Q: But when we do guess, we have a sense to guess right.

A: But do not do it often.

Q: You are not prepared to say whether that fish was made especially to swallow a man or not?

A: The Bible doesn't say, so I am not prepared to say.

Q: You don't know whether that was fixed up specially for the purpose?

A: No, the Bible doesn't say.

Q: But do you believe he made them—that he made such a fish and that it was big enough to swallow Jonah?

A: Yes, sir. Let me add: One miracle is just as easy to believe as another.

Q: It is for me.
A: It is for me.
Q: Just as hard.
A: It is hard to believe for you, but easy for me. A miracle is a thing performed beyond what man can perform. When you get beyond what man can do, you get within the realm of miracles; and it is just as easy to believe the miracle of Jonah as any other miracle in the Bible.
Q: Perfectly easy to believe that Jonah swallowed the whale?
A: If the Bible said so; the Bible doesn't make as extreme statements as evolutionists do.
Q: That may be a question, Mr. Bryan, about some of those you have known.
A: The only thing is, you have a definition of fact that includes imagination.
Q: And you have a definition that excludes everything but imagination, everything but imagination.
Stewart: I object to that as argumentative.
Bryan: You—
Darrow: The witness must not argue with me, either.

Could Joshua Command the Sun to Stand Still?

(Transcript)

To a rationalist such as Darrow, the story of Joshua commanding the sun to stand still, as the Bible relates in the Book of Joshua (10:12), was still more incredible. By now, it was clear that Darrow was going to rehash most of the standard skeptic's arguments that he had learned as a youth in the late nineteenth century.

Darrow: Do you consider the story of Joshua and the sun a miracle?
Bryan: I think it is.
Q: Do you believe Joshua made the sun stand still?
A: I believe what the Bible says. I suppose you mean that the earth stood still?
Q: I don't know. I am talking about the Bible now.

A: I accept the Bible absolutely.
Q: The Bible says Joshua commanded the sun to stand still for the purpose of lengthening the day, doesn't it, and you believe it?
A: I do.
Q: Do you believe at that time the entire sun went around the earth?
A: No, I believe that the earth goes around the sun.
Q: Do you believe that the men who wrote it thought that the day could be lengthened or that the sun could be stopped?
A: I don't know what they thought.
Q: You don't know?
A: I think they wrote the fact without expressing their own thoughts.

. . .

Darrow: Have you an opinion as to whether—whoever wrote the book, I believe it is, Joshua, the Book of Joshua, thought the sun went around the earth or not?
Bryan: I believe that he was inspired.
Q: Can you answer my question?
A: When you let me finish the statement.
Q: It is a simple question but finish it.
A: You cannot measure the length of my answer by the length of your question.
Q: No, except that the answer be longer.
(Laughter in the courtyard.)
A: I believe that the Bible is inspired, an inspired author. Whether one who wrote as he was directed to write understood the things he was writing about, I don't know.
Q: Whoever inspired it? Do you think whoever inspired it believed that the sun went around the earth?
A: I believe it was inspired by the Almighty, and he may have used language that could be understood at that time—
Q: Was—
A (cont.): —instead of using language that could not be understood until Darrow was born.
(Laughter and applause in the courtyard.)
Q: So, it might not, it might have been subject to construction, might it not?
A: It might have been used in language that could be understood then.
Q: That means it is subject to construction?
A: That is your construction. I am answering your question.
Q: Is that correct?

A: That is my answer to it.
Q: Can you answer?
A: I might say, Isaiah spoke of God sitting upon the circle of the earth.
Q: I am not talking about Isaiah.
The Court: Let him illustrate, if he wants to.
Darrow: Is it your opinion that passage was subject to construction?
Bryan: Well, I think anybody can put his own construction upon it, but I do not mean that necessarily that is a correct construction. I have answered the question.
Q: Don't you believe that in order to lengthen the day it would have been construed that the earth stood still?
A: I would not attempt to say what would have been necessary, but I know this, that I can take a glass of water that would fall to the ground without the strength of my hand and to the extent of the glass of water I can overcome the law of gravitation and lift it up. Whereas without my hand it would fall to the ground. If my puny hand can overcome the law of gravitation, the most universally understood, to that extent, I would not set power to the hand of Almighty God that made the universe.
Q: I read that years ago. Can you answer my question directly? If the day was lengthened by stopping either the earth or the sun, it must have been the earth?
A: Well, I should say so.
Q: Yes? But it was language that was understood at that time, and we now know that the sun stood still as it was with the earth. We know also the sun does not stand still?
A: Well, it is relatively so, as Mr. Einstein would say.
Q: I ask you if it does stand still?
A: You know as well as I know.
Q: Better. You have no doubt about it?
A: No. And the earth moves around.
Q: Yes?
A: But I think there is nothing improper if you will protect the Lord against your criticism.
Q: I suppose he needs it?
A: He was using language at that time the people understood.
Q: And that you call "interpretation."
A: No, sir; I would not call it interpretation.
Q: I say, you would call it interpretation at this time, to say it meant something then?
A: You may use your own language to describe what I have to say, and I will use mine in answering.

Q: Now, Mr. Bryan, have you ever pondered what would have happened to the earth if it had stood still?
A: No.
Q: You have not?
A: No; the God I believe in could have taken care of that, Mr. Darrow.
Q: I see. Have you ever pondered what would naturally happen to the earth if it stood still suddenly?
A: No.
Q: Don't you know it would have been converted into a molten mass of matter?
A: You testify to that when you get on the stand, I will give you a chance.
Q: Don't you believe it?
A: I would want to hear expert testimony on that.
Q: You have never investigated that subject?
A: I don't think I have ever had the question asked.
Q: Or ever thought of it?
A: I have been too busy on things that I thought were of more importance than that.

. . .

Did the Flood Wipe Out Civilization?

(Transcript)

As tempers grew shorter, Darrow attempted to probe Bryan's position on whether the Flood related in Genesis could have wiped out all living creatures except those saved in Noah's ark. Here, as elsewhere in his testimony, Bryan noted that he had always concerned himself more with reforming society for the future than with exploring society's past, and he seemed almost unconcerned with the implications of the Flood. Was Darrow's questioning fair? What was his intent with these questions?

Interestingly, "scientific creationists" at the turn of the twenty-first century stake much of their argument on the power of the biblical deluge to have altered the geological record so that the 6,000-year-old earth only appears to be 4 billion years older.

Stewart: Your Honor, he is perfectly able to take care of this but we are attaining no evidence. This is not competent evidence.

Bryan: These gentlemen have not had much chance—they did not come here to try this case. They came here to try revealed religion. I am here to defend it, and they can ask me any question they please

The Court: All right.

(Applause from the courtyard.)

Darrow: Great applause from the bleachers.

Bryan: From those whom you call "yokels."

Darrow: I have never called them yokels.

Bryan: That is the ignorance of Tennessee, the bigotry.

Darrow: You mean who are applauding you? (Applause.)

Bryan: Those are the people whom you insult.

Darrow: You insult every man of science and learning in the world because he does not believe in your fool religion!

The Court: I will not stand for that.

. . .

Darrow: How long ago was the Flood, Mr. Bryan?

Bryan: Let me see Ussher's calculation about it[3]. . . . It is given here, as 2348 years B.C.

Q: Well, 2348 years B.C. You believe that all the living things that were not contained in the ark were destroyed?

A: I think the fish may have lived.

Q: Outside of the fish?

A: I cannot say.

Q: You cannot say?

A: No, except that just as it is, I have no proof to the contrary.

Q: I am asking you whether you believe?

A: I do.

Q: That all living things outside of the fish were destroyed?

A: What I say about the fish is merely a matter of humor.

. . .

Darrow: You are not satisfied there is any civilization that can be traced back 5,000 years?

[3]In 1650, the Irish archbishop James Ussher used astronomy and the ages of subjects in the Old Testament to calculate the approximate date of the biblical creation as 4004 B.C.E. In later years, Ussher's calculations were often bound with editions of the Bible.

Bryan: I would not want to say there is because I have no evidence of it that is satisfactory.

Q: Would you say there is not?

A: Well, so far as I know, but when the scientists differ, from 24,000,000 to 306,000,000 in their opinion, as to how long ago life came here. I want them nearer, to come nearer together before they demand of me to give up my belief in the Bible.

Q: Do you say that you do not believe that there were any civilizations on this earth that reach back beyond 5,000 years?

A: I am not satisfied by any evidence that I have seen.

. . .

Darrow: Let me make this definite. You believe that every civilization on the earth and every living thing, except possibly the fishes, that came out of the ark were wiped out by the Flood?

Bryan: At that time.

Q: At that time. And then, whatever human beings, including all the tribes, that inhabited the world, and have inhabited the world, and who run their pedigree straight back, and all the animals, have come onto the earth since the Flood?

A: Yes.

Q: Within 4,200 years. Do you know a scientific man on the face of the earth that believes any such thing?

A: I cannot say, but I know some scientific men who dispute entirely the antiquity of man as testified to by other scientific men.

Q: Oh, that does not answer the question. Do you know of a single scientific man on the face of the earth that believes any such thing as you stated, about the antiquity of man?

A: I don't think I have ever asked one the direct question.

Q: Quite important, isn't it?

A: Well, I don't know as it is.

Q: It might not be?

A: If I had nothing else to do except speculate on what our remote ancestors were and what our remote descendants have been, but I have been more interested in Christians going on right now, to make it much more important than speculation on either the past or the future.

Q: You have never had any interest in the age of the various races and people and civilization and animals that exist upon the earth today? Is that right?

A: I have never felt a great deal of interest in the effort that has been made to dispute the Bible by the speculations of men, or the investigations of men.

Q: Are you the only human being on earth who knows what the Bible means?

Stewart: I object.

The Court: Sustained.

Darrow: You do know that there are thousands of people who profess to be Christians who believe the earth is much more ancient and that the human race is much more ancient?

Bryan: I think there may be.

Q: And you never have investigated to find out how long man has been on the earth?

A: I have never found it necessary.

Q: For any reason, whatever it is?

A: To examine every speculation; but if I had done it I never would have done anything else.

Q: I ask for a direct answer.

A: I do not expect to find out all those things, and I do not expect to find out about races.

Q: I didn't ask you that. Now, I ask you if you know if it was interesting enough, or important enough for you to try to find out about how old these ancient civilizations were?

A: No; I have not made a study of it.

Q: Don't you know that the ancient civilizations of China are 6,000 or 7,000 years old, at the very least?

A: No; but they would not run back beyond the creation, according to the Bible, 6,000 years.

. . .

Darrow: You have never in all your life made any attempt to find out about the other peoples of the earth—how old their civilizations are—how long they had existed on the earth, have you?

Bryan: No, sir. I have been so well satisfied with the Christian religion, that I have spent no time trying to find arguments against it.

Q: Were you afraid you might find some?

A: No, sir. I am not afraid now that you will show me any. . . . I have all the information I want to live by and to die by.

Q: And that's all you are interested in?

A: I am not looking for any more on religion.

Q: You don't care how old the earth is, how old man is, and how long the animals have been here?

A: I am not so much interested in that.
Q: You have never made any investigation to find out?
A: No, sir, I have never.
Q: All right.

. . .

Darrow Questions Bryan on Genesis

(Transcript)

After touching on various Old Testament miracles for more than an hour, Darrow finally came to the crux of his questioning: What was Bryan's interpretation of the story of the divine creation in the Bible—specifically, the age of the earth—as related in the Book of Genesis? Note that Bryan's admission that the biblical days of creation might have lasted much longer than twenty-four hours apiece was a long-held position that Bryan shared with many other fundamentalists. Do you think Bryan's answers are consistent with his belief in biblical literalism? Does this testimony seem damaging to you?

Darrow: Mr. Bryan, could you tell me how old the earth is?
Bryan: No, sir, I couldn't.
Q: Could you come anywhere near it?
A: I wouldn't attempt to. I could possibly come as near as the scientists do, but I had rather be more accurate before I give a guess.
Q: You don't think much of scientists, do you?
A: Yes, sir, I do, sir.
Q: Is there any scientist in the world you think much of?
A: I do.
Q: Who?
A: Well, I think the bulk of the scientists—
Q: I don't want that kind of answer, Mr. Bryan, who are they?
A: I will give you George M. Price, for instance.[4]

[4]George McCready Price, a Flood geologist, was an early proponent of the "young earth" theory of creation. Like his brethren in the Seventh-day Adventists, Price believed that God had created the earth in seven days of twenty-four hours each, and he

Q: Who is he?
A: Professor of geology in a college.
Q: Where?
A: He was out near Lincoln, Nebraska.
Q: How close to Lincoln, Nebraska?
A: About three or four miles. He is now in a college out in California.
Q: Where is the college?
A: At Lodi.
Q: That is a small college?
A: I didn't know you had to judge a man by the size of the college—I thought you judged him by the size of the man.
Q: I thought the size of the college made some difference.
A: It might raise a presumption in the minds of some, but I think I would rather find out what he believed.
Q: You would rather find out whether his belief corresponds with your views or prejudices or whatever they are before you said how good he was?
A: Well, you know the word "prejudice" is—
Q: Well, belief, then.
A: I don't think I am any more prejudiced for the Bible than you are against it.
Q: Well, I don't know.
A: Well, I don't know either. It is my guess.
Q: You mentioned Price because he is the only human being in the world so far as you know that signs his name as a geologist that believes like you do?
A: No, there is a man named Wright, who taught at Oberlin.[5]
Q: I will get to Mr. Wright in a moment. Who publishes his book?
A: I can't tell you. I can get you the book.
Q: Don't you know? Don't you know it is Revell & Co., Chicago?[6]
A: I couldn't say.
Q: He [Revell] publishes yours, doesn't he?
A: Yes, sir.

---

explained discrepancies between the "young earth" and the fossil record by pointing to the possible impact of the Old Testament Flood. On Price, see Ronald L. Numbers, *The Creationists* (New York: Alfred A. Knopf, 1992), 72–101. See also George McCready Price, *The New Geology* (Mountain View, Calif.: Pacific Press Publishing, 1923).

[5]Bryan refers to Chauncey Wright, Price's ally in the "young earth" interpretation of creation.

[6]Revell & Co. was a well-known publisher of conservative evangelical works.

Stewart: Will you let me make an exception? I don't think it is pertinent about who publishes a book.
Darrow: He has quoted a man that every scientist in this country knows is a mountebank and a pretender and not a geologist at all.
The Court: You can ask him about the man, but don't ask him about who publishes the book.
Darrow: Do you know anything about the college he is in?
Bryan: No, I can't tell you.
Q: Do you know how old his book is?
A: No, sir, it is a recent book.
Q: Do you know anything about his training?
A: No, I can't say on that.
Q: Do you know of any geologist on the face of the earth who ever recognized him?
A: I couldn't say.
Q: Do you think he is all right? How old does he say the earth is?
A: I am not sure that I would I insist on some particular geologist that you picked out recognizing him before I would consider him worthy if he agreed with your views.
Q: You would consider him worthy if he agreed with your views?
A: Well, I think his argument is very good

. . .

Darrow: Have you any idea how old the earth is?
Bryan: No.
Q: The book you have introduced in evidence tells you, doesn't it?
A: I don't think it does, Mr. Darrow.
Q: Let's see whether it does; is this the one?
A: That is the one, I think.
Q: It says B.C. 4004?
A: That is Bishop Ussher's calculation.
Q: That is printed in the Bible you introduced?
A: Yes, sir.
Q: And numerous other Bibles?
A: Yes, sir.

. . .

Darrow: Would you say that the earth was only 4,000 years old?
Bryan: Oh, no; I think it is much older than that.
Q: How much?
A: I couldn't say.

Q: Do you say whether the Bible itself says it is older than that?

A: I don't think the Bible says itself whether it is older or not.

Q: Do you think the earth was made in six days?

A: Not six days of twenty-four hours.[7]

Q: Doesn't it say so?

A: No, sir.

Stewart: I want to interpose another objection. What is the purpose of this examination?

Bryan: The purpose is to cast ridicule on everybody who believes in the Bible, and I am perfectly willing that the world shall know that these gentlemen have no other purpose than ridiculing every Christian who believes in the Bible.

Darrow: We have the purpose of preventing bigots and ignoramuses from controlling the education of the United States and you know it, and that is all.

Bryan: I am glad to bring out that statement. I want the world to know that this evidence is not for the view Mr. Darrow and his associates have filed affidavits here stating, the purposes of which I understand it, is to show that the Bible story is not true.

Malone: Mr. Bryan seems anxious to get some evidence in the record that would tend to show that those affidavits are not true.

Bryan: I am not trying to get anything into the record. I am simply trying to protect the word of God against the greatest atheist or agnostic in the United States! (Prolonged applause.) I want the papers to know I am not afraid to get on the stand in front of him and let him do his worst! I want the world to know! (Prolonged applause.)

Darrow: I wish I could get a picture of these clappers.

Stewart: I am not afraid of Mr. Bryan being perfectly able to take care of himself, but this examination cannot be a legal examination and it cannot be worth a thing in the world, and, your Honor, I respectfully except to it, and call on your Honor, in the name of all that is legal, to stop this examination and stop it here.

Hays: I rather sympathize with the general, but Mr. Bryan is produced as a witness because he is a student of the Bible and he presumably

[7]Bryan here revealed his belief in the "day-age" theory of Genesis, a fairly conventional thesis among fundamentalists at the time. Only decades later would the "young earth" theory of creation begin to supplant the "day-age" theory and the even more popular "gap" theory, which claimed that a gap of perhaps thousands of years existed between the first chapter of Genesis and the creation of Adam and Eve; see Ronald L. Numbers, *Darwinism Comes to America* (Cambridge: Harvard University Press, 1998), 80–82.

understands what the Bible means. He is one of the foremost students in the United States, and we hope to show Mr. Bryan, who is a student of the Bible, what the Bible really means in connection with evolution. Mr. Bryan has already stated that the world is not merely 6,000 years old and that is very helpful to us, and where your evidence is coming from, this Bible, which goes to the jury, is that the world started in 4004 B.C.

Bryan: You think the Bible says that?

Hays: The one you have taken in evidence says that.

Bryan: I don't concede that it does.

Hays: You know that that chronology is made up by adding together all of the ages of the people in the Bible, counting their ages; and now then, let us show the next stage from a Bible student, that these things are not to be taken literally, but that each man is entitled to his own interpretation.

Stewart: The court makes the interpretation.

Hays: But the court is entitled to information on what is the interpretation of an expert Bible student.

. . .

The Court: Of course, it is incompetent testimony before the jury. The only reason I am allowing this to go in at all is that they may have it in the appellate courts as showing what the affidavit would be.[8]

Bryan: The reason I am answering is not for the benefit of the superior court. It is to keep these gentlemen from saying I was afraid to meet them and let them question me, and I want the Christian world to know that any atheist, agnostic, unbeliever, can question me any time as to my belief in God, and I will answer him.

Darrow: I want to take an exception to this conduct of this witness. He may be very popular down here in the hills. I do not need to have his explanation for his answer.

The Court: Yes.

Bryan: If I had not, I would not have answered the question.

Hays: May I be heard? I do not want your Honor to think we are asking questions of Mr. Bryan with the expectation that the higher court will not say that those questions are proper testimony. The reason I state that is this: your law speaks for the Bible. Your law does not say the literal interpretation of the Bible. If Mr. Bryan,

[8]That is, the discussion was to help inform the appellate court on what the defense's expert witnesses would have said if they had been allowed to testify.

who is a student of the Bible, will state that everything in the Bible need not be interpreted literally, that each man must judge for himself; if he will state that, of course, then your Honor would charge the jury [that] we are not bound by a literal interpretation of the Bible. If I have made my argument clear enough for the attorney general to understand, I will retire.

Stewart: I will admit you have frequently been difficult of comprehension, and I think you are as much to blame as I am.

Hays: I know I am.

. . .

Bryan: Your Honor, they have not asked a question legally, and the only reason they have asked any question is for the purpose, as the question about Jonah was asked, for a chance to give this agnostic an opportunity to criticize a believer in the word of God; and I answered the question in order to shut his mouth so that he cannot go out and tell his atheistic friends that I would not answer his question. That is the only reason, no more reason in the world.

. . .

Darrow: Do you believe that the first woman was Eve?

Bryan: Yes.

Q: Do you believe she was literally made out of Adam's rib?

A: I do.

Q: Did you ever discover where Cain got his wife?

A: No, sir; I leave the agnostics to hunt for her.

Q: You have never found out?

A: I have never tried to find.

Q: You have never tried to find?

A: No.

Q: The Bible says he got one, doesn't it? Were there other people on the earth at that time?

A: I cannot say.

Q: You cannot say. Did that ever enter your consideration?

A: Never bothered me.

Q: There were no others recorded, but Cain got a wife.

A: That is what the Bible says.

Q: Where she came from you do not know. All right. Does the statement, "The morning and the evening were the first day," and, "The morning and the evening were the second day," mean anything to you?

A: I do not think it necessarily means a twenty-four-hour day.
Q: You do not?
A: No.
Q: What do you consider it to be?
A: I have not attempted to explain it. If you will take the second chapter—let me have the book. (Examining Bible.) The fourth verse of the second chapter says: "These are the generations of the heavens and of the earth, when they were created in the day that the Lord God made the earth and the heavens." The word "day" there in the very next chapter is used to describe a period. I do not see that there is any necessity for construing the words, "the evening and the morning," as meaning necessarily a twenty-four-hour day, "in the day when the Lord made the heaven and the earth."
Q: Then, when the Bible said, for instance, "And God called the firmament heaven. And the evening and the morning were the second day," that does not necessarily mean twenty-four hours?
A: I do not think it necessarily does.
Q: Do you think it does or does not?
A: I know a great many think so.
Q: What do you think?
A: I do not think it does.
Q: You think those were not literal days?
A: I do not think they were twenty-four-hour days.
Q: What do you think about it?
A: That is my opinion—I do not know that my opinion is better on that subject than those who think it does.
Q: You do not think that?
A: No. But I think it would be just as easy for the kind of God we believe in to make the earth in six days as in six years or in 6,000,000 years or in 600,000,000 years. I do not think it important whether we believe one or the other.
Q: Do you think those were literal days?
A: My impression is they were periods, but I would not attempt to argue as against anybody who wanted to believe in literal days.
Q: Have you any idea of the length of the periods?
A: No; I don't.

. . .

Darrow: The creation might have been going on for a very long time?
Bryan: It might have continued for millions of years.

Q: Yes. All right. Do you believe the story of the temptation of Eve by the serpent?

A: I do.

Q: Do you believe that after Eve ate the apple, or gave it to Adam, whichever way it was, that God cursed Eve, and at that time decreed that all womankind thenceforth and forever should suffer the pains of childbirth in the reproduction of the earth?

A: I believe what it says, and I believe the fact as fully—

Q: That is what it says, doesn't it?

. . .

Bryan: Your Honor, I think I can shorten this testimony. The only purpose Mr. Darrow has is to slur at the Bible, but I will answer his question. I will answer it all at once, and I have no objection in the world. I want the world to know that this man, who does not believe in a God, is trying to use a court in Tennessee—

Darrow: I object to that!

Bryan (cont.): —to slur at it, and while it will require time, I am willing to take it!

Darrow: I object to your statement. I am examining you on your fool ideas that no intelligent Christian on earth believes!

The Court: Court is adjourned until 9 o'clock tomorrow morning.

NEW YORK TIMES

Laughter at Bryan's Expense

July 21, 1925

Although Bryan's testimony surely did not go as well as he had hoped, neither did it go as poorly as legend seems to have it. The myth of Darrow breaking Bryan's heart under the pitiless Tennessee sun grew out of reports such as this, from a New York Times *correspondent with strong defense sympathies. Does this report reflect what you learned from the transcript? Why or why not?*

New York Times, 21 July 1925, 1.

So-called Fundamentalists of Tennessee sat under the trees of the Rhea County Court House lawn today listening to William J. Bryan defend his faith in the "literal inerrancy" of the Bible, and laughed.

Clarence Darrow, agnostic and skeptic, has called the leader of the Fundamentalists to the stand in an effort to establish by the testimony of Mr. Bryan himself that the Bible need not be interpreted literally, so that the defense might argue before the jury that Mr. Scopes did not teach a theory of evolution which contradicts the Bible.

The greatest crowd of the trial had come in anticipation of hearing Messrs. Bryan and Darrow speak, and it got more than it expected. It saw Darrow and Bryan in actual conflict—Mr. Darrow's rationalism in combat with Mr. Bryan's faith—and forgot for the moment that Bryan's faith was its own. The crowd saw only the battle, appreciated only the blows one dealt the other and laughed with and at both.

To the crowd spread under the trees watching the amazing spectacle on the platform the fight seemed a fair one. There was no pity for the helplessness of the believer come so suddenly and so unexpectedly upon a moment when he could not reconcile statements of the Bible with generally accepted facts. There was no pity for his admissions of ignorance of things boys and girls learn in high school, his floundering confessions that he knew practically nothing of geology, biology, philology, little of comparative religion, and little even of ancient history.

These Tennesseans were enjoying a fight. That an ideal of a great man, a biblical scholar, an authority on religion, was being dispelled seemed to make no difference. They grinned with amusement and expectation, until the next blow by one side or the other came, and then they guffawed again. And finally, when Mr. Bryan, pressed harder and harder by Mr. Darrow, confessed he did not believe everything in the Bible should be taken literally, the crowd howled.

8

Eighth Day's Proceedings

Tuesday, July 21, 1925

Attorney General Tom Stewart had been outraged by Clarence Darrow's cross-examination of William Jennings Bryan on day seven and reached an agreement with Bryan and Judge John T. Raulston before court opened on day eight to expunge Bryan's testimony and put a halt to any further cross-examinations. With no strategies left, Darrow asked the court to instruct the jury to find a guilty verdict so the defense would be able to appeal the case to a higher court. By giving up his own closing argument in this way, Darrow also ensured that Bryan would not be allowed to deliver the closing speech that he had been working on for weeks. Instead of closing arguments, the final day of the Scopes trial concluded with farewell remarks from counsel on both sides, a brief sermon by Judge Raulston, and the only words that the defendant, John Thomas Scopes, uttered in court during the trial.

Court Strikes Bryan's Testimony

(Transcript)

Recognizing that he had given the defense attorneys too much latitude in allowing Darrow to question Bryan, Judge Raulston removed Bryan's testimony from the court record. Bryan was ambivalent about the judge's ruling. What was Bryan's concern? Does his response shed light on his decision the previous day to take the stand?

The Court: Let's have order. Since the beginning of this trial the judge of this court has had some big problems to pass upon. Of course, there is no way for me to know whether I decided these questions correctly or not until the courts of last resort speak. . . . I fear that I may have committed error on yesterday in my over-zeal to ascertain if there was anything in the proof that was offered that might aid the higher courts in determining whether or not I had committed error in my former decrees. . . . The only question we have now is whether or not this teacher, this accused, this defendant, taught that man descended from a lower order of animals. As I see it, after due deliberation, I feel that Mr. Bryan's testimony cannot aid the higher court in determining that question. If the question before the higher court involved the issue as to what evolution was or as to how God created man, or created the earth, or created the universe, this testimony might be relevant, but those questions are not before the court, and so taking this view of it, I am pleased to expunge this testimony, given by Mr. Bryan on yesterday, from the records of this court and it will not be further considered.

. . .

William Jennings Bryan (p): May it please the court.

The Court: I will hear you, Mr. Bryan.

Bryan: At the conclusion of your decision to expunge the testimony given by me upon the record I didn't have time to ask you a question. I fully agree with the court that the testimony taken yesterday was not legitimate or proper. I simply wanted the court to understand that I was not in position to raise an objection at that time myself nor was I willing to have it raised for me without asserting my willingness to be cross-examined. I also stated that if I was to take the witness stand I would ask that the others take the witness stand also, that I might put certain questions to them. Now the testimony was ended and I assume that you expunge the questions as well as the answers.

The Court: Yes, sir.

Bryan: That it isn't a reflection upon the answers any more than it is upon the questions.

The Court: I expunged the whole proceedings.

Bryan: Now I had not reached the point where I could make a statement to answer the charges made by the counsel for the defense as to my ignorance and my bigotry.

Clarence Darrow (d): I object, your Honor. Now what's all this about?

The Court: Why do you want to make this, Col. Bryan?

Bryan: I just want to finish my sentence.

Darrow: Why can't he go outside on the lawn?

Bryan: I am not asking to make a statement here.

The Court: I will hear what you say.

Bryan: I shall have to trust to the justness of the press, which reported what was said yesterday, to report what I will say, not to the court, but to the press in answer to the charge scattered broadcast over the world and I shall also avail myself of the opportunity to give to the press, not to the court, the questions that I would have asked had I been permitted to call the attorneys on the other side.

Darrow: I think it would be better, Mr. Bryan, for you to take us out also with the press and ask us the questions and then the press will have both the questions and the answers.

Bryan: The gentleman who represents the defense, not only differs from me, but he differs from the court very often in the manner of procedure. I simply want to make that statement and say that I shall have to avail myself of the press without having the dignity of its being presented in the court, but I think it is hardly fair for them to bring into the limelight my views on religion and stand behind a dark lantern that throws light on other people, but conceals themselves. I think it is only fair that the country should know the religious attitude of the people who come down here to deprive the people of Tennessee of the right to run their own schools.

Darrow: I object to that.

The Court: I overrule the objection.

Bryan: That is all.

. . .

Jury Reaches a Verdict; Scopes Speaks

(Transcript)

The defense had no more arguments, and it had planned all along to appeal the case to a higher court, so Darrow basically asked the jury to return a guilty verdict. Why do you think Darrow placed so much faith in the higher courts?

Darrow: May I say a few words to the jury? Gentlemen of the jury, we are sorry to have not had a chance to say anything to you. We will do it some other time. Now, we came down here to offer evidence in this case and the court has held under the law that the evidence we had is not admissible, so all we can do is to take an exception and carry it to a higher court to see whether the evidence is admissible or not. As far as this case stands before the jury, the court has told you very plainly that if you think my client taught that man descended from a lower order of animals, you will find him guilty, and you heard the testimony of the boys on that question and heard read the books, and there is no dispute about the facts. Scopes did not go on the stand, because he could not deny the statements made by the boys. I do not know how you may feel—I am not especially interested in it—but this case and this law will never be decided until it gets to a higher court, and it cannot get to a higher court probably, very well, unless you bring in a verdict. So, I do not want any of you to think we are going to find any fault with you as to your verdict. I am frank to say, while we think it is wrong, and we ought to have been permitted to put in our evidence, the court felt otherwise, as he had a right to hold. We cannot argue to you gentlemen under the instructions given by the court—we cannot even explain to you that we think you should return a verdict of not guilty. We do not see how you could. We do not ask it. We think we will save our point and take it to the higher court and settle whether the law is good, and also whether he should have permitted the evidence. I guess that is plain enough.

Atty. Gen. Tom Stewart (p): That is satisfactory.

(Jury is excused and returns nine minutes later.)

The Court: Mr. Foreman, will you tell us whether you have agreed on a verdict?

Foreman: Yes, sir. We have, your honor.

The Court: What do you find?

Foreman: We have found for the state, found the defendant guilty.

. . .

The Court: Mr. Scopes, the jury has found you guilty under this indictment, charging you with having taught in the schools of Rhea County, in violation of what is commonly known as the anti-evolution statute. . . . The statute makes this an offense punishable by fine of not less than $100 nor more than $500. The court now fixes your fine at $100, and imposes that fine upon you—

John Randolph Neal (d): May it please your Honor, we want to be heard a moment.

The Court: Have you anything to say, Mr. Scopes, as to why the court should not impose punishment upon you?

John T. Scopes: Your Honor, I feel that I have been convicted of violating an unjust statute. I will continue in the future, as I have in the past, to oppose this law in any way I can. Any other action would be in violation of my ideal of academic freedom—that is, to teach the truth as guaranteed in our Constitution, of personal and religious freedom. I think the fine is unjust.

. . .

Farewell Remarks

(Transcript)

With the verdict in, the participants in the trial had an opportunity to reflect on the meaning of their dispute. Compare Bryan's and Darrow's valedictories. Do they seem consistent with your view of the men? What was the basis of Bryan's optimism?

Bryan: I don't know that there is any special reason why I should add to what has been said, and yet the subject has been presented from so many viewpoints that I hope the court will pardon me if I mention a viewpoint that has not been referred to. Dayton is the center and the seat of this trial largely by circumstance. We are told that more words have been sent across the ocean by cable to Europe and Australia about this trial than has ever been sent by cable in regard to anything else happening in the United States. That isn't because the trial is held in Dayton. It isn't because a schoolteacher has been subjected to the danger of a fine from $100 to $500, but I think illustrates how people can be drawn into prominence by attaching themselves to a great cause. Causes stir the world. It is because it goes deep. It is because it extends wide, and because it reaches into the future beyond the power of man to see. Here has been fought out a little case of little consequence as a case, but the world is interested because it raises an issue, and that issue will some day be settled right, whether it is settled on our side or the other side. It is going to be settled right. There can be no settlement of a great cause without discussion, and people will not discuss a cause until their attention is drawn to it, and the value of this trial is not in any incident of the trial, it is not because of anybody who is attached to it, either in an official way or as counsel on either side. Human beings are mighty small, your Honor. We are apt to magnify the personal element and we sometimes become inflated with our importance, but the world little cares for man as an individual. He is born, he works, he dies, but causes go on forever, and we who participated in this case may congratulate ourselves that we have attached ourselves to a mighty issue. . . .

The people will determine this issue. They will take sides upon this issue, they will state the question involved in this issue, they will examine the information—not so much that which has been brought out here, for very little has been brought out here, but this case will stimulate investigation and investigation will bring out information, and the facts will be known, and upon the facts, as ascertained, the decision will be rendered, and I think, my friends, and your Honor, that if we are actuated by the spirit that should actuate every one of us, no matter what our views may be, we ought not only desire, but pray, that that which is right will prevail, whether it be our way or somebody else's. (Applause.)

. . .

Darrow: Of course, there is much that Mr. Bryan has said that is true. And nature—nature, I refer to, does not choose any special setting for mere events. I fancy that the place where the Magna Charta was wrested from the barons in England was a very small place, probably not as big as Dayton.[1] But events come along as they come along. I think this case will be remembered because it is the first case of this sort since we stopped trying people in America for witchcraft, because here we have done our best to turn back the tide that has sought to force itself upon this—upon this modern world, of testing every fact in science by a religious dictum. That is all I care to say.

. . .

The Court: Now, we spoke—Dayton has been referred to—that the law—that something big could not come out of Dayton. Why, my friends, the greatest Man that has ever walked on the face of the earth, the Man that left the portals of heaven, the Man that came down from heaven to earth that man might live, was born in a little

[1]Darrow misread his history slightly. In 1215, at Runnymede, England, a number of English barons forced King John to grant a series of rights to the nobility by signing the Magna Carta, a document generally considered the foundation of constitutional democracy in western Europe.

town, and he lived and spent his life among a simple, unpretentious people.

. . .

Now, my friends, the people in America are great people. We are great in the South, and they are great in the North. We are great because we are willing to lay down our differences when we fight the battle out and be friends. And, let me tell you, there are two things in this world that are indestructible, that man cannot destroy, or no force in the world can destroy.

One is truth. You may crush it to the earth but it will rise again. It is indestructible, and the causes of the law of God. Another thing indestructible in America and in Europe and everywhere else, is the word of God, that he has given to man, that man may use it as a waybill to the other world. Indestructible, my friends, by any force because it is the word of the Man, of the forces that created the universe, and he has said in his word that "My word will not perish" but will live forever.

. . .

We will adjourn. And Brother Jones will pronounce the benediction.

Dr. Jones: May the grace of our Lord Jesus Christ, the love of God and the communion and fellowship of the Holy Ghost abide with you all. Amen.

The Court: The court will adjourn sine die.

H. L. MENCKEN

Battle Now Over; Genesis Triumphant and Ready for New Jousts

July 18, 1925

The Scopes trial fitted perfectly into H. L. Mencken's vision of the United States—especially the southern and rural United States—as a benighted land of ignorance and conformity. The presence of Bryan, whom the libertarian Mencken had always reviled as a reforming busy-

H. L. Mencken, "Battle Now Over, Mencken Sees; Genesis Triumphant and Ready for New Jousts," *Baltimore Evening Sun,* 18 July 1925, 1.

body, only made the trial a more inviting target for the writer's sharp pen. The following selection, written while Mencken was leaving Dayton before the trial's end, conveys the pungency of Mencken's writing and demonstrates his genius for developing a self-image for "sophisticated" city dwellers in contrast to his stereotype of their rural southern brethren.

All that remains of the great cause of the State of Tennessee against the infidel Scopes is the formal business of bumping off the defendant. There may be some legal jousting on Monday and some gaudy oratory on Tuesday, but the main battle is over, with Genesis completely triumphant. . . .

More interesting than the hollow buffoonery that remains will be the effect upon the people of Tennessee, the actual prisoners at the bar. That the more civilized of them are in a highly feverish condition of mind must be patent to every visitor. The guffaws that roll in from all sides give them great pain. They are full of bitter protests and valiant projects. They prepare, it appears, to organize, hoist the black flag and offer the fundamentalists of the dung-hills a battle to the death. They will not cease until the last Baptist preacher is in flight over the mountains, and the ordinary intellectual decencies of Christendom are triumphantly restored.

With the best will in the world I find it impossible to accept this tall talk with anything resembling confidence. The intelligentsia of Tennessee had their chance and let it get away from them. When the old mountebank Bryan first invaded the State with his balderdash they were unanimously silent. When he began to round up converts in the back country they offered him no challenge. When the Legislature passed the anti-evolution bill and the Governor signed it, they contented themselves with murmuring pianissimo [softly]. . . .

The Scopes trial, from the start, has been carried on in a manner exactly fitted to the anti-evolution law and the simian imbecility under it. There hasn't been the slightest pretense to decorum. The rustic judge, a candidate for re-election, has postured before the yokels like a clown in a ten-cent side show, and almost every word he has uttered has been an undisguised appeal to their prejudices and superstitions. The chief prosecuting attorney, beginning like a competent lawyer and a man of self-respect, ended like a convert at a Billy Sunday[2] revival. It fell to him, finally, to make a clear and astonishing statement of the theory of justice prevailing under fundamentalism. What he said, in

[2]Billy Sunday (1862–1935) was a popular traveling evangelist and fundamentalist.

brief, was that a man accused of infidelity had no rights whatever under Tennessee law.

This is probably not true yet, but it will become true inevitably if the Bryan murrain [plague] is not arrested. The Bryan of today is not to be mistaken for the political rabble rouser of two decades ago. That earlier Bryan may have been grossly in error, but at least he kept his errors within the bounds of reason; it was still possible to follow him without yielding up all intelligence. The Bryan of today, old, disappointed and embittered, is a far different bird. He realizes at last that the glories of this world are not for him, and he takes refuge, peasant-like, in religious hallucinations. They depart from sense altogether. They are not merely silly; they are downright idiotic. And being idiotic, they appeal with irresistible force to the poor half-wits upon whom the old charlatan now preys.

When I heard him, in open court, denounce the notion that man is a mammal, I was genuinely staggered and so was every other stranger in the courtroom. People looked at one another in blank amazement. But the native fundamentalists, it quickly appeared, saw nothing absurd in his words. The attorneys for the prosecution smiled approval, the crowd applauded, the very judge on the bench beamed his acquiescence. And the same thing happened when he denounced all education as corrupting and began arguing incredibly that a farmer who read the Bible knew more than any scientist in the world. Such dreadful bilge, heard of far away, may seem only ridiculous. But it takes on a different smack, I assure you, when one hears it discharged formally in a court of law and sees it accepted as wisdom by judge and jury.

Darrow has lost this case. It was lost long before he came to Dayton. But it seems to me that he has nevertheless performed a great public service by fighting it to a finish and in a perfectly serious way. Let no one mistake it for comedy, farcical though it may be in all its details. It serves notice on the country that Neanderthal man is organizing in these forlorn backwaters of the land, led by a fanatic, rid of sense, and devoid of conscience. Tennessee, challenging him too timorously and too late, now sees its courts converted into campmeetings and its Bill of Rights made a mock of by its sworn officers of the law. There are other States that had better look to their arsenals before the Hun is at their gates.

PART THREE

The Scopes Trial and the Culture of the 1920s: The Documents

1

Cartoonists Draw the Scopes Trial

The Scopes trial was a monthlong frolic for editorial cartoonists. The circus atmosphere of the trial, the monkey motif, the celebrity attorneys—all were inviting targets for satire. Newspapers have used illustrations for centuries both to appeal to less literate readers and to deliver a much richer message in a smaller space. The Scopes cartoons embodied this mixture of motives. How did the cartoonists in the following pages convey their meaning? Do you see recurring themes in the cartoons? How did the cartoonists' messages differ from the regular newspaper and magazine accounts of the trial? Do you think the cartoon form in general affected what the cartoonists could say? Which cartoons do you find most effective and why?

DORMAN

No Wonder the Monkeys Are Worried

June 29, 1925

Here is an example of the most common Scopes trial motif—a couple of monkeys observing the follies of modern America and questioning whether they could actually be related to humans. Such "monkey-superior" cartoons offered a nice inversion of the evolutionary ladder that placed humans above other primates, but they seldom commented directly on the trial itself. What was the target of this cartoonist's satire?

Nashville Tennessean, 29 June 1925, 4.

ROGERS

Disbelievers in the Evolution Theory

June 20, 1925

The "monkey-superior" motif found much sharper expression in the *Chicago Defender,* an African American newspaper notable for its unbending attitude toward racism. Rather than satirizing such minor vices as high taxes or loose morals, this cartoonist aimed his pen directly at the persistence of whites lynching African Americans in the 1920s. Although the cartoonist was surely thinking about the American South as the heartland both of antievolutionism and of racist lynching, he also drew the U.S. Capitol in the background. Why? Compare this cartoon both with the other cartoons and with the documents on race and the Scopes trial in part three, chapter 2.

Chicago Defender, 20 June 1925, sec. 2, p. 12.

CROSS

Unduly Excited

June 25, 1925

Despite their own role in sensationalizing the trial, many Tennessee newspapers officially deplored the "ballyhoo" surrounding the Scopes trial. Interestingly, this cartoon, published more than two weeks before the trial began, forecast fairly accurately the course of the trial. What was this cartoonist's message? Is this a pro-evolution or antievolution cartoon?

Nashville Tennessean, 25 June 1925, 4.

CARGILL

Education in the Higher Branches

1925

Education in the higher branches !

Prompted by the Butler law, this cartoonist commented more broadly on the post–World War I wave of laws regulating what could be taught in the public schools (see also the documents on educational freedom and the Scopes trial in part three, chapter 3). Look carefully at the imagery here: How is "higher education" represented? Is this a heroic picture? How does the cartoonist portray the "state legislature"? What do you think Bryan would have said about this cartoon?

Wall Street Journal, n.d., reprinted in *Outlook,* 1 July 1925, 319.

ALLEY

The Light of Economic Liberty

May 7, 1925

Published well before the trial controversy began, the cartoon on page 177 nevertheless conveys the "boosterish" attitude common in Tennessee and other border states. Look at the list of positive attributes the cartoonist discerned in the South. How do these fit together? How does this cartoon fit with attacks by H. L. Mencken and other northern reporters on the economic backwardness of the South? Do you think the cartoonist would have considered the Butler law a sign of backwardness? In this light, why do you think the southern *Manufacturers' Record* might have considered the Dayton trial to have been "one of the South's supremest advertisements, and an advertisement which will do boundless good"?[1]

[1]"Why the Dayton Trial Will Resound [*sic*] to the South's Good," *Manufacturers' Record,* 20 August 1925, 70, quoted in Willard B. Gatewood Jr., *Preachers, Pedagogues, and Politicians: The Evolution Controversy in North Carolina* (Chapel Hill: University of North Carolina Press, 1966), 354.

THE LIGHT OF ECONOMIC LIBERTY.

BALTIMORE SUN

Waiting

July 17, 1925

Waiting

How is William Jennings Bryan portrayed in this somber cartoon? How does this cartoon differ in tone from the others?

Baltimore Sun, 17 July 1925, 10.

ALLEY

What Manner of Material So Enduring?

May 3, 1925

WHAT MANNER OF MATERIAL SO ENDURING?

Echoing in form the cartoonist's portrayal of "The Light of Economic Liberty" (see page 177), this cartoon depicts the author's faith in the Bible's eternal strength against "Hate," "Atheism," "Liberalism," and other threats. Do you think it is a commentary on modern culture generally? Where would evolution have fit in this picture?

Memphis Commercial Appeal, 3 May 1925, 1. Copyright, The Commercial Appeal, Memphis, TN. Used with permission.

2

Race and the Scopes Trial

Although participants in the Scopes trial seldom invoked race explicitly, the debate over evolution offered a window into racial thought in 1920s America. On the one side, scientific racists used Darwinism to justify their argument that some races were superior and some inferior and to support their fight for eugenics programs that would reward the "wellborn" and restrict reproduction among the "feebleminded" and "unfit" of various races. On the other side, African American activists such as W. E. B. Du Bois and their allies often saw science as an ally in their struggle to prove the worthiness of the "African race" and condemned the white South's attempt to outlaw evolutionary teaching as part and parcel of its attempt to keep African American citizens in ignorance. In between these two poles dwelled a number of deeply religious African Americans, who sought to sort out for themselves their multiple allegiances to conservative Christianity and racial equality.

CHICAGO DEFENDER

If Monkeys Could Speak

May 23, 1925

The Chicago Defender *was one of the major African American newspapers in the country, noteworthy for, among other things, its uncompromising condemnation of white supremacy in the South. How does this editorial differ from, say, H. L. Mencken's commentary beginning on page 168?*

"If Monkeys Could Speak," *Chicago Defender,* 23 May 1925, sec. 2, p. 12.

In Tennessee a schoolteacher is being tried for teaching evolution to his pupils. If convicted, a prison term awaits him; he will be branded as an ordinary felon and thrown into a cell with robbers, gunmen, thugs, rapists and murderers. He will wear a striped suit, learn the lock-step and spend a few years reducing rocks to a more serviceable size.

That is the South's way. Anything which conflicts with the South's idea of her own importance, anything which tends to break down her doctrine of white superiority, she fights. If truths are introduced and these truths do not conform to what southern grandfathers believed, then it must be suppressed.

The Tennessee legislators who passed the law making it a crime to teach Darwinism in that state probably have never read the text themselves and all they know about the subject is that the entire human race is supposed to have started from a common origin. Therein lies their difficulty. Admit that premise and they will have to admit that there is no fundamental difference between themselves and the race they pretend to despise. Such admission would, of course, play havoc with the existing standards of living in the South.

And so, encouraged by America's champion long distance presidential "white hope," William Jennings Bryan, Tennessee blazes the trail making ignorance compulsory. Florida, Mr. Bryan's adopted home, follows by a close margin.

There never was a surer "back to the monkey" sign than in Tennessee's present trend. It is too bad the monkeys cannot speak and show the South just how ridiculous she is becoming in her efforts to convince the world that she is "superior."

W. E. B. DU BOIS

Dayton Is *America*

September 1925

W. E. B. Du Bois (1868–1963) was one of the United States' greatest intellectuals. From his position as editor of the Crisis, *the propaganda organ for the National Association for the Advancement of Colored People (NAACP), Du Bois for decades kept up a running commentary on the multitudinous ways in which white America attempted to undermine African Americans. How does Du Bois seem to differ from the mostly white journalists covering the trial? In what ways does he echo their concerns? How does he differ from the editorialist in the* Chicago Defender*?*

One hundred per cent Americans are now endeavoring to persuade hilarious and sarcastic Europe that Dayton, Tennessee, is a huge joke and very, very exceptional. And in proof of all this the learned American press is emitting huge guffaws and peals of Brobdingnagian[1] laughter combined with streaming tears. But few are deceived, even of those who joke and slap each other on the back. The truth is and we know it: Dayton, Tennessee, is America: a great, ignorant, simple-minded land, curiously compounded of brutality, bigotry, religious faith and demagoguery, and capable not simply of mistakes but of persecution, lynching, murder and idiotic blundering, as well as charity, missions, love and hope.

This is America and America is what it is because we believe in Ignorance. The whole modern Nordic civilization of which America is a great and leading branch has sold its soul to Ignorance. Its leading priests profess a religious faith which they do not believe and which they know, and every man of intelligence knows, they do not and cannot believe; and then when a knot of back-woodsmen led by some cheap demagogues try to drive out error in a logical way they learn to their own intense surprise that what the world was thinking and doing

[1]The Brobdingnagians were giants in Jonathan Swift's *Gulliver's Travels*. As an adjective, the word means "colossally large."

W. E. B. Du Bois, "Scopes," *Crisis,* Sept. 1925, 218.

had in some unaccountable way been kept from them. Either, then, they have been deceived or are being attacked. They resent it and with the proper demagogue to lead they are ready to drive out heretics and defend the Truth as they have received it with gun and fagots.

Who is to blame? They that know; they that teach; they that have; they that sit silent and enjoy; great universities that close their doors to the mob; great scientists who prostitute truth to prejudice; great preachers who quibble with faith and facts; great rulers of wealth who fear understanding; and voluptuaries who have no wish to be disturbed by real democracy.

The folk who leave white Tennessee in blank and ridiculous ignorance of what science has taught the world since 1859 are the same ones who would leave black Tennessee and black America with just as little education as is consistent with fairly efficient labor and reasonable contentment; who rave over the 18th Amendment and are dumb over the 15th;[2] who permit lynching and make bastardy legal in order to render their race "pure." It is such folk who, when in sudden darkness they descry the awful faces of the Fanatic, the Fury and the Fool, try to hide the vision with gales of laughter.

But Dayton, Tennessee, is no laughing matter. It is menace and warning. It is a challenge to Religion, Science and Democracy.

[2]The Eighteenth Amendment, passed in 1919, prohibited the manufacture or sale of alcoholic beverages and found its main support among native-born, rural, white, Protestant reformers such as William Jennings Bryan. The Fifteenth Amendment, one of the "civil rights amendments" adopted in 1870, was supposed to guarantee African American males the right to vote, but by 1925 almost every southern state, including Bryan's adopted state of Florida, had effectively stripped African Americans of their ability to vote.

REVEREND JOHN W. NORRIS

African Methodist Episcopal Church Minister Stands with Bryan

October 1925

The Reverend John W. Norris, a Baltimore minister of the African Methodist Episcopal Church, embodied the more theologically conservative side of this all-black denomination. Note the way in which he ties his condemnation of slavery to a condemnation of evolution.

The Bible and Evolution do not agree. They do not agree because the Bible is a fact and Evolution is not a fact. Evolution is a theory. . . . Theory is an open field of speculation. The ablest minds have been out in that endless field of speculation. They have in thousands of years found a few things they call facts. The Bible was not found out there in those speculative fields, but direct from the Word of God. Hence the Bible comes to us along a path of inspiration. This holy book brings such truths as happened when there was not a man on earth. . . .

Mr. Darwin was a man of great mind, but God was of **greater Mind**. God was unchangeable and all He made was unchangeable. . . . Adam below the angels and above the lower order of animal life. Everything above man he was to fear, and everything below man was to fear him. Everything above man was to be his master, and everything below the man the man was to master, and also master himself. No man has ever been mastered by man. Man cannot be mastered, never was mastered and never will be mastered. No slave was ever mastered. They had a master, but they were never mastered. If so, please tell me when.

Now, from what did this man evolve? Not a monkey, for the monkey was among the things and creatures mastered by the man. Man was a special creature to rule all other creatures. Slavery was wrong because man was never made to be a slave. No nation on earth ever ruled its slaves only by force. This shows that the man was made a

John W. Norris, "Evolution Not a Fact—The Bible a Fact," *A.M.E. Church Review,* Oct. 1925, 323–24.

special brain-case creature. He was given a brain case so he would be able to rule himself and all other created creatures. . . . There is no other animal on this globe or any other globe so equipped. In no sense are there any connecting links below the man that would link him on to other animals.

P. W. CHAMBERLAIN

Racial Hierarchy Proves Evolution

July 13, 1925

This letter to the editor of the Baltimore Sun*—sent, presumably, by a white writer—conveys some of the common belief that the races of the world were arranged in a hierarchy, with Anglo-Saxons at the top and persons of African or Pacific Island descent near the bottom, close to the dividing line between humans and other primates.*

The opponents of the theory of evolution . . . are the ones that make the claim man descends from the monkey—not the men of science—and when they visualize evolution, it is by making a comparison between an educated, well-groomed and dignified gentleman and one of those Ateles monkeys that the Italian organ grinders carry in the streets, and their minds become horrified at the revolting idea of any blood relationship between the two; the probability is that those persons have never seen the lowest type of humanity, such as the vermin eaters, Fuegians, or the lower still wife eaters, Australian savages.

There is actually more difference between the white gentleman and those savages than between those savages and the higher apes.

Baltimore Evening Sun, 13 July 1925, sec. 2, p. 13.

GEORGE W. HUNTER

Race and Eugenics in A Civic Biology

1914

George W. Hunter, a prominent biology teacher in New York City, was also the author of one of the most widely used biology textbooks in the early part of the twentieth century. A Civic Biology *was the textbook that John T. Scopes used to lecture the students in Dayton on evolution. In these passages, Hunter uses "race" to signify both the human race as a whole and the pseudoscientific groupings of people into "races"—a notion that had been growing in popularity since the late nineteenth century. The "eugenics" movement that Hunter alludes to was a crusade led by "old stock" Americans to encourage reproduction among the "better people"—generally people like themselves—and to halt reproduction by "inferior" people, defined variously in medical, legal, moral, and racial terms. What were the racial lessons, conscious or unconscious, conveyed by* A Civic Biology*? What were the implications of these racial concepts? Besides evolution, do you see elements in* A Civic Biology *that William Jennings Bryan might have found objectionable, especially in the discussion of eugenics? How do you think W. E. B. Du Bois might have responded to the Hunter text?*

Racial Hierarchy

Evolution of Man. -Undoubtedly there once lived upon the earth races of men who were much lower in their mental organization than the present inhabitants. If we follow the early history of man upon the earth, we find that at first he must have been little better than one of the lower animals. He was a nomad, wandering from place to place, feeding upon whatever living things he could kill with his hands. Gradually he must have learned to use weapons, and thus kill his prey, first using rough stone implements for this purpose. As man became more civilized, implements of bronze and of iron were used. About this time the subjugation and domestication of animals began to take place. Man then began to cultivate the fields, and to have a fixed place

George W. Hunter, *A Civic Biology* (New York: American Book Co., 1914), 195–96, 261–63.

of abode other than a cave. The beginnings of civilization were long ago, but even to-day the earth is not entirely civilized.

The Races of Man. -At the present time there exist upon the earth five races or varieties of man, each very different from the other in instincts, social customs, and, to an extent, in structure. These are the Ethiopian or negro type, originating in Africa; the Malay or brown race, from the islands of the Pacific; the American Indian; the Mongolian or yellow race, including the natives of China, Japan, and the Eskimos; and finally, the highest type of all, the Caucasians, represented by the civilized white inhabitants of Europe and America. . . .

Eugenics

Improvement of Man. -If the stock of domesticated animals can be improved, it is not unfair to ask if the health and vigor of the future generations of men and women on the earth might not be improved by applying to them the laws of selection. This improvement of the future race has a number of factors in which we as individuals may play a part. These are personal hygiene, selection of healthy mates, and the betterment of the environment.

Personal Hygiene. -In the first place, good health is the one greatest asset in life. We may be born with a poor bodily machine, but if we learn to recognize its defects and care for it properly, we may make it do its required work effectively. If certain muscles are poorly developed, then by proper exercise we may make them stronger. If our eyes have some defect, we can have it remedied by wearing glasses. If certain drugs or alcohol lower the efficiency of the machine, we can avoid their use. With proper *care* a poorly developed body may be improved and do effective work.

Eugenics. -When people marry there are certain things that the individual as well as the race should demand. The most important of these is freedom from germ diseases which might be handed down to the offspring. Tuberculosis, that dread white plague which is still responsible for almost one seventh of all deaths, epilepsy, and feeble-mindedness are handicaps which it is not only unfair but criminal to hand down to posterity. The science of being well born is called *eugenics*.

The Jukes. -Studies have been made on a number of different families in this country, in which mental and moral defects were present in one or both of the original parents. The "Jukes" family is a notorious example. The first mother is known as "Margaret, the mother of criminals." In seventy-five years the progeny of the original generation has cost the state of New York over a million and a quarter of dollars, besides giving over to the care of prisons and asylums considerably over a hundred feeble-minded, alcoholic, immoral, or criminal persons. Another case recently studied is the "Kallikak" family. This family has been traced to the union of Martin Kallikak, a young soldier of the War of the Revolution, with a feeble-minded girl. She had a feeble-minded son from whom there have been to the present time 480 descendants. Of these 33 were sexually immoral, 24 confirmed drunkards, 3 epileptics, and 143 *feeble-minded.* The man who started this terrible line of immorality and feeble-mindedness later married a normal Quaker girl. From this couple a line of 496 descendants have come, with *no* cases of feeble-mindedness. The evidence and the moral speak for themselves!

Parasitism and Its Cost to Society. -Hundreds of families such as those described above exist to-day, spreading disease, immorality, and crime to all parts of this country. The cost to society of such families is very severe. Just as certain animals or plants become parasitic on other plants or animals, these families have become parasitic on society. They not only do harm to others by corrupting, stealing, or spreading disease, but they are actually protected and cared for by the state out of public money. Largely for them the poorhouse and the asylum exist. They take from society, but they give nothing in return. They are true parasites.

The Remedy. -If such people were lower animals, we would probably kill them off to prevent them from spreading. Humanity will not allow this, but we do have the remedy of separating the sexes in asylums or other places and in various ways preventing intermarriage and the possibilities of perpetuating such a low and degenerate race. Remedies of this sort have been tried successfully in Europe and are now meeting with success in this country.

3

Educational Freedom and the Scopes Trial

At the heart of the struggle over evolutionary teaching was the question of who should determine what would be taught in the schools. William Jennings Bryan and his allies argued that local majorities—especially overwhelming majorities such as those that supported antievolutionism in Tennessee—should have the right to determine what was taught in the schools, while the American Civil Liberties Union (ACLU) and its allies appealed to the dawning concept of academic freedom to justify the continued teaching of evolution in Tennessee. What were their competing visions of education in American society? Do you agree that an inevitable tension exists between academic freedom and majority rule?

WILLIAM JENNINGS BRYAN

Who Shall Control Our Schools?

June 1925

William Jennings Bryan was, of course, the most important figure in the antievolution crusade, but he also had earned a reputation as the political leader of the "plain people" in the United States—the farmers and the poor, who made up a majority of the Populist party in the 1890s and who bulked large in the Democratic party thereafter. Note the ways in which Bryan's argument over the schools fits with his broader commitment to democratic rule.

William Jennings Bryan, "Who Shall Control?" (June 1925) in William Jennings Bryan and Mary Baird Bryan, *The Memoirs of William Jennings Bryan* (Philadelphia: United Publishers of America, 1925), 526–28.

The first question to be decided is: Who shall control our public schools? We have something like twenty-six millions of children in the public schools and spend over one billion and seven hundred thousand dollars a year upon these schools. As the training of children is the chief work of each generation, the parents are interested in the things to be taught the children.

Four sources of control have been suggested. The first is the people, speaking through their legislatures. That would seem to be the natural source of control. The people are sovereigns and governments derive their just powers from the consent of the governed. . . . Legislatures regulate marriage and divorce, property rights, descent of property, care of children, and all other matters between citizens. Why are our legislatures not competent to decide what kind of schools are needed, the requirements of teachers, and the kind of instruction that shall be given?

If not the legislatures, then who shall control? Boards of Education? It is the legislature that authorizes the election of boards and defines their duties, and boards are elected by the people or appointed by officials elected by the people. All authority goes back at last to the people; they are the final source of authority.

Some have suggested that the scientists should decide what shall be taught. How many scientists are there? . . . The American Society for the Advancement of Science has about eleven thousand members, but that includes Canadians as well as citizens of the United States. If the number is put at eleven thousand, it makes about one scientist for every ten thousand people—a pretty little oligarchy to put in control of the education of all the children, especially when Professor [James H.] Leuba declares that over half of the scientists agree with him in the belief that there is no personal God and no personal immortality.

The fourth source suggested is the teacher. Some say, let the teacher be supreme and teach anything that seems best to him. The proposition needs only be stated to be rejected as absurd. The teacher is an employee and receives a salary; employees take directions from their employers, and the teacher is no exception to the rule. . . . No teacher would be permitted to go from the South and teach in a northern school that the northern statesmen and soldiers of the Civil War were traitors; neither would a northern teacher be permitted to go from the North and teach in a southern school that the southern soldiers and statesmen were traitors. . . . [A] teacher must respect the wishes of his employers on all subjects upon which the employers have a deep-seated conviction. The same logic would suggest that a teacher receiving pay in dollars on which is stamped, "In God We Trust," should not be permitted to teach the children that there is no God. Neither should he be allowed to accept employment in a Christian community and teach that the Bible is untrue.

That is the Tennessee case. Evolution disputes the Bible record of man's creation, and the logic of the evolution eliminates as false the miracles of the Bible, including the virgin birth and the bodily resurrection of Christ. Christians are compelled to build their own colleges in which to teach Christianity; why not require agnostics and atheists to build their own colleges if they want to teach agnosticism or atheism?

The Tennessee case is represented by some as an attempt to stifle freedom of conscience and freedom of speech, but the charge is seen to be absurd when the case is analyzed. Professor Scopes, the defendant in the Tennessee case, has a right to think as he pleases—the law does not attempt to regulate his thinking. Professor Scopes can also say anything he pleases—the law does not interfere with his freedom of speech. As an individual, Professor Scopes is perfectly free to think and speak as he likes and the Christians of Tennessee will protect him in the enjoyment of these inalienable rights. But that is not the Tennessee case and has nothing to do with it.

Professor Scopes was not arrested for doing anything as an individual. He was arrested for violating a law as a *representative* of the *state* and as an employee in a school. As a representative, he has no right to misrepresent; as an employee, he is compelled to act under the direction of his employers and has no right to defy instructions and still claim his salary. The right of free speech cannot be stretched as far as Professor Scopes is trying to stretch it. A man cannot demand a salary for saying what his employers do not want said, and he cannot require his employers to furnish him with an audience to talk to, especially an audience of children or young people, when he wants to say what the parents do not want said. The duty of a parent to protect his children is more sacred than the right of teachers to teach what parents do not want taught, especially when the speaker demands pay for his teaching and insists on being furnished with an audience to talk to. Professor Scopes can think whatever he wants about evolution, but he has no right to force his opinion upon students against the wishes of the tax payers and parents.

And, I may add, Professor Scopes is doing more harm to teachers than to anyone else. If he establishes the doctrine that a teacher can say anything he likes to the students, regardless of the wishes of his employers, who are the parents and tax payers, it will become necessary to enquire what teachers think before they are employed. . . . Professor Scopes has raised a question of the very first magnitude and the ones most likely to suffer by the raising of the issue are those who think they can ignore the right of the people to have what they want in government, including the kind of education they want.

AMERICAN CIVIL LIBERTIES UNION

Postwar Threats to Academic Freedom

1931

The precursor of the ACLU, the National Civil Liberties Union, had been founded during the Great War and became dedicated to protecting the rights of labor, including teachers, and the right to free speech, particularly for radicals who were meeting stern popular repression during the war. Were the ACLU and the defense team serious about full academic freedom, or was this merely a strategy for keeping evolution in the classroom?

The great essential to education is freedom—freedom in presenting and studying all the facts, and freedom of teachers to believe as they see fit and to express their beliefs like other citizens. It holds that, when for any reason this freedom is curtailed,—real education itself is crippled.

The professed objects of our educational system have always been freedom from propaganda for private interests, liberty for teachers outside their classrooms, and the training of children without reference to any economic dogma. . . . The restrictions on teaching in our public schools relate to our basic institutions and beliefs—religion, patriotism and the economic order.

During the hysteria of war, the pattern for interference with education was set, and majority dogmas became firmly entrenched. The

American Civil Liberties Union Committee on Academic Freedom, *The Gag on Teaching* (New York: ACLU, 1931), 4–5.

dogmas of conventional patriotism developed first as part of the war propaganda, evidenced in the laws for the teaching of the Constitution, flag-saluting, special oaths of loyalty from teachers, and the revision of history textbooks. Then came the efforts of the Ku Klux Klan and the Fundamentalists in the name of Protestantism to outlaw evolution, compel the reading of the Bible (Protestant version) and, in one state, to ban all private (meaning Catholic) schools. . . .

The tendencies to restrict freedom of teaching can be fought only by constant agitation, repeal of the present restrictive laws, opposition to specific measures and cases of discrimination and by the growth of teachers' unions to protect teachers' liberties.

AMERICAN FEDERATION OF TEACHERS

Concern over Intolerance

July 18, 1925

The American Federation of Teachers was a more militant organization of educators in comparison to the much larger National Education Association, which never expressed itself clearly on the matter of the Butler law in Tennessee.

The following resolution was adopted by the American Federation of Teachers, assembled in convention from June 29 to July 2:

The American Federation of Teachers is deeply concerned about the effect of the Tennessee anti-evolution law on the development of enlightenment in teaching in this country.

In certain states of the union teaching as a constructive social function has been menaced, and may be menaced again, by misguided legislative authority that fears to trust the intelligence, the public spirit and the devotion to duty of the profession whose obligation it is, and whose desire it is, to serve the people by training the children for intelligent citizenship. The reactionary Lusk school laws in the state of

"Resolution Adopted by the American Federation of Teachers," *School and Society,* 18 July 1925, 74–75.

New York, abolished in 1923 after a trial of two years, the Green Bill of California proposed in 1921 and also dealing with the matter of controlling the opinions of teachers, as well as the numerous bills in several states that have been designed to censor the writing and the teaching of history in the schools—all reflect the same unfortunate suspicion and mistrust of educational intelligence which the Tennessee anti-evolution law betrays.[1] As public school teachers, and other teachers, representing many states, east, west, north and south, we, the delegates to the Ninth Annual Convention of the American Federation of Teachers, in convention assembled, deplore the continuance in our national life of the spirit of unenlightened legislative dictatorship.

As public-spirited members of our profession, we raise no objection to legislative or other inquiry into the prevailing customs, the aims and the qualifications of teachers anywhere. On the contrary, we welcome from all quarters investigations of teachers and of school systems. But we insist that attention be given to the conditions that relate for good or ill to the improvement, nay, to the very life, of teaching as a necessary activity of organized society. Ineffective as teaching may have been in much of our educational work, progress is to be expected only where there is freedom not only to think, but also to follow with the understanding and development of thought in every field of human endeavor. . . .

As teachers we especially fear the effect of the present wave of intolerance in education on the task of providing the schools with enlightened teachers. Without freedom in the intellectual life, and without the inspiration of uncensored discovery and discussion, there could ultimately be no scholarship, no schools at all and no education. The minds that now seek an outlet in education would be driven off into other fields, if, indeed they could find a reason for existence anywhere.

[1]New York's Lusk laws grew out of that state's Joint Committee to Investigate Seditious Activities. The laws, which were in force from 1921 to 1923, required teachers to take loyalty oaths.

AMERICAN ASSOCIATION OF UNIVERSITY PROFESSORS

University Faculty Define Academic Freedom

1915

"Academic freedom" initially was a concept developed by and confined to college and university faculty members. This 1915 statement from the American Association of University Professors was the first major outline of the justification for academic freedom. Although academic freedom fitted well with college professors' desire to be considered "professionals," its relevance to high schools was and is a matter of greater debate. How does the following reasoning apply to the Scopes trial? How would academic freedom apply today if a high school biology instructor wanted to teach antievolution theory instead of evolution?

The importance of academic freedom is most clearly perceived in the light of the purposes for which the universities exist. These are three in number:

A. To promote inquiry and advance the sum of human knowledge.
B. To provide general instruction to the students.
C. To develop experts for various branches of the public service.

Let us consider each of these. In the earlier stages of a nation's intellectual development, the chief concern of educational institutions is to train the growing generation and to diffuse the already accepted knowledge. It is only slowly that there comes to be provided in the highest institutions of learning the opportunity for the gradual wresting from nature of her intimate secrets. The modern university is becoming more and more the home of scientific research. . . . The first condition of progress is complete and unlimited freedom to pursue inquiry and publish its results. Such freedom is the breath in the nostrils of all scientific activity.

American Association of University Professors, *Report of the Committee on Academic Freedom and Tenure* (n.p., 1915).

The second function—which for a long time was the only function—of the American college or university is to provide instruction for students. It is scarcely open to question that freedom of utterance is as important to the teacher as it is to the investigator. No man can be a successful teacher unless he enjoys the respect of his students, and their confidence in his intellectual integrity. It is clear, however, that this confidence will be impaired if there is suspicion on the part of the student that the teacher is not expressing himself fully or frankly, or that college and university teachers in general are a repressed and intimidated class who dare not speak with that candor and courage which youth always demands in those whom it is to esteem. . . .

Since there are no rights without corresponding duties, the consideration heretofore set down with respect to the freedom of the academic teacher entail certain correlative obligations. The claim to freedom of teaching is made in the interest of the integrity and of the progress of scientific inquiry; it is, therefore, only those who carry on their work in the temper of the scientific inquirer who may justly assert this claim. The liberty of the scholar within the university to set forth his conclusions, be they what they may, is conditioned by their being conclusions gained by a scholar's method and held in a scholar's spirit; that is to say, they must be the fruits of competent and patient and sincere inquiry, and they should be set forth with dignity, courtesy, and temperateness of language. The university teacher . . . should above all, remember that his business is not to provide his students with ready-made conclusions, but to train them to think for themselves, and to provide them access to those materials which they need if they are to think intelligently. . . .

It is, it will be seen, in no sense the contention of this committee that academic freedom implies that individual teachers should be exempt from all restraints as to the matter or manner of their utterances, either within or without the university. Such restraints as are necessary should in the main, your committee holds, be self-imposed, or enforced by the public opinion of the profession. But there may, undoubtedly, arise occasional cases in which the aberrations of individuals may require to be checked by definite disciplinary action. What this report chiefly maintains is that such action can not with safety be taken by bodies not composed of members of the academic profession. Lay governing boards are competent to judge concerning charges of habitual neglect of assigned duties, on the part of individual teachers, and concerning charges of grave moral delinquency. But in matters of opinion, and of the utterance of opinion, such boards cannot intervene without destroying, to the extent of their intervention, the essential nature of a university—without converting it from a place dedicated to openness of mind, in which the conclusions expressed are the tested conclusions of trained scholars, into a place barred against the access of new light, and precommitted to the opinions or prejudices of men who have not been set apart or expressly trained for the scholar's duties.

R. S. WOODWORTH

Tennessee Can Dictate Curriculum, Not Answers

August 29, 1925

The author of this letter to School and Society, *a faculty member at Columbia University, attempts to reconcile majoritarianism with academic freedom by emphasizing the separate responsibilities of legislators and educators. Does this separation seem useful? Do you accept the author's distinction between the curriculum and its conclusions? Do you think people who argue this way truly support free inquiry, or just free inquiry that reaches the conclusions they already believe?*

"What shall be taught" means first the curriculum, the subjects that shall be taught, but in the end, as applied in the Tennessee statute, it means the facts and conclusions that shall be taught. To prescribe the curriculum is to determine what questions shall be taken up in the schools, while the Tennessee statute presumes to fix the answers that shall be given. Now it is one thing to order that certain questions shall or shall not be taken up in the schools, and quite a different thing to order that certain answers shall, or shall not, be given to those questions. Certainly a much stronger case could be made for the right of the legislature, or of its creatures, to prescribe the topics and

---

R. S. Woodworth, "The Scopes Case and the 'Constitutional Rights' of the Teacher," *School and Society,* 29 Aug. 1925, 274–75.

questions which should be considered, than for its right to put into the mouth of its teachers the answers which they must give. . . .

A person who is duly and legally employed by a public agency to teach a certain branch of knowledge has a duty, and a correlative right, to teach that branch of knowledge. As the questions proper to the subject arise, it is his duty, and his right, to answer according to the state of knowledge in that subject.

4

The Scopes Trial and the "New Woman"

Antievolutionists opposed Darwinism in part because they suspected that it was helping to remove the moral supports of society and pushing America down into an amoral materialism. For many Americans, the most palpable sign of this moral decline was the new behavior of youths, especially the heavy-petting, hard-drinking, fast-driving young women who came to be called flappers. At the same time, more traditional Americans looked to women, especially mothers, as society's last bulwark against moral decline, and women who took seriously this role bulked large in the antievolution forces.

FATHER HUGH L. McMENAMIN

A Catholic Priest Argues Women Are Surrendering Their Moral Duty

October 1927

Hugh L. McMenamin was rector of the Catholic Cathedral in Denver, and although his Catholicism set him apart significantly from the Protestant leadership of the antievolution crusade, the arguments McMenamin made about women's role in the erosion of American morality were fairly typical of adult commentators in the 1920s. On which side of the Scopes trial would you have expected to find McMenamin? Why?

Hugh L. McMenamin, "Evils of Woman's Revolt against the Old Standards," *Current History,* Oct. 1927, 30–32.

Look about you. The theatre, the magazine, the current fiction, the ball room, the night clubs and the joy-rides—all give evidence of an ever-increasing disregard for even the rudiments of decency in dress, deportment, conventions and conduct. Little by little the bars have been lowered, leaving out the few influences that held society in restraint. One need be neither prude nor puritan to feel that something is passing in the hearts and in the minds of the women of today that is leaving them cold and unwomanly. I know it is said that if a man may indulge freely in alcohol so may she; if he may witness prize-fights so may she; if he may harangue a crowd from a corner soap box so may she; if he may go about half naked so may she. But the moment she does so she has stepped down from the pedestal before which man was accustomed to worship and he is left without an ideal. . . .

We may try to deceive ourselves and close our eyes to the prevailing flapper conduct. We may call boldness greater self-reliance, brazenness greater self-assertion, license greater freedom and try to pardon immodesty in dress by calling it style and fashion, but the fact remains that deep down in our hearts we feel a sense of shame and pity.

When women can gaze upon and indulge in the voluptuous dance of the hour; when young girls can sit beside their youthful escorts and listen to the suggestive drama, their idle hours absorbed in sex-saturated fiction; when women, both married and single, find their recreation in drinking and petting parties; when mothers clothe their daughters in a manner that exposes their physical charms to the voluptuous gaze of every passing libertine; when they can enter the contract of marriage with the avowed purpose of having no children, then surely the "New Woman" is different, and it is a libel on the generation that has gone to hold the contrary. . . .

Modern economic conditions, with the mania for speedy profits, have been a powerful factor in producing the "New Woman," inasmuch as they have dragged her into the commercial world and made her economically independent. It is quite impossible for a woman to engage successfully in business and politics and at the same time create a happy home. A woman cannot be a mother and a typist at the same time, and unfortunately she elects to be merely a wife, and out of that condition have arisen those temples of race suicide—our modern apartment houses—and the consequent grinding of the divorce mill.[1]

[1]"Race suicide" was a phrase that Theodore Roosevelt had coined at the turn of the century to convey his alarm that the "better sorts" of Americans were not having enough children, while the "worse sorts" seemed to be reproducing at an extraordinary rate and thereby threatened to dominate society in the future.

REGINA MALONE

A Flapper Responds to Attacks on Youths

July 1926

Regina Malone was in her early twenties when she wrote this response to the generalized attacks on youthful morality. Consider the ways in which each side of the Scopes trial might have viewed her justification of youthful behavior and attitudes. How might these social changes be related to the antievolution controversy?

The syllabus of crimes charged against this "fabulous monster," the Younger Generation, might read as follows: It has exhibited a general independence of thought and action not compatible, according to its accusers, with those ideals and traditions which are the foundation of true family life. It has shown a flagrant contempt for parents and parental guidance. It has displayed, even flaunted, its disregard of morals—indicated in its lack of manners, its dancing, its drinking, its "petting," and its intimate relationships with men. It has chosen entirely to disregard religion; or, still worse, it has dared to attack the firmly established religious beliefs of its ancestors.

Let us consider these charges in detail.

Is independence a crime? Logically, an age of freedom always follows a period of artificiality and repression, just as an era of romance succeeds an epoch of pedantry and didacticism. Sure our history shows that attempts at religious, political, economic, or other kinds of reform would have been abortive if the dissenting voice of popular opinion had been heeded. Is not this independence of our Youth of today little more than a swing of pendulum from Victorianism, with its laughable prudery and absurd conventions, to an ultra-sophisticated and brutally frank age of Modernism? It is only by juxtaposition and contrast that either age appears exaggerated.

Turning now to our revolt against parental guidance, has not the very nature of that authority made the revolt inevitable? . . . We have the paradox of a Youth, taught beauty and idealism, sent to war; a Youth, taught temperance, inflicted with Prohibition (a paradox within

---

Regina Malone, "The Fabulous Monster," *Forum,* July 1926, 26–30.

a paradox); a Youth, reared in an atmosphere of rigid morality, forced to see the indifferent morals of its elders flung before its eyes. . . . The sin of our parents' age was the mortal sin of evasion, of refusing to face life as it is. . . .

Which brings us to a more serious phase of the Youth question: our attitude toward sex. We no longer spell the word with a capital letter; and it is as frankly discussed as automobiles or the advantage of cold storage over moth balls. Why should our elders consider our interest in this subject a sign of unnaturalness or perversion? Should not it constitute the chief concern of those in whose hands the future generation lies? Is not this desire and ability to procreate the primary function of every human being? . . .

Finally we come to religion. The younger members of society have thrown religion overboard,—that is, religion as conceived by their elders. No longer do we believe in a Deity moulded in the form of a police inspector. But our own faith in an Infinite Being possessed of infinite comprehension is too great to leave us stranded high and dry on the rocks of unbelief. As we sought, and are finding freedom in other channels, so will we find it in religious ones.

MRS. E. P. BLAIR

A Tennessee Woman Calls for Battle against Evolutionist Outsiders

June 29, 1925

Mrs. E. P. Blair of Nashville became a fixture in the local newspapers during the dispute over the Butler Act. Consider Mrs. Blair's image of a mother's role and the way it might fit with Hugh McMenamin's in the first selection in this chapter. Is Mrs. Blair one of the New Women of the 1920s? Why or why not? Consider as well her view of the out-of-state counsel for the Scopes defense.

Mrs. E. P. Blair, "The Battle Hymn of Tennessee," *Nashville Tennessean,* 29 June 1925, 2.

Between Truth and Error, Right and Wrong,
The fight is on.
For country, God, and mother's song
It must be won!
Go sound the alarm, go gather your forces,
Oh Tennessee!
Land of the pioneer, home of the volunteer,
The daring, the free.

Now Error, the monster, calls forth her cohorts
From sea to sea.
They come from earth's four corners down
To Tennessee.
They challenge your power to rule your own
Your rights deny.
They scoff at you, ridicule you,
Your laws defy.

Their forces are clad in garments great,
Of science and law.
With the camouflage cloak of knowledge
To hide their claw.
So look at the havoc and heartache of nations
Where they have passed through.
Their blasting breath has meant instant death
To the noble and true.

God made this His battleground, for you've
Been wise and true.
Earth's unborn, its children, mothers and nations
Are calling to you.
So Tennessee, light your candle of wisdom!
Your altar of prayer!
And the God of Truth fire and inspire you
To do and to dare!

MRS. JESSE SPARKS

A Tennessee Mother Writes to Support the Butler Act

July 3, 1925

Mrs. Jesse Sparks lived in the small town of Pope, Tennessee. Her letter to the Nashville Tennessean *exemplified the support the common people of Tennessee gave to the antievolution crusade. Do you think it was significant that Mrs. Sparks was a woman? How might this argument have been different if the writer had been male?*

Editor of the *Tennessean:*

At the time the bill prohibiting the teaching of evolution in our public schools was passed by our legislature I could not see why the mothers in greater number were not conveying their appreciation to the members for this act of safeguarding their children from one of the destructive forces which combined with other evils if left unchecked will destroy our civilization. I for one felt grateful for their standing for the right against all criticism. And grateful, too, that we have a Christian man for governor who will defend the Word of God against this so-called science.

Then there have been a number of people writing through your paper defending the veracity of the Bible, the reading of which brings a ray of hope for the future in these times when ministers of the gospel are engulfed in material things. . . .

The Bible tells us that the gates of hell shall not prevail against the church. Therefore we know there will always be standard-bearers for the cross of Christ. But in these times of materialism I am constrained to thank God deep down in my heart for Mrs. Blair and every other one whose voice is raised for the uplift of humanity and the coming of God's kingdom.

MRS. JESSE SPARKS
POPE, TENNESSEE.

Mrs. Jesse Sparks, letter to the editor, *Nashville Tennessean,* 3 July 1925, 4.

5

Religious Alternatives in the 1920s

The struggle between fundamentalists and modernists was not the only religious story of the 1920s. In the face of an apparent general decline in religion, a number of religious Americans launched unconventional crusades to bring believers back to worship. As the following two passages illustrate, these missionary efforts often involved a fusion of religion and Jazz Age culture. Consider how these efforts fit with what you know about fundamentalism and the 1920s. Do you think these religious leaders succeeded in placing religion on a stronger footing?

SARAH COMSTOCK

Performing for the Lord: Sister Aimee Semple McPherson

December 1927

"Sister" Aimee Semple McPherson (1890–1944) was one of the extraordinary figures of the 1920s. A consummate Evangelical performer, McPherson launched a phenomenally successful revival in Los Angeles in the early 1920s and soon built her own church, Angelus Temple, as a house of worship for the Foursquare Gospel. She built her successes on spectacular services and sermons and billed herself as "the world's most pulchritudinous evangelist." Although her theology was not rigid, McPherson leaned toward fundamentalism. How does she fit with the

Sarah Comstock, "Aimee Semple McPherson: Prima Donna of Revivalism," *Harper's Magazine,* Dec. 1927, 11–19.

image of the New Woman of the 1920s? How does she seem to fit with the culture generally? Do you see her as a fundamentalist? What is the author's opinion of McPherson?

There is a blare of trumpets, and the murmur of more than five thousand people hushes sharply. A baton flickers—"The Stars and Stripes" flings itself in long red and white streamers of sound. Glances swing abruptly toward a staircase which comes down to the flower-decked platform. A figure descends—plump, tripping, balancing an armload of roses.

"There she is! That's her!"

"That's *her!*"

The plump one trips forward to center stage, lifts the bouquet, her face wreathed in a garland of interwoven roses and smiles. Upon it plays the calcium[1]—violet light, pink light, blue light, golden light. And now the vast gathering rises to its feet, breaks into clapping. . . . This was my first sight of Aimee Semple McPherson. . . . Her Sunday evening service is a complete vaudeville program, entirely new each week, brimful of surprises for the eager who are willing to battle in the throng for entrance. In this show-devouring city no entertainment compares in popularity with that of Angelus Temple. . . .

It is in what she terms "illustrations" that she gives full vent to her showman's genius. These are her master effort, a novel and highly original use that she makes of properties, lights, stage noises, and mechanical devices to point her message. Heaven and Hell, sinner and saint, Satan, the fleshpots[2] of Egypt, angels of Paradise and temptations of a bejazzed world are made visual by actors, costumes, and theatrical tricks of any and every sort that may occur to her ingenious mind. . . .

On this particular evening her analogy pertains to the sea.

"Look at the little pleasure boat!" She turns to the background of tossing waves. "Here it comes, sailing along, having a grand time!"

Forth sails the little boat, which represents the gay and reckless one who ignores the warning to repent. It crosses the background of painted waves somewhat jerkily, but entirely to the satisfaction of the enraptured spectators.

[1]*calcium:* calcium light, or limelight; an early type of stage light in which lime was heated to incandescence, producing brilliant illumination.

[2]*fleshpots:* places of lascivious entertainment.

"Yes, it's having a grand time, all right. But here comes the pirate ship—oh, the old pirate'll get you, little pleasure boat! I'm sorry for you, but it's too late!"

And now the pirate ship, emblem of Satan, hurries forward, overtakes the gay craft. A struggle—then down goes the victim, crashing, capsizing, while a rejoicing mob applauds—not the triumph of Evil, but the triumph of Sister the Showman. . . .

One of the first questions raised by the observant and non-partisan visitor concerns the audience. . . . A glance about shows that they are largely represented by the Middle-West farmer or small-townsman and his family who have come to form so large a proportion of Los Angeles' population. On every hand are old men and women, seamed, withered, shapeless, big jointed from a lifetime of hard labor with corn and pigs. The men wear what would be their Sunday-best in Iowa. The women are often gaudy in the short, tight, adolescent garb that some salesperson has foisted upon them, and their gray hair is bobbed. The couples drag tired old bones to the Temple and listen as if at the gates of Heaven itself. . . .

In the main her sermons . . . are mired hopelessly in a slough of analogy and metaphor (frequently much mixed), in hackneyed phrases, and in the type of sentimentalism styled as "sob sister." "The Scarlet Thread" is "considered to be the most magnificent of all Sister McPherson's superb sermons" according to its own foreword. It is a mass of commonplaces, melodrama, tawdriness, and cheap emotionalism. . . . Aimee McPherson's power lies not here. Rather, it is the remarkable combination of showman and actress in her gifts which attracts and holds the multitude. . . .

Mrs. McPherson's creed is clearly defined. Heaven is an "indescribably glorious habitation" where the righteous will be presented at the Throne "without spot or wrinkle"; and "wherein hosts of attending angels sweep their harps." Hell is "a place of outer darkness, and there into a lake that burns with fire and brimstone shall be cast the unbelieving, the abominable, the murderers, sorcerers, idolaters, and liars." It is needless to say in what light she regards Mr. Darwin. One trembles for him. Garden of Eden, serpent and apple are her origin of species, and her pictures of the Hereafter are authoritative.

BRUCE BARTON

Jesus as Business Executive

1925

In 1925, a New York advertising executive named Bruce Barton published a best-selling book, The Man Nobody Knows, *that treated Jesus as the founder of modern business—a fun-loving, powerful executive who blended in well with the business culture of the 1920s. In this selection, Barton reminisces in the third person about his childhood dissatisfaction with religion and his decision as an adult to describe the "real" life of Jesus. How do you think the fundamentalists felt about Barton's descriptions of Jesus? Where does Barton's approach fit into the controversy between modernists and fundamentalists? Where does it fit with what you know about the culture of the 1920s? How does this passage relate to the question of gender during the Scopes trial?*

Love Jesus! The little boy looked up at the picture which hung on the Sunday-school wall. It showed a pale young man with flabby forearms and a sad expression. . . . Jesus was the "lamb of God." The little boy did not know what that meant, but it sounded like Mary's little lamb. Something for girls—sissified. Jesus was also "meek and lowly," a "man of sorrows and acquainted with grief." . . .

Years went by and the boy grew up and became a business man.

He began to wonder about Jesus. . . . He said, "I will read what the men who knew Jesus personally said about him. I will read about him as though he were a new historical character, about whom I had never heard anything at all."

The man was amazed.

A physical weakling! Where did they get that idea? Jesus pushed a plane and swung an adze; he was a successful carpenter. He slept outdoors and spent his days walking around his favorite lake. His muscles were so strong that when he drove the money-changers out, nobody dared to oppose him!

A kill-joy! He was the most popular dinner guest in Jerusalem! The criticism which proper people made was that he spent too much time

Bruce Barton, *The Man Nobody Knows: A Discovery of the Real Jesus* (New York: Bobbs-Merrill Company, 1925), preface.

with publicans [tax collectors] and sinners (very good fellows, on the whole, the man thought) and enjoyed society too much. They called him a "wine bibber and a gluttonous man."

A failure! He picked up twelve men from the bottom ranks of business and forged them into an organization that conquered the world.

When the man had finished his reading he exclaimed, "This is a man nobody knows.

"Some day," said he, "some one will write a book about Jesus. Every business man will read it and send it to his partners and his salesmen. For it will tell the story of the founder of modern business."

6

An Invasion of "Outsiders"?

Ben McKenzie and the other prosecutors during the Scopes trial often complained that "foreign attorneys" were invading Tennessee to subvert the will of the local majority. Why do you think local sentiment was so strong over this issue? One of the following passages is from a fundamentalist reflecting on the Scopes trial in 1925. The other is from a Native American scholar and activist fighting for Indian independence in the 1990s. Think about the similarities and differences between the two readings. Are the authors reacting to similar "invasions"? How do these passages fit with the readings on academic freedom in chapter 3, part three, particularly William Jennings Bryan's question, "Who shall control our public schools?"

REVEREND JOHN ROACH STRATON

A Fundamentalist Defends Tennessee against Outside Invasion

December 26, 1925

This passage was written by John Roach Straton, one of the prominent fundamentalist ministers who traveled the nation in the 1920s to do battle with modernism, modernity, and evolution. Straton agreed with Bryan that a large majority of Tennesseans supported the Butler law. Do you agree with Straton that the question of majority rule was at the heart of the Scopes trial? How do you feel about his suggestion that

John Roach Straton, "The Most Sinister Movement in the United States," *American Fundamentalist,* 26 Dec. 1925, 8–9, reprinted in Willard B. Gatewood Jr., *Preachers, Pedagogues, and Politicians: The Evolution Controversy in North Carolina* (Chapel Hill: University of North Carolina Press, 1966), 355–57.

Tennessee (and perhaps the South in general) was being invaded? Would you feel the same way if Tennessee were a different country? What does Straton see as dividing Tennessee from the cities of the North?

The real issue at Dayton and everywhere today is: "Whether the religion of the Bible shall be ruled out of the schools and the religion of evolution, with its ruinous results—shall be ruled into the schools by law." The issue is whether the taxpayers—the mothers and fathers of the children—shall be made to support the false and materialistic religion, namely evolution, in the schools, while Christianity is ruled out, and thereby denied their children.

And with this goes the even deeper issue of whether the majority shall really have the right to rule in America, or whether we are to be ruled by an insignificant minority—an "aristocracy" . . . of skeptical schoolmen and agnostics.

That is the exact issue in this country today. And that it is a very real and urgent issue is proved by the recent invasion of the sovereign state of Tennessee by a group of outside agnostics, atheists, Unitarian preachers, skeptical scientists, and political revolutionists. These uninvited men—including Clarence Darrow, the world's greatest unbeliever, and Dudley Malone, the world's greatest religious What-Is-It,—these and the other samples of our proposed "aristocracy" of would-be rulers, swarmed down to Dayton during the Scopes trial and brazenly tried to nullify the laws and overthrow the political and religious faiths of a great, enlightened, prosperous, and peaceful people.

And the only redeeming feature in all that unlovely parade of human vanity, arrogant self-sufficiency, religious unbelief, and anti-American defiance of majority rule was the courtesy, hospitality (even to unwelcome guests), forbearance, patience, and Christlike fortitude displayed by the noble judge, and the Christian prosecuting attorneys and people of Tennessee!

There was an element of profound natural irony in the entire situation. Darrow, Malone, and the other members of the Evolutionist Bund vicariously left their own communities and bravely sallied forth, like Don Quixote, to defeat the windmills and save other communities from themselves.

They left New York and Chicago, where real religion is being most neglected, where law, consequently, is most defied, where vice and crime are most rampant, and where the follies and ruinous immoralities of the rising generation—debauched already by religious modernism and a Godless materialistic science—smell to high heaven, and they went to save from itself a community where women are still honored, where men are still chivalric, where laws are still respected, where home life is still sweet, where the marriage vow is still sacred, and where man is still regarded, not as a descendant of the slime and beasts of the jungle, but as a child of God, with the wisdom and love of a divine Revelation in his hands, to guide him on life's rugged road, to give him the knowledge of a Savior from his sins, and to plant in his heart the hope of heaven to cheer him on his upward way!

And that is the sort of community which Darrow, Malone, and company left Chicago and New York to save!

Think of the illogic of it! and the nerve of it! and the colossal vanity of it!

Little wonder it is recorded in Holy Writ that "He that sitteth in the Heavens shall laugh" at the follies of men! And surely the very battlements of Heaven must have rocked with laughter at the spectacle of Clarence Darrow, Dudley Malone, and their company of cocksure evolutionists going down to save the South from itself!

It is all the other way around! The religious faith and the robust conservatism of the chivalric South and the sturdy West will have to save America from the sins and shams and shames that are now menacing her splendid life!

VINE DELORIA JR.

A Modern Native American Scholar Decries the Invasion of European Science

1995

The historian Vine Deloria Jr. came to fame as the author of Custer Died for Your Sins *(1969), a classic "revisionist" work that contested the dominant white account of American westward expansion in favor of looking at the "invasion" from the Native American perspective.*

Vine Deloria Jr., *Red Earth, White Lies: Native Americans and the Myth of Scientific Fact* (New York: Scribner, 1995), 14–19.

In these passages from Red Earth, White Lies *(1995), Deloria argues that the Euro-American invasion involved more than just land. It brought a new way of seeing the earth and its history, and this European perspective threatens the survival of American Indian culture. Euro-American geologists, Deloria argues later in the book, have seriously misinterpreted the age of the earth, and he comes close to echoing a "young-earth" creationism, because that accords more closely with the oral tradition of numerous native tribes and traditional native ways of viewing the world.*

Do you see a difference between Deloria's attempt to protect Indian ways of seeing against modern science and the fundamentalists' defense of their faith at Dayton? Is one more justified than the other? Why or why not? How would you respond if Deloria called for tribal high schools to teach only Native American creation stories and not Darwinian evolution?

The push for education in the last generation has done more to erode the sense of Indian identity than any integration program the government previously attempted. The irony of the situation is that Indians truly believed that by seeking a better life for their children through education, much could be accomplished. College and graduate education, however, have now created a generation of technicians and professionals who also happen to have Indian blood. . . .

Three areas . . . may prove fatal to Indian efforts to remain faithful to whatever traditions are still being practiced . . . in science, in religion, and in forms of social interaction. . . .

These three areas of conflict and misunderstanding were present at the beginning of colonial discovery days; they have defined the terms of the conflict between the indigenous peoples and the invaders for more than five hundred years. . . . Our view of government, our allegiance to high spiritual powers, and our understanding of our world will continue to guide our thoughts and activities in the future unless we are able to move beyond present notions into a more mature understanding of our planet, its history, and the rest of the universe. Much of Western science must go, all of Western religion should go, and if we are in any way successful in ridding ourselves of these burdens, we will find that we can fundamentally change government so that it will function more sensibly and enable us to solve our problems.

Science and religion are inherited ways of believing certain things about the world. A good many of our problems today are a result of the perpetuation of dreadfully outmoded beliefs derived from the Near Eastern/European past which do not correspond to what our science is discovering today or to the remembered experiences of non-Western peoples across the globe. Even the purest forms of scientific and religious expression are rooted in the unconscious metaphysics of the past, and critical examination of the roots of the basic doctrines in these areas will reveal the inadequacy of our beliefs. . . .

When Europeans arrived on these shores they brought with them a powerful technology. . . . Mechanical devices from the musket to the iron kettle to the railroad made it a certainty that Indians would lose the military battle to maintain their independence. Technology made it certain that no tribe would be able to maintain its beliefs in the spiritual world when it was apparent that whites had breached certain fundamental ways of living in that spiritual world. . . . Whites had already traded spiritual insight for material comfort, and once trade of material things characterized the Indian relationship with whites, Indians would soon lose much of their spiritual heritage also. . . . Behind and beneath technology . . . lurk a large number of misperceptions, badly directed emphases, and unresolved philosophical problems. As Western civilization grew and took dominance over the world, it failed to resolve basic issues. A view of the natural world as primarily physical matter with little spiritual content took hold and became the practical metaphysics for human affairs. . . .

In our society we have been trained to believe that scientists search for, examine, and articulate truths about the natural world and about ourselves. They don't. But they do search for, take captive, and protect the social and economic status of scientists. As many lies are told to protect scientific doctrine as were ever told to protect "the church." . . .

Regardless of what Indians have said regarding their origins, their migrations, their experiences with birds, animals, lands, waters, mountains, and other peoples, the scientists have maintained a stranglehold on the definitions of what respectable and reliable human experiences are. The Indian explanation is always cast aside as a superstition, precluding Indians from having an acceptable status as human beings, and reducing them in the eyes of educated people to a pre-human level of ignorance.

A Chronology of Events Related to the Scopes Trial (1859–1999)

1859 Charles Darwin publishes *Origin of Species.*

1900 Rediscovery of Gregor Mendel's genetic experiments bolsters evolutionary arguments.

1910–1915 Conservative theologians publish *The Fundamentals,* an influential series of pamphlets supporting biblical inerrancy, the veracity of miracles, and other positions that were to become central to the fundamentalist movement; antievolutionism is not yet a central concern.

1914–1918 First World War—United States enters in the spring of 1917; National Civil Liberties Bureau—later the American Civil Liberties Union (ACLU)—is founded in 1917; numerous states pass laws requiring prayer and/or reading of the Bible in the public schools.

1919 "Red Summer" of radical and labor agitation—and violent reactions against it—convulses the nation; more than six thousand people meet for the first convention of the World's Christian Fundamentals Association (WCFA), an interdenominational group soon to become the leading force in antievolutionism; states ratify the Eighteenth Amendment—the "Prohibition amendment"; veterans of the Great War found the American Legion.

1920 States ratify the Nineteenth Amendment, giving women the right to vote.

1921 New York State passes the Lusk laws requiring certificates of loyalty from teachers; similar laws spread across the country.

1922 Kentucky legislature narrowly rejects the first statewide antievolution bill.

1923 With William Jennings Bryan's support, Florida legislature condemns teaching of evolution in public schools, but the resolution has no enforcement power; Oklahoma prohibits mention of evolution in state-adopted textbooks (act repealed in 1926); antievolution bill fails in West Virginia.

1925 *January 20* Tennessee representative John Washington Butler sponsors a bill prohibiting the teaching of evolution in the public schools. State House of Representatives quickly passes the bill, 71 to 5.

March 13 Tennessee Senate passes the Butler bill by a vote of 24 to 6.

March 23 Governor Austin Peay signs the Butler bill into law; ACLU soon places advertisements seeking a test case.

May 5 Constable in Dayton, Tennessee, places John Thomas Scopes under arrest for violating the Butler law; William Jennings Bryan joins the prosecution, prompting Clarence Darrow and Arthur Garfield Hays to volunteer for Scopes's defense.

July 10–21 Scopes trial takes place in Dayton, Tennessee; Scopes is convicted of violating the Butler law and is fined $100.

July 25 Bryan dies in Dayton, Tennessee.

Also in 1925 Texas governor Miriam "Ma" Ferguson bans evolution from the state's official school textbooks; antievolution statutes are defeated in North Carolina, Florida, Georgia, and West Virginia; the *New Yorker* magazine commences publication for the "caviar sophisticate"; Alain Locke's anthology, *The New Negro,* publicizes the Harlem Renaissance; Bruce Barton publishes *The Man Nobody Knows,* about Jesus as business executive.

1926 Mississippi legislature bans teaching of evolution in the public schools; antievolution bills fail in Kentucky and Louisiana.

1927 Antievolution bills are proposed and defeated in Alabama, Arkansas, California, Delaware, Florida, Georgia, Kansas, Kentucky, Maine, Minnesota, Missouri, New Hampshire, North Carolina, North Dakota, Oklahoma, Oregon, South Carolina, Washington, and West Virginia.

1928 Arkansas passes an antievolution statute by popular referendum, 108,991 to 63,406.

1947 In *Everson v. Board of Education,* U.S. Supreme Court first applies its interpretation of the establishment clause to the states. Decisions over the following decades will progressively raise the "wall of separation" between church and state.

1960 Hollywood puts out a film version of *Inherit the Wind,* a 1955 play by Jerome Lawrence and Robert E. Lee that uses the setting of the Scopes trial to condemn the McCarthyite attack on left-wing freedom of speech in the 1950s.

1961 Publication of John C. Whitcomb Jr. and Henry M. Morris's *The Genesis Flood* inaugurates the modern movement for the teaching of creationism rather than evolution.

1967 Tennessee legislature repeals the Butler law.

1968 U.S. Supreme Court's *Epperson* decision strikes down the Arkansas antievolution statute as a violation of the First Amendment's separation of church and state.

1987 U.S. Supreme Court in *Edwards v. Aguillard* holds that creation science is primarily a religion and not a science, and thus a Louisiana state law mandating "equal time" for creationism and evolution violates the constitution.

1990 Seventh Circuit Court of Appeals in *Webster v. New Lenox School District* finds that a public school district may legally prevent a teacher from teaching creation science without violating the teacher's free speech rights.

1994 Ninth Circuit Court of Appeals in *Peloza v. Capistrano School District* rejects plaintiff's argument that evolutionism is a "religion." The school district may therefore require that biology teachers instruct in evolution without violating a teacher's First Amendment right to free exercise of religion.

1999 State Board of Education in Kansas removes evolution from state tests for high school students, leaving the teaching of the subject up to "local option." Measure is repealed the next year. Evolution does not appear in state educational standards in Illinois, Arkansas, Kentucky, Tennessee, Mississippi, and Georgia, and is mentioned slightly in Missouri, Florida, and South Carolina. Other states require that textbooks bear a disclaimer that evolution is a theory and not a fact. Evolution disputes take place primarily at the school district level.

Questions for Consideration

1. Why was this debate over a scientific and educational matter so passionate on both sides? What other issues were involved? What seemed to be at stake for the defense? For the prosecution?
2. In what ways was the Scopes trial fundamentally an argument over democracy and majority rule? Do you agree with Bryan that "the hand that writes the check rules the schools"? How would you support his statement? Could you make the same argument today? Why or why not?
3. Was the Scopes trial ultimately a conflict of personalities? A regional conflict? A religious conflict? A cultural conflict? How did these forces interact with one another? Which do you see as dominant?
4. How did southerners, and Tennesseans in particular, seek to portray themselves to the rest of America? Was their support of the Butler law compatible with their dreams of economic growth? How would you have tried to "sell" Tennessee to the rest of the nation in 1925?
5. Describe the conflicting arguments over the admissibility of expert testimony. Was this purely a legal conflict, or did it have a theological component as well?
6. Consider a situation in which a high school biology instructor in the early twenty-first century decides that she wants to teach biblical creation rather than evolution. Should she be protected by the same arguments about academic and religious freedom that Scopes's defense team invoked? Why or why not?
7. What role did women play in the antievolution conflict and in the Scopes trial? Was this a conflict over female roles as well as a conflict over science and religion?
8. Do you find the reporting on the trial to be objective or biased? What image of Dayton and the South did the reporters create? How would you construct a narrative of the trial or of a particular day's arguments from the point of view of a Bryan supporter? Does this alternative seem equally valid?

9. Why did the defense call Bryan to the witness stand on day seven? Why did Bryan accept? Do you think Bryan's testimony helped or hurt his cause?
10. Did participants in the trial hold differing views of the purpose of education? How did these differing views fit with their regional and cultural backgrounds?
11. Explain Bryan's argument that teaching evolution in the public schools infringes on the students' religious freedom. Do you find the argument convincing? Why or why not? Where does Scopes fit into the tradition of church-state separation in the United States?
12. Do you see Bryan's role in the antievolution movement as consistent with his earlier career in liberal reform? Why or why not?
13. How does the Scopes trial fit with the rest of what you know about culture in the Jazz Age?

Selected Bibliography

Beale, Howard K. *A History of Freedom of Teaching in American Schools.* 1941. Reprint, New York: Octagon Books, 1966.

Bellomy, Donald C. "Social Darwinism Revisited." *Perspectives in American History,* n.s., 1 (1984): 1–130.

Blee, Kathleen M. *Women of the Klan: Racism and Gender in the 1920s.* Berkeley: University of California Press, 1991.

Carpenter, Joel. *Revive Us Again: The Reawakening of American Fundamentalism.* New York: Oxford University Press, 1997.

Coben, Stanley. *Rebellion against Victorianism: The Impetus for Cultural Change in 1920s America.* New York: Oxford University Press, 1991.

Cohen, Lizabeth. *Making a New Deal: Industrial Workers in Chicago, 1919–1939.* New York: Cambridge University Press, 1990.

Conkin, Paul. *When All the Gods Trembled: Darwinism, Scopes, and American Intellectuals.* New York: Rowman & Littlefield, 1998.

Cottrell, Robert B. *Roger Nash Baldwin and the American Civil Liberties Union.* New York: Columbia University Press, 2000.

Cremin, Lawrence. *American Education, the Metropolitan Experience, 1876–1980.* New York: Harper & Row, 1988.

Darrow, Clarence. *The Story of My Life.* New York: Scribner's, 1932.

Douglas, Ann. *Terrible Honesty: Mongrel Manhattan in the 1920s.* New York: Farrar, Straus and Giroux, 1995.

Fass, Paula. *The Damned and the Beautiful: American Youth in the 1920s.* New York: Oxford University Press, 1977.

Fleming, Donald. *John William Draper and the Religion of Science.* Philadelphia: University of Pennsylvania Press, 1950.

Fraser, James W. *Religion and Public Education in a Multicultural America.* New York: St. Martin's Press, 1999.

Gatewood, Willard B., Jr. *Preachers, Pedagogues, and Politicians: The Evolution Controversy in North Carolina.* Chapel Hill: University of North Carolina Press, 1966.

Gould, Stephen Jay. *Bully for Brontosaurus: Reflections in Natural History.* New York: W. W. Norton & Co., 1991.

Hutchison, William R. *The Modernist Impulse in American Protestantism.* Cambridge: Harvard University Press, 1976.

Keith, Jeanette. *Country People in the New South: Tennessee's Upper Cumberland.* Chapel Hill: University of North Carolina Press, 1995.

Kevles, Daniel. *In the Name of Eugenics: Genetics and the Uses of Human Heredity.* New ed. Cambridge: Harvard University Press, 1995.

Lacey, Michael J., ed. *Religion and Twentieth-Century American Intellectual Life.* New York: Wilson Center and Cambridge University Press, 1989.

Larson, Edward J. *Summer for the Gods: The Scopes Trial and America's Continuing Debate over Science and Religion.* New York: Basic Books, 1997.

———. *Trial and Error: The American Controversy over Creation and Evolution.* New York: Oxford University Press, 1985.

Levine, Lawrence W. *Defender of the Faith: William Jennings Bryan: The Last Decade, 1915–1925.* New York: Oxford University Press, 1965.

Levy, Leonard. *The Establishment Clause: Religion and the First Amendment.* 2nd ed., rev. Chapel Hill: University of North Carolina Press, 1994.

Lippmann, Walter. *American Inquisitors: A Commentary on Dayton and Chicago.* New York: Macmillan, 1928.

MacLean, Nancy. *Behind the Mask of Chivalry: The Making of the Second Ku Klux Klan.* New York: Oxford University Press, 1994.

Marsden, George M. *Fundamentalism and American Culture: The Shaping of Twentieth-Century Evangelicalism: 1870–1925.* New York: Oxford University Press, 1980.

———. *Understanding Fundamentalism and Evangelicalism.* Grand Rapids, Mich.: William B. Eerdmans Publishing, 1991.

Mayr, Ernst. *The Growth of Biological Thought: Diversity, Evolution, and Inheritance.* Cambridge: Belknap Press of Harvard University Press, 1982.

Moore, James R. *The Post-Darwinian Controversies: A Study of the Protestant Struggle to Come to Terms with Darwin in Great Britain and America, 1870–1900.* New York: Cambridge University Press, 1979.

Numbers, Ronald L. *The Creationists.* New York: Alfred A. Knopf, 1992.

———. *Darwinism Comes to America.* Cambridge: Harvard University Press, 1998.

Numbers, Ronald L., and John Stenhouse, eds. *Disseminating Darwinism: The Role of Place, Race, Religion, and Gender.* Cambridge: Cambridge University Press, 1999.

Scopes, John T., and James Presley. *Center of the Storm: Memoirs of John T. Scopes.* New York: Holt, Rinehart and Winston, 1967.

Index